D0564588

Beyond Anxiety & Phobia

Edmund J. Bourne, Ph.D.

NEW HARBINGER PUBLICATIONS, INC.

Publisher's Note

This publication is designed to provide accurate and authoritative information in regard to the subject matter covered. It is sold with the understanding that the publisher is not engaged in rendering psychological, financial, legal, or other professional services. If expert assistance or counseling is needed, the services of a competent professional should be sought.

Portions of this book were previously published under the title *Healing Fear*.

Distributed in Canada by Raincoast Books

New Harbinger Publications, Inc.
5674 Shattuck Avenue
Oakland, CA 94609

Cover design by SHELBY DESIGNS & ILLUSTRATES
Edited by Angela Watrous
Text design by Michele Waters

Library of Congress Catalog Card Number: 00-134863

ISBN-10 1-57224-229-9
ISBN-13 978-1-57224-229-6

Printed in the United States of America on recycled paper

New Harbinger Publications' website address: www.newharbinger.com

10 09 08

15 14 13 12 11 10 9

Grateful acknowledgment to:

Matt McKay, for his patience and flexibility in working with me throughout the project

Carole Honeychurch and Angela Watrous, for skillful and sensitive editing

Amy Shoup, for her contribution to the cover design

Michele Waters, for the text design

Tom Rucker, Sita Packer, and Steve Prakken, for reviewing early versions of the book

and to

Jane Lunstrum, who processed the entire manuscript and made valuable editorial contributions.

In moments of separation,
Adrift from ourselves or each other,
Our restless minds
Too quickly conjure fearful images—
Like bad dreams we mistake as real.

Though we see it not,
Each of us seeks to return
To a common ground
That lies deep within and beyond us.
A place—long remembered—
Where we all can meet
Beyond visible and verbal differences
Where each may feel safe,
Take heart,
And remember the quiet love
That enfolds us all.

Contents

Appendices

Introduction

For the past fifteen years I have used cognitive-behavioral therapy to help people overcome problems with panic, phobias, and anxiety. With panic attacks, I teach them to do abdominal breathing, let go of catastrophic thoughts, and habituate to panic-provoking body sensations. With phobias, I assist them in facing avoided situations gradually, in small increments, until they stop avoiding. With worries and general anxiety, I teach relaxation skills and work with counterproductive self-talk and beliefs. About fifty percent of the time, my clients either are already taking medication or I refer them for medication, particularly SSRIs such as Paxil or Zoloft. When their problems are severe, they seem to benefit most from a combination of cognitive-behavioral therapy and medication.

Several years ago, at the time of writing my first book, *The Anxiety & Phobia Workbook,* I noticed that a substantial portion of my clients achieved only a partial improvement from cognitive-behavioral therapy (CBT) and/or medication, not the high degree of recovery they had initially hoped for. Quite a few also relapsed six months to two years after receiving effective treatment. Why did these clients fail to adequately benefit? In some cases, it was because they did not continue to practice basic cognitive-behavioral skills such as relaxation, challenging negative self-talk, or exposure on a consistent basis following treatment. In other cases, they didn't take medication when needed or the right medication long enough. In quite a few cases, however, I got the distinct impression that my clients needed help beyond what CBT and medication could offer. They were practicing all the right skills, but their lives hadn't really changed and their symptoms would periodically recur. Certainly they received some benefit from conventional treatment, but not enough to feel completely recovered.

What more was required? It became apparent to me that many of them needed to modify basic personality traits such as perfectionism, codependency, or a fear of abandonment. Others need to resolve long-standing interpersonal conflicts with partners or family members that contributed to their anxiety. Still others needed to change their diet, particularly with respect to caffeine, sugar, and junk food consumption. Finally, some needed to get out of a dead-end career and find a broader meaning or purpose to their life. The second half of *The Anxiety & Phobia Workbook* touched briefly on all of these issues, offering chapters on such topics as anxiety-prone personality traits, self-esteem, life purpose, and spirituality.

During the 1990s about fifty books appeared in the anxiety disorders field, refining and elaborating the standard cognitive-behavioral and pharmacological approaches to treatment in considerable detail. Many fine books for both lay people and professionals are now available. Yet, I've continued to see very few writings that address the broader issues of personality, lifestyle, meaning, and spirituality, and particularly how such issues impact problems people have with anxiety.

Because I feel that these issues are important, I decided to devote an entire book to them. *Beyond Anxiety & Phobia* expands considerably on the topics broached in *The Anxiety & Phobia Workbook* and introduces several entirely new topics. I felt there was a need for such a book, as a counterpoint to the many books that present conventional cognitive-behavioral and medication approaches. While mainstream treatment really does work and is often helpful, there are many other approaches to try beyond conventional ones if you feel the latter have not offered you the degree of recovery you wish.

This book offers ten approaches that are "complementary" to the conventional treatment methods you'll find in most books on anxiety disorders. Some of these approaches directly address topics such as simplifying your lifestyle and environment, overcoming anxiety-prone personality traits, and the need for meaning and a sense of purpose in your life. Others could best be described as "alternative" approaches. They define a counterpoint to mainstream CBT and medication treatment methods, and are also characterized by the term "alternative" within the field of medicine. A brief description of each of these approaches follows.

Simplify your life—Your anxiety difficulties may be hard to overcome because your lifestyle is too complicated. Relaxation and cognitive-behavioral techniques can only help so much if you create too much to do in too short a time, too many expenses to meet, too long and stressful a commute, or too many e-mails and phone calls to answer. Chapter 2 makes a case for simplfying your lifestyle and environment as a way to reduce anxiety.

Address core personality issues—Underlying your issues with panic, phobias, or generalized anxiety are certain core fears, such as the fear of abandonment, fear of rejection, fear of losing control, fear of injury or death, and fear of confinement. These fears often originate from early trauma or dysfunctional relationships with your parents in childhood. Working to overcome them can help you get to the "root" of your issues with anxiety. Addressing core fears can also help resolve interpersonal conflicts that keep you anxious or stressed. For example, if you let go of a core fear of rejection, you may learn to stop giving yourself away in order to please or accommodate others. Chapter 5 takes up the topic of core fears and anxiety-prone personality traits in detail.

Discover and express your unique life purpose—When life feels pointless or meaningless, many of us seek outward forms of stimulation, including various types of addictions, to fill the gap. None of these provides any lasting solution. Anxiety arising from a sense of meaninglessness can be healed when you get in touch with your own unique creative purpose or "mission" for being here on earth. Each of us has one or several such purposes, and they always involve making a contribution to the welfare of something or someone beyond ourselves. Find your unique purpose and you'll regain an enthusiasm for life that comes from within. Chapter 6 explores this topic.

I believe these three areas are critical for many people to achieve a satisfactory and lasting recovery from anxiety disorders. Beyond these, there are several other "alternative" approaches that may help you in your efforts toward recovery. All of them have been beneficial to my clients as well as to me personally.

Herbs and supplements—You may find natural, nonprescription remedies such as kava, St.-John's-wort, SAM-e, or calcium-magnesium to be helpful in reducing anxiety, depression, and enhancing well-being in general (see chapter 3).

Energy balance disciplines—A variety of practices exist to help promote deep relaxation and release blocks to the natural flow of your "life energy" or vitality. Daily practice of yoga, t'ai chi, or chi gung promotes mind-body integration, enhances your energy, and promotes a sense of well-being. Healing arts such as acupuncture, massage or chiropractic, when received on a regular basis, have a similar effect (see chapter 3).

Diet—What you eat affects your mood, anxiety level, and overall well-being. Eliminating caffeine, sugar, and food allergens from your diet will help you to calm down. So will eating more whole and unprocessed foods, more protein relative to carbohydrate, and more vegetable rather than animal-based food items (see chapter 4).

Meditation—The world's oldest method for attaining peace of mind can enable you to access a quiet place of serenity deep within yourself. It can also help you develop a capacity to witness instead of always reacting to the ups and downs of daily life (see chapter 7).

Spirituality—Spirituality, the most profound of all healing approaches, empowers you to align with the creative intelligence of the universe. You learn that you don't have to work out your life entirely on your own but can turn to a Higher Power for strength, solace, and inner peace (see chapters 8 and 9).

Create your vision—What you believe in and commit to with your whole heart tends to come to you. By holding a vision of your recovery and using visualizations or affirmations to reinforce that vision on a regular basis, you will eventually realize the freedom from fear and peace of mind you seek (see chapter 10).

Love—Authentic love can always overcome fear or anxiety because it originates from a place in yourself that is deeper than fear. Fear is largely an illusion of your conditioned mind that disconnects you from yourself and others. Love is a gift of your soul that can bridge and heal all forms of separation (see chapter 11).

To sum up, this book presents a variety of approaches that can complement a basic program of cognitive-behavioral therapy and/or medication to overcome problems with anxiety. Looking at both mainstream and complementary approaches (indicated below) will give you an idea of the full spectrum of treatment for anxiety that is available.

Mainstream Approaches

- Abdominal breathing
- Relaxation training
- Physical exercise
- Replacing catastrophic with realistic thoughts
- Habituation to body sensations associated with anxiety
- Exposure—gradually and incrementally facing phobic situations
- Reducing sensitivity to perceived threats
- Increasing perceived ability to cope
- Medications

Complementary Approaches

- Simplifying your life
- Addressing anxiety-prone personality traits
- Finding meaning and life purpose
- Energy balance disciplines
- Diet
- Meditation
- Spirituality
- Creating your vision of recovery
- Love
- Herbs and supplements

Your own program for recovery will likely draw from both categories of approaches. Different people respond to different methods. There is no shortcut to determine which approaches are optimal for you except by trying many to see what works best. If you have just begun to seek help for your problem, I recommend working with mainstream approaches first, as described in *The Anxiety & Phobia Workbook.* If you are looking for something beyond the mainstream, or if you've already tried conventional treatments, then this book is a good place to start.

Recovering from an anxiety disorder requires persistence, effort, and commitment. If you are strongly self-motivated, you may develop your own recovery program drawing from the variety of approaches just listed. However, you may prefer not to go it alone. You may, in fact, find it helpful to work with a therapist who specializes in treating anxiety disorders. Such a therapist can provide guidance, support, and structure, enabling you to fine-tune the concepts and strategies found in this book or others. You may also find support groups or treatment groups for anxiety disorders to be quite valuable, if available in your area. For a list of therapists who specialize in treating anxiety disorders, please see the *National Professional Membership Directory*, available from the Anxiety Disorders Association of America, or you can call the ADAA or go to www.adaa.org (see appendix 1).

I wish you the best in your efforts to overcome your difficulties with anxiety. There is much help available, and I believe that a high level of recovery is always possible if you're sincerely motivated and committed to achieving it.

1

New Help for Anxiety and Phobias

The last two decades of the twentieth century saw an explosion of knowledge about different types of problems with anxiety and how to treat them. Seven major types of anxiety disorders were described:

Panic Disorder—Sudden episodes of acute, intense anxiety that appear to come out of the blue.

Agoraphobia—A fear of panic attacks in situations that are perceived to be far from safety or a safe place (such as home), or from which escape might be difficult (such as driving on a freeway or waiting in line at the grocery store). Such fear can lead to avoidance of a wide range of situations.

Social Phobia—A fear of embarrassment or humiliation in situations where you are exposed to the scrutiny of others or must perform.

Specific Phobia—A strong fear and avoidance of one particular object or situation (such as spiders, water, thunderstorms, elevators, or flying).

Generalized Anxiety Disorder—Chronic anxiety and worry for at least six months about two or more issues or activities (such as work or health).

Obsessive-Compulsive Disorder—Recurring obsessions (repetitive thoughts) and/or compulsions (rituals performed to dispel anxiety) that are severe enough to be time-consuming or cause marked distress.

Post-traumatic Stress Disorder—Development of anxiety and other symptoms following an acute and intense trauma (such as a natural disaster, assault, rape, or accident) or after witnessing an event that involves death or injury to another person.

Researchers and clinicians in both the United States and Britain have developed effective methods for treating these difficulties. Cognitive-behavioral therapy (CBT), the marriage of Aaron Beck's cognitive therapy and Joseph Wolpe's systematic desensitization, became and remains to this day the dominant and most helpful psychological treatment for all of the anxiety disorders. Research and clinical experience has consistently demonstrated the efficacy of CBT. In its present form, cognitive-behavioral therapy consists of a combination of approximately six strategies, including:

- *Abdominal Breathing Training*—Learning to breathe more slowly from your abdomen
- *Muscle Relaxation Training*—Learning to deeply relax all the muscles of your body
- *Cognitive Therapy*—Replacing catastrophic, fearful thoughts with more realistic, constructive thoughts
- *Interoceptive Exposure*—Desensitizing to internal sensations of anxiety
- *In Vivo Exposure*—Gradually facing phobic situations that have been avoided, often with a support person
- *Exposure and Response Prevention*—Refraining from compulsive behaviors when exposed to situations that would ordinarily provoke them.

With the advent of short-acting, high-potency tranquilizers in the 80s and selective serotonin reuptake inhibitor (SSRI) medications in the 90s, psychiatry has also developed effective psychopharmacological treatments for all of the anxiety disorders. Current clinical practice often combines cognitive-behavioral therapy and medication, especially in the case of panic disorder, social phobia, and obsessive-compulsive disorder. Medications appear particularly helpful when anxiety symptoms are in the moderate to severe range of intensity.

The fact is that cognitive-behavioral therapy and medications work. Countless people all over the world have been helped by either one or a combination of both of these approaches. Research and clinical practice have repeatedly supported their efficacy. No self-respecting clinician who is knowledgeable about anxiety disorders fails to utilize them.

Why, then, this book? Why present a book that offers a new perspective beyond the mainstream approaches adopted by most clinicians? The reason is simply this: not everyone who receives cognitive-behavioral therapy and/or medication achieves satisfactory recovery. And there are some persons who, having received good treatment, get better for a while and then relapse. Thus it appears that, at least sometimes, something more than CBT and medication is needed to ensure a lasting and high level of recovery.

At the time of writing my first book, *The Anxiety & Phobia Workbook*, I recognized that the technologies of cognitive-behavioral therapy and psychopharmacology, while very helpful, might not always be sufficient. If, for example, people didn't change their lifestyles, work on overcoming anxiety-prone personality traits (such as perfectionism), address interpersonal conflicts at home or work, or find some larger meaning in their life, they might continue to remain anxious in spite of the best efforts of their cognitive-behavioral therapists and psychiatrists. While these themes are touched on in *The Anxiety & Phobia Workbook*, the purpose of *Beyond Anxiety & Phobia* is to explore such issues in depth. The remaining chapters of this book focus on lifestyle, environmental, and personality issues that can affect anxiety disorders while also looking at the existential and spiritual dimensions of anxiety. I've become convinced, over twenty years of clinical practice, that these issues often don't receive the attention they deserve by clinicians who specialize in using cognitive-behavioral therapy or medications.

Two points of contrast exist between the approach taken in this book and the approach of cognitive-behavioral therapy. First, CBT breaks down problems with anxiety into their component parts and then seeks to treat each component. For example, if you have panic attacks with agoraphobia, you learn: 1) strategies to reduce physiological anxiety, such as abdominal breathing and progressive muscle relaxation, 2) techniques to change fear-provoking thoughts (cognitive therapy), and 3) techniques for overcoming phobic avoidance behavior (graded exposure). All of these methods can go a long way toward helping you overcome your problems with panic and phobias. Yet in some cases, however helpful, they aren't enough. What if a major source of your anxiety comes from the fact that your lifestyle is continually driven and rushed? Or if much of your anxiety arises from an ongoing conflict with your employer, partner, or authority figures in general? Or, again, what if an underlying lack of meaning or purpose in your life is contributing to both anxiety and depression?

Rather than offering specific techniques to address physiology, thoughts, and behavior, the approach taken in this book deals with the whole person. As you read through the following chapters, you'll be examining such issues as:

- how to simplify your life to achieve greater peace of mind
- how to address difficult personality issues that create anxiety
- what "alternative" therapies might be helpful
- how learning to meditate regularly can reduce worry
- how finding your unique life purpose and embracing a more spiritual outlook might offer a deep healing in your life

All of this is not intended to replace the effective help you can get from cognitive-behavioral therapy and medication. My purpose here is to supplement these approaches by offering a holistic perspective—a way of addressing the problem of anxiety from a standpoint that views you as a whole person.

A second point of contrast between the approach of this book and conventional treatment is the view it takes of anxiety symptoms. Symptoms are usually viewed as something to be gotten rid of. The aim of treatment is to find strategies for reducing or eliminating panic attacks, phobic avoidance, generalized anxiety, or obsessions and compulsions. While I have no argument with the importance and validity of reducing symptoms, I also want to encourage you to regard your symptoms as a *sign*. Symptoms are not random and arbitrary—they contain a message. The question to ask yourself is: *What does the fact that I developed an anxiety disorder* mean? *What are my body and mind trying to tell me?* And most important, *What changes are being called for in order for me to recover?*

You didn't develop an anxiety disorder out of the blue. It happened because of an accumulation of stress over a long time—or perhaps just one major stressor—*in combination with* your genetic makeup; your childhood; and your particular lifestyle, priorities, personality, and interpersonal situation as an adult. Yes, of course, you want to get rid of your symptoms. But you might also view your symptoms as an ally.

Your symptoms are calling you to understand yourself better—to really examine yourself and figure out what changes you need to make in yourself and your life to feel better. Look at it this way: If your anxiety disorder didn't stop you in your tracks and call you to pay attention, you might have gone on in your habitual ways until something even more serious happened. I often tell my clients that an anxiety disorder functions in much the same way as ulcers or migraine headaches. Your body is giving you a warning signal that you need to make some changes. The change required may be to deal with a long-standing personality pattern, resolve an interpersonal conflict, make a shift in your priorities and values, and/or find new meaning in your life. When you figure out what is needed and make the necessary changes, your *whole life* works better and you start to feel better. Your problem with panic, phobias, or obsessive worry will certainly get better, and so also may your depression, headaches, insomnia, and/or tendency to be short-tempered or irritable. *All of you* gets better.

In this book, you'll be asked to do what you need to do to reduce your symptoms, but also let them convey to you their implicit message.

Why Don't People Who Receive Help Get Better?

As mentioned, the purpose of this book is to provide some new perspectives to help people with anxiety improve their likelihood of recovery and reduce the risk of relapse. Approximately 30–40 percent of people who receive state-of-the-art treatment for their anxiety problems have limited recovery. They do not experience the relief they were hoping to find. Of those people who *do* initially derive benefit from treatment, a significant percentage relapse after a period of time. In some cases the relapse is a temporary response to increased stress and may be overcome; in other, less fortunate cases, it seems to be enduring.

Why do some persons not get better in spite of good treatment? Why do others relapse? I've thought quite a bit about this problem and have come up with what I believe to be five major reasons. In presenting them, I'm assuming that the treatment offered was appropriate, the kind that helps many people: a well-administered course of cognitive-behavioral therapy and/or medication. If you've not gotten better because you've not received appropriate treatment (i.e., your therapist sat and just talked with you or tried some other form of treatment instead of cognitive-behavioral therapy), you need to keep looking until you find effective help. So keep in mind that the reasons that follow assume you've already had proper treatment but have not improved as much as you would like.

1. *You don't continue to practice the basic techniques and strategies of cognitive behavioral therapy.*

Recovery from panic, phobias, obsessions and compulsions, or general anxiety requires consistent effort over a period of time. You need to make time each day to practice deep muscle relaxation, engage in aerobic exercise, challenge and counter anxiety-provoking self-talk, and incrementally face internal anxiety sensations or avoided external situations. If you're unable or unwilling to make such an effort during a course of cognitive-behavioral therapy, you will probably not benefit much from it. And if you don't keep up with the basic practices of relaxation, exercise, and exposure following the completion of therapy, you increase your risk of relapse. Recovery from an anxiety disorder requires a permanent change in lifestyle, with time allocated each day for practicing skills that keep anxiety and phobias from recurring.

If you find you're having difficulty maintaining a commitment to the daily practices that can ensure your long-term recovery, there are a couple of things you might do. First, you might arrange with your therapist to have periodic "booster sessions" (after you've finished therapy) to help you stay on track with your recovery program. Second, if you live in a large metropolitan area, you can attend an anxiety disorders support group. Such a group needs to be a place where the focus is on what everybody is doing to maintain or enhance recovery—not just venting about their problems. If you don't have a support group in your area, you can find support through message boards and chat rooms online (see appendix 1).

2. *You do not take medication when it's needed or stop taking it before it has offered its full benefit.*

Often prescription medication is unnecessary. However, if your problem is relatively severe, you may well need to combine medication with cognitive-behavioral therapy to get the best results. By "severe," I mean that your problem meets at least one of the following criteria:

- Your anxiety is disruptive enough that it's difficult for you to get to work and/or function on your job (or it has caused you to stop working).
- Your anxiety interferes with your ability to maintain fulfilling and close relationships with family members and/or significant others (or it prevents you from establishing a relationship with any significant other).
- Your anxiety causes you significant distress 50 percent of the time you're awake. It's not just a major nuisance or irritation—you often feel overwhelmed and find it hard to get through the day.

If you believe your anxiety problem meets any one or more of these criteria, it's likely you may benefit from a trial of medication such as an SSRI like Paxil, Zoloft, or Celexa, or perhaps the medication Buspar. Not to try medications because you're afraid or philosophically opposed to them may hamper your recovery if your situation is severe. Over the years I've witnessed quite a few clients who remained stuck for years until they finally decided to try medication.

Detailed guidelines for when to use medication and which ones to use can be found in the chapter "Medication" in *The Anxiety & Phobia Workbook*. You can also obtain a referral to a psychiatrist in your area skilled in treating anxiety disorders by contacting the ADAA at 301-231-9350 or going to their Web site www.adaa.org.

Another problem with medication is the failure to take it long enough. Research has found, for example, that the most effective period of time to take antidepressant medication (i.e. Tofranil, Paxil, Zoloft, Serzone, Celexa, etc.) if you have panic disorders is about eighteen months. Rates of relapse were found to be 70 percent for a group who took these medications six months and only 30 percent for another group who took the medications for eighteen months.

My theory is that staying on medication longer enables the brain to recover and regenerate from the initial trauma caused by severe anxiety symptoms. That is, the initial trauma of an anxiety disorder actually *may* have physical effects on the brain. Unfortunately, the longer severe anxiety symptoms persist untreated, the greater the potential for trauma. And the greater the trauma, the more likely anxiety symptoms will become chronic. Beginning medication sooner rather than later can help mitigate such traumatic effects. Then staying on the medication at least eighteen months—or in some cases even longer—allows the brain an opportunity to rest and regenerate. Hopefully there will be more research in the future to evaluate this theory. The above observation applies primarily to the use of SSRIs (Prozac, Paxil, Zoloft, Luvox, Serzone, Celexa) and tricyclic (Pamelor, Norpramin, Sinequan) antidepressants. Relapse rates following the use of high-potency tranquilizers such as Xanax or Klonopin tend to be very high—even after taking these medications for several years—if you haven't learned any other skills or made lifestyle changes to help overcome your problem.

3. *You don't modify your lifestyle in a way that supports greater peace and ease in your life.*

Even if you've received cognitive-behavioral therapy and have taken the proper medication(s), your recovery may still be limited if your lifestyle is so complicated and busy that you continually keep yourself at a high level of stress. Anxiety disorders are caused by three factors: heredity, personality (based on childhood experience), and cumulative stress. You can't do much about your genetic makeup or your early childhood, but you can do a lot to mitigate stress in your life. If you reduce and manage your stress, you will reduce your vulnerability to anxiety. It's that simple. Stress arises from both external and internal factors. External stress factors include things like work demands, rush-hour commutes, smog, food additives, negative relatives, and noise pollution. These type of stressors usually require external solutions. Internal stress factors have to do with your own attitudes, such as overemphasizing success at the cost of everything else, or a tendency to cram too many things into too short a time. They require internal solutions—basically shifting your attitudes and priorities. Many persons do not recover from panic or anxiety until they are willing to place as much importance on their peace of mind and health as they do on career success and material accomplishment.

The chapter following this one, "Simplify Your Life," offers some strategies that appear to fall more on the "external" side of stress management. However, implementing them also requires a shift in attitude. In that chapter I speak first about my own personal experience in reducing stress by making my life quite a bit simpler. Then I go on to suggest a number of ways you might attempt to simplify your own life. In so doing you will change the *structure* of your life in a direction that promotes more peace, ease, and harmony. When you seriously want more peace in your life, you are usually willing to make some fairly major changes toward simplification. Such changes may have as large an impact in reducing your vulnerability to anxiety as relying on cognitive-behavioral therapy or medication. They did so for me.

4. *You fail to address personality and interpersonal issues that perpetuate anxiety.*

Cognitive therapy and exposure may help you to change panic-provoking thoughts and face your fears. However, they may not modify core personality traits that predispose you to be anxious in the first place. If you grew up with perfectionistic, overly controlling parents, for example, you're likely to be perfectionistic yourself. Nothing in yourself or your life ever quite meets your overdrawn standards, and so you set yourself up for continuous stress. Or if your parents were highly critical of you, you may have grown up with an excessive need to please and win approval. If you spend your life trying to please others at the expense of your own personal needs, you're likely to harbor a lot of unexpressed resentment and thus be more prone to anxiety. Insecurity, overdependency, overcautiousness, and the excessive need for control are additional personality issues common to people with anxiety disorders. Such core personality traits are often associated with interpersonal problems, i.e., perhaps you expect too much of your spouse (perfectionism) or you don't ask enough (excessive need to please). Or you may resent your parents' attempts to control you, but you don't assert your needs with them.

Chapter 5, "Address Your Personality Issues," examines six major issues that I've observed among people with anxiety problems:

- Excessive need to please (fear of rejection)
- Insecurity and overdependency (fear of abandonment)
- Overcontrol
- Perfectionism
- Overcautiousness (fear of illness, injury, or death)
- Fear of confinement

The chapter offers brief self-tests for each issue so you can evaluate where you stand. Then guidelines are presented for working on and remedying each of these facets of what I would call the "anxiety-prone personality."

5. *Existential Issues*

The problem at the root of your anxiety may lie still deeper than personality. Anxiety may persist in spite of therapy and medication because you experience a sense of emptiness or meaninglessness about your life. In present times, with so many conflicting values and a loss of traditional authorities such as the church or social mores, it's easy to feel adrift and confused. The very pace of modern life can lead to feelings of confusion, if not outright chaos.

What has been called "existential anxiety" does not respond to cognitive-behavioral therapy and demands a different kind of approach.

If your life feels meaningless or without direction, perhaps you need to discover your own unique gifts and creativity, and then find a way to meaningfully express them in the world. I believe each of us has a unique gift to offer—a unique contribution to make. Chapter 6, "Find Your Unique Purpose," examines how to do this. You will find a questionnaire there to help stimulate reflection about what your own unique purpose or "mission" for your life might be. Guidelines are offered for implementing that purpose, once you've become clear about it. If your life feels empty or purposeless, this may be the first chapter you want to read.

Of the five reasons described, which, if any, apply to you? Especially if you've already sought help for your anxiety difficulties, but haven't recovered as much as you would like, what else do you feel you might need to consider?

The purpose of this book is to give you a wide array of approaches that might help beyond cognitive-behavioral therapy and medication. So I will offer three additional perspectives that you may find quite beneficial:

- Alternative therapies
- Meditation
- Spirituality

These perspectives have been helpful for me personally, as well as for many of my clients.

Alternative Therapies

In recent years there has been a strong public interest in alternative health approaches. Problems with mainstream medicine and managed care insurance coverage have led increasing numbers of people to explore what alternative health practices have to offer. This is no less true for people suffering from anxiety disorders. A substantial number of my clients seek to try natural methods before relying on prescription drugs. Others who already take medications want to try out herbs, acupuncture, massage, or other such alternative approaches. The basic idea behind such efforts is simple: *restoring the body to wholeness should help overcome anxiety*. Alternative therapies in general aim to heal the whole person. As such, they can be of considerable benefit to anxiety sufferers. While they are unlikely to ever replace first-line treatment with cognitive-behavioral therapy, they can be quite useful as adjuncts to CBT. Enough so, in fact, that I felt they deserve a separate chapter in this book.

Chapter 3 examines a variety of alternative approaches. Probably the best known of these is the use of herbs and supplements to treat both anxiety and depression. Natural tranquilizers such as kava, valerian, and passionflower have brought benefit to many people experiencing anxiety. Natural antidepressants such as St.-John's-wort, SAM-e, and tryptophan can be quite helpful for the depression that often accompanies anxiety disorders, as well as have some impact on the anxiety itself. Herbs and supplements work best for anxiety/depression in the *mild to moderate range*. Anxiety at this level is a nuisance and discomfort in your life, but does not cause serious distress or interfere with your ability to function. Depression in the mild to moderate range means you feel "down," discouraged, or pessimistic, but you haven't lost your appetite, don't have severe sleep problems every night, and you aren't thinking about suicide often. More severe problems with anxiety and depression are best treated with a combination of therapy and medication.

Beyond herbs and supplements, disciplines such as yoga or t'ai chi can help to reduce muscle tension and "blocked energy" that often contribute to anxiety. Regular practice leads to greater ease and flexibility in your body, improved energy, and an overall sense of wellness. Making a commitment to get a deep-muscle massage every week can go a long way toward reducing chronic skeletal muscle tension, which will certainly help relieve anxiety. Acupuncture enhances relaxation, improves energy, and has been demonstrated to help chronic depression. Chiropractic treatments can relieve stress and muscle tension by releasing locked-up joints.

Last, but certainly not least among alternative approaches, is diet. Chapter 4 takes up the topic of diet in detail. The first and most important dietary guideline for anxiety disorders is to eliminate caffeine (and other stimulants such as nicotine or ephedrine). Beyond that, many other nutritional issues can play a role in anxiety disorders, including hypoglycemia, food allergies, overacidity of your body, insufficient protein, insufficient fluid intake, and eating too much processed "junk" food. Chapter 4 presents fourteen dietary guidelines that can help reduce anxiety.

In the future, alternative, holistic modalities will be increasingly accepted as a part of mainstream treatment. Until that time, I encourage you to learn more about these approaches and explore any you feel drawn to. The references at the end of chapters 3 and 4 list many useful books to help get you started.

Meditation

Some people consider meditation just another alternative treatment. In truth, it's the most ancient and still one of the most valuable approaches for overcoming generalized anxiety and worry. The practice of meditation originated in the Far East about four thousand years ago. It's aim was simple: to reduce suffering by transcending or moving beyond the overactive, restless mind. The traditions in which meditation developed held the view that all of us have, by nature, a quiet, serene place deep inside that is always present, yet is clouded over and hidden beneath the constant activity of the mind. If you can quiet down your mind through the practice of meditation, this place/state of quiet serenity deep inside has the chance to emerge.

Regular practice of meditation does lead to increased peace and serenity. Of all the deep relaxation techniques, meditation is probably the most potent if practiced on a daily basis. Research has found numerous major benefits of regular meditation practice including decreases in stress, anxiety, blood pressure, and psychosomatic complaints, as well as increases in alertness, energy, and self-esteem. The topic of meditation is taken up in chapter 7.

Probably the most important benefit of practicing meditation is the development of mindfulness. If the word "mindfulness" sounds like it has too much to do with the mind, substitute the word "awareness." Cultivating mindfulness means a fundamental change in your *relationship* or stance toward everything that happens in your ongoing experience of life. It means that you develop increased ability to *witness* rather than just *react* to whatever you're feeling in each moment. Instead of being buffeted about by every impulse, desire, fear, anger, regret, judgment, etc., that you feel, you learn simply to "be with" all the elements of your immediate experience without resistance or judgment. Mindfulness is not about being detached from your feelings; it's about being consciously aware of them so that you're free to choose how to act (rather than react) in each moment. With regard to anxiety, mindfulness overcomes worry. To worry is to live in the future. Your mind reacts with anxiety to a perceived threat or danger that hasn't really happened and, in most cases, is not likely to happen. Mindfulness redirects you to live more in the present moment, simply observing your mind's tendency to create fantasies of perceived threat rather than getting caught up in them.

Meditation has been a profound approach for helping many of my clients and myself personally to reduce worry. I believe it should be a standard part of treatment for generalized anxiety. It is important enough to merit its own chapter in this book.

Spirituality and Anxiety

The religions of the world are not silent on the subject of anxiety. All of them, in one way or another, provide beliefs and practices for attaining inner peace. And peace of mind can certainly be viewed as an ultimate remedy for fear, worry, and anxiety. Most religions also view unconditional love (or compassion) as one of the highest human states of consciousness possible. Some of these traditions regard such love as the essential nature of their deity. Like inner peace, unconditional love can also be understood as something opposite to and capable of overcoming fear.

A comparative study of how various world religions define the path to peace and compassion would be quite interesting, but is beyond the scope of this book. You may already feel strongly aligned with one particular religion, perhaps finding solace and inner peace that can help conquer anxiety through the beliefs and practices of that particular faith. For our purposes here, though, I choose to focus on spirituality rather than on any one particular religion. Spirituality is a common denominator that spans different world religions. Such religions propose various doctrines and belief systems about the nature of a Higher Power and humanity's relationship with it. Spirituality, on the other hand, refers to a *common experience* of a holy or transcendent reality that inspires all of the various religious traditions. There are many names for this transcendent reality, the most popular in our culture being God. No matter what religion you are born into, you are capable of having an experience where you come into contact with a "something" that transcends your personal self and the human order of things. For our purposes here, I want to refrain from speculating on the nature of that something. I'm more concerned with how cultivating a relationship with it (call it a Higher Power or God or whatever you feel most comfortable with) can have a healing effect on anxiety.

Beyond all of the mainstream methods for overcoming anxiety, developing your spirituality is an additional, powerful resource for healing your difficulties with fear and indeed transforming your entire life. Spirituality has been an important part of the path to recovery from anxiety for me personally, as well as for quite a few of my clients. It has also been a central part of the recovery of millions of persons worldwide who have successfully overcome addictions through 12-step programs. An important intent of this book is to give spirituality its proper place in the anxiety disorders field. As has already begun to happen in the field of medicine, the anxiety disorders field is beginning to move toward a new paradigm where scientifically based approaches to treatment are seen as complementary—not in conflict—with holistic and spiritually based approaches.

Three chapters of this book directly focus on how spiritual principles and practices can help overcome anxiety. Chapter 8, "Letting Go," is divided into two parts. The first addresses letting go of worry in daily life; the second considers letting go of a problem that may seem insoluble to the care of your Higher Power or God. Relying on a Higher Power for assistance in no way diminishes your responsibility to do all you can to work on your problem through available methods. Recovery can be fostered through a *combination* of doing all the necessary "footwork" (specifically, cognitive-behavioral homework) *and* trusting in assistance from a Higher Power. This is valid for the many persons who work through 12-step programs to overcome their addictions, and I believe it is equally applicable to persons struggling with anxiety disorders.

Chapter 9 explores spirituality as an important way to change your very way of looking at your problem with anxiety. To me this is a special form of "cognitive therapy": cognitive therapy at a philosophical or philosophy-of-life level. Fundamental changes in attitude tend to accompany increased involvement in spirituality, such as greater faith in the possibility of recovery, an increased sense of inner security, peace of mind, a relaxing of perfectionistic standards and the need to control, and improved self-worth. Questionnaires are offered for exploring both your concept of a Higher Power as well as the nature of your personal spiritual experiences. Finally, I invite you to explore your personal views about life and reality by offering twelve of my own ideas about spirituality. These ideas have been points of departure for discussion with my clients and are intended to stimulate your thinking about your own religious views. They may lead you to revise the way you look at your problem with anxiety.

Chapter 10, "Create Your Vision," builds on the idea that what you believe in and srongly commit to will tend to come to you. The notion that human beings can "create their reality"—attract to themselves what they believe in most strongly—is best understood from a spiritual perspective (conventional science tends to view such an idea as "magical thinking"). When you sincerely commit to a goal—and that goal is for your highest good—your Higher Power (however you choose to define such a power) will assist you in achieving it. Chapter 10 offers step-by-step procedures for applying this principle to overcoming problems with anxiety.

Finally, chapter 11, "Love," introduces the idea that authentic love is a most profound and enduring solution to the problem of anxiety. By "authentic love," I mean the kind of unconditional love that arises in moments of genuine compassion, forgiveness, or spontaneous generosity. Cultivating authentic love toward yourself and others is a direct way to overcome anxiety. Love cancels out anxiety in the same way light dispels darkness. Love is more powerful than fear, because it goes much deeper. Love resides at the foundation of your being, at a place where all of us are interconnected with each other and everything else in the universe. Fear, on the other hand, is a conditioned response learned early on to avoid situations that pose a threat. As such, it does not run as deep as love. Love arises whenever you fully, heartfully accept a connection with someone or something other than yourself; anxiety, by contrast, arises out of a *separation* or *disconnection* from others—or a separation within your own being. As you open your heart and deepen your capacity to love, it becomes easier to dispel anxiety. You simply become "larger" than the anxiety, which is created by your conditioned mind. In those moments when you're anxious, if you are able to come from your heart ("take heart"), your perception of things becomes clearer and any unrealistic fears are exposed as the illusions that they are.

It's my hope that the spiritual perspective developed in the last few chapters of this book may be helpful to you. As you read through these chapters, take what fits for you and discard what does not. The diverse religions and creeds of the world reflect the countless ways in which human beings have approached the spiritual dimension of life. There is no one right way, and each person must define the nature and scope of spirituality for him or herself.

The purpose of this book is to provide a wide range of approaches to overcoming anxiety that acknowledge yet go beyond existing, mainstream methods. In my experience, such a comprehensive strategy has the best chance of helping people achieve a full and lasting recovery—and a more fulfilling and peaceful quality of life over the long term. Rather than replacing cognitive-behavioral therapy and psychopharmacology, this book seeks to complement current treatment with an alternative model based on the metaphor of healing. I believe that such an approach is needed not only in the field of anxiety disorders, but in psychology in general, as well as in medicine, politics, international relations, and particularly in our attitude toward the earth's environment as we embark on a new century. Scientific and holistic perspectives on ourselves and our world no longer need to clash, but can best complement each other. I, for one, believe that it is through a collaboration of both types of perspectives that we as humans can find lasting solutions to our problems, both at the individual and collective level.

2

Simplify Your Life

Living more simply is a potent way to overcome difficulties with anxiety. It is a way to make peace of mind a priority in your life. To simplify your life is to live more consciously and with a minimum of needless distractions. It is to establish a more direct and unencumbered relationship with all aspects of your life: family, work, community, nature, the cosmos, and yourself.

To simplify your life does not mean to live in poverty. Poverty is involuntary and disabling, whereas the choice for simplicity is one that is voluntary and empowering. Simplicity is finding the right balance between austerity and excess. It's somewhere between a log cabin in the forest and an estate in the suburbs. Simplicity can even be achieved in an urban environment, if living in the country is unrealistic. Above all, simple living does not mean doing away with modern comforts and conveniences to prove your ability to live apart from twentieth-century technology. Gandhi made an interesting statement about denying the material side of life: "As long as you derive inner help and comfort from anything, you should keep it. If you were to give it up in a mood of self-sacrifice or out of a stern sense of duty, you would continue to want it back, and that unsatisfied want would make trouble for you."

There is no precise formula defining what constitutes living simply. Each individual needs to discover his or her own ways to reduce complexity and unnecessary encumbrances. One author who has thought a lot about simplicity, Duane Elgin (1993), proposes the following list. Those who choose to simplify their lives:

- Invest the time and energy freed up by simpler living in activities with their partner, children, and friends (walking, making music together, sharing a meal, camping, etc.)

- Work on developing the full spectrum of their potentials: physical (running, biking, hiking, etc.), emotional (learning the skills of intimacy and sharing feelings in important relationships), mental (engaging in lifelong learning by reading, taking classes, etc.), and spiritual (learning to move through life with a quiet mind and compassionate heart)

- Feel an intimate connection with the earth and a reverential concern for nature
- Feel a compassionate concern for the world's poor
- Lower their overall level of personal consumption—buy less clothing, for example (with more attention to what is functional, durable, aesthetic, and less concern with passing fads, fashions, and seasonal styles)
- Alter their patterns of consumption in favor of products that are durable, easy to repair, nonpolluting in their manufacture and use, energy-efficient, functional, and aesthetic
- Shift their diet away from highly processed foods, meat, and sugar toward foods that are more natural, healthy, and simple
- Reduce undue clutter and complexity in their personal lives by giving away or selling those possessions that are seldom used and could be used productively by others (clothing, books, furniture, appliances, tools, etc.)
- Recycle metal, glass, and paper and to cut back on consumption of items that are wasteful of nonrenewable resources
- Develop personal skills that contribute to greater self-reliance and reduce dependence upon experts to handle life's ordinary demands (basic carpentry, plumbing, appliance repair, etc.)
- Prefer smaller-scale, more human-sized living and working environments that foster a sense of community, face-to-face contact, and mutual caring
- Participate in holistic health-care practices that emphasize preventive medicine and the healing powers of the body when assisted by the mind
- Change transportation modes in favor of public transit, car pooling, smaller and more fuel-efficient autos, living closer to work, riding a bike, and walking

In recent years increasing numbers of persons have favored simplifying their lives. After thirty years of economic expansion and material growth, the decade of the 90s was, for many, a time of downsizing. According to a survey conducted in 1991 and quoted by Duane Elgin in *Voluntary Simplicity*:

- 69 percent of the people surveyed said they would like to "slow down and live a more relaxed life," in contrast to only 19 percent who said they would like to "live a more exciting, faster-paced life."
- 61 percent agreed that "earning a living today requires so much effort that it's difficult to find time to enjoy life."

- When asked about their priorities, 89 percent said it was more important these days to spend time with their families.
- Only 13 percent saw importance in keeping up with fashion trends and just 7 percent thought it was worth bothering to shop for status-symbol products.

A poll published in June 1997 in *USA Today* illustrated the fact that by mid-decade (1995) 28 percent of Americans reported they had deliberately made life changes during the preceding five years that resulted in less income, with 87 percent of them reporting satisfaction with the change.

How I Simplified My Life

The trend toward simplification is one in which I've participated. For much of my adult life, I bought into the complexity of life in modern society. There was much that I thought I needed when, in fact, I actually didn't. Over a period of a year, I made a number of changes—both large and small—that served to reduce the unnecessary complications in my life. I will offer you my personal life-simplification program as an inspiration to create your own, realizing that not all of the items on my list may be feasible or even desirable for you.

Moving to a Small Town

After almost twenty-five years of living in large, urban metropolitan areas, I decided to move to a small town of fewer than twenty thousand people. I found that I felt a greater sense of ease in an area where there were no freeways and only rare episodes of traffic congestion. Everything I needed was within easy driving distance, and it took only five minutes to drive out of town to open countryside. Just having a lower population density in itself made a significant difference in the ambiance of the surrounding environment.

I realize that the opportunity to move to a smaller town may not be available or desirable for you. Perhaps your problem with anxiety requires that you confront driving on freeways or dealing with traffic congestion. If so, my sympathies are with you and I hope you may benefit from some of the other strategies to follow.

Downsizing Your Living Situation

Presently, I'm living in a small condominium, a considerable downsizing from the house where I once lived. It's simply not possible for me to accumulate a large number of possessions because there's no room for them. While it was an adjustment at first, I find I'm quite comfortable in smaller quarters. It takes less than an hour to clean and is a whole lot less expensive to maintain.

Letting Go of Things You Don't Need

When I chose to move to a smaller home, I realized much of what I'd previously owned would have to go. Since I wanted to make a fresh start in my life, I decided to let go of almost everything, including about 95 percent of the furniture, clothes, and books I'd accumulated for three decades. I felt a tremendous sense of freedom and exhilaration in letting go of so many things that I didn't really use or need. In letting go of so much of what was associated with my past, I allowed myself a wide open space to recreate my life.

As a general rule, if you want to reduce clutter, I suggest you consider letting go of everything you haven't used in more than a year, except, of course, items that have sentimental value.

Doing What You Want for a Living

For many years I thought I needed to see twenty to twenty-five clients per week in order to support my lifestyle. The energy expenditure required for such a practice exceeded my personal resources (twenty-five clients equals at least fifty hours' work when you include case preparation, letter writing, telephone calls, insurance billing, and so on). I didn't leave myself enough time for rest and recreation, and, over time, I paid an increasing price. Besides, there was little time left to write, which is what I enjoyed doing most.

Now I've reduced my expenditures to the point where I only do eight to ten phone consultations per week out of my home and have plenty of time for rest, recreation, and writing. The difference in the way I feel—the sense of ease in my life—is enormous.

Doing what you truly want may require time, risk, and effort. It may take one to two years to gain the retraining or retooling you need to begin a new career. Then you may have to endure some time at an entry level before your new line of work meets your financial needs. In my estimation—and those of others who have done it—the time, effort, and disruption involved are worth it.

Reducing Your Commute

Reducing or eliminating your commute to work is one of the most significant changes you can make to simplify your life. It doesn't take much reflection to see the extent to which negotiating rush hour traffic on a daily basis can add to stress. Moving closer to where you work or choosing to live in a smaller town can help reduce your commute. At the very least, if you have to commute over a long distance, you can try to arrange for flexible hours (to avoid rush hour) or have a comfortable car with a tape deck. At this time, nearly 15 percent of Americans work out of their homes, and the number is rising. If you can figure out a consulting service or computer-based job you can do out of your home, you can join them.

Reducing Exposure to TV

How much time during the day do you spend in front of a screen? When I was a child there were three channels on the TV, and I had to get up out of my chair and walk over to the TV to switch from one to another. These days the average household has two to three TVs, each with an average of forty to sixty channels. As if this were not enough, sixty million American households have computers offering an endless array of child and adult games as well as Internet access to thousands of topics and virtually millions of Web sites. Granted, there are many good programs on TV, and the Internet is a wonderful tool for communicating information. My concern is with the sheer complexity of having so many options, all of which involve a passive stance of either witnessing entertainment or absorbing information. While life in front of the screen can be a distraction from anxiety, I wonder how it can contribute to rebuilding a deeper connection with nature, others, or oneself. If anxiety arises from too much stimulation and an experience of disconnection on multiple levels, then it seems to me that time in front of the screen might be done in moderation. Personally, I rarely watch TV and use the Internet in moderation. I prefer the simplicity of spending my time in nature, reading a good book, or developing my creative outlets in writing and music.

Living Close to Nature

Anxiety states are often associated with feelings of disembodiment. Being ungrounded and out of touch with your feelings and physical body is especially evident in the sensations of depersonalization that can accompany acute anxiety or panic. This disconnection can be aggravated in situations that involve being literally disconnected from the earth, such as riding in a car, being high up in a tall building, or flying. It may also be aggravated in situations where you are bombarded with so many stimuli that your awareness is scattered or dispersed, such as a grocery store, shopping mall, or social gathering.

Taking a walk in the woods or a park is a simple act that can help reverse the tendency to feel disembodied. Being in close proximity to the earth—its sights, sounds, smells, and energies—can help you to remain more easily connected with yourself. Choosing to live in such a setting, if possible, allows you to reestablish a connection with earth—something that much of modern civilization seems to have lost—on an ongoing basis.

Taming the Telephone

It surprises me to learn that there are people who feel they "should" answer the phone virtually every time it rings, regardless of the time of day or the mood they're in at the time. Whether it's a creditor, a sales solicitation, or a cantankerous relative, some people feel it is an almost sacred obligation to answer every call. For me personally, I have found that life is more simple, peaceful, and easy when I don't have to listen to the phone ring. If I'm in the middle of a meal, a writing project, or meditating, I don't have to worry who might be calling. I used to have an answering machine, but its clicking was only a small improvement over a phone. Now my voice mail faithfully collects all of my messages without my having to hear anything. Then I'm free to respond to them at my leisure. While some readers may feel that I'm not appropriately responsive to my callers, I would rather call them when I'm in the mood to offer them my full and best attention.

Delegating Menial Chores

How many menial chores would you delegate to someone else if money were not an issue? In my own situation, I've been able to simplify my life by delegating most house cleaning, typing, billing, and tax preparation, among other things. Even delegating one activity you don't like to do can make a difference in the sense of ease you bring to your day-to-day life. If money is an issue, is there something your children could learn to do just about as well as you? Can you allow other family members to help with the cooking, yard upkeep, or housecleaning?

Learning to Say "No"

Learning to say no was a major issue in my own case. For many years friends, family, and clients pretty much could rely on me to be available to them on demand, and I prided myself for being so consistently "helpful." The end result of many years of this codependent lifestyle was serious burnout and exhaustion. Presently I've learned to carefully evaluate each request I receive as to whether it's serving both my highest interest and the other person's highest interest to respond. Life has definitely been simpler and easier as I've learned to set limits that are consistent with my available energies and capabilities. I feel I can offer my best to others when I am not overextending myself to do so.

There are many other ways you might choose to simplify your life. For example, you can reduce the amount of junk mail you receive by writing to an organization called Stop The Mail at P.O. Box 9008, Farmingdale, NY 11735. Request that your name not be sold to mailing list companies, and you will likely reduce your junk mail by up to 75 percent. Or you can eliminate all of your credit cards except for one, as I did. Having one card comes in handy for making telephone purchases or renting a car.

Apart from that, you will save yourself a lot of monthly bills as well as annual fees by reducing your number of credit cards.

About one hundred other ways to simplify your life are clearly described in an excellent book entitled *Simplify Your Life* by Elaine St. James (1994). The author offers a wide range of life-simplification strategies in the areas of work, relationships, finances, health, household, and leisure time. If you're serious about making your lifestyle more simple and easy, this book is an invaluable remedy for the frenzied pace and high complexity of modern life.

Now it's your turn. Take some time to think about ways in which you might simplify your life. Use the following questionnaire to assist your deliberation.

Simplify Your Life Questionnaire

1. On a 1 to 10 scale, with "1" representing a high degree of simplicity and "10" representing a high degree of complexity, where would you rate your own lifestyle at present?

2. Have you made any changes in your living arrangements in the past year toward simplicity? If so, what changes?

3. What changes toward simplifying your life would you like to make in general?

4. What changes toward simplifying your life are you *willing* to make in the next year?

5. Check off any of the following simplification strategies you would be willing to try or initiate in the next two months:

   ____ Reduce the clutter in your home

   ____ Move to a smaller house

   ____ Move to a smaller town

____ Move close to shopping resources so you can do all of your errands quickly

____ Buy less clothing, with attention to what is functional, durable, and aesthetic—rather than fashionable

____ Drive a simple, fuel-efficient car

____ Reduce dependence on your TV

____ Reduce dependence on outside entertainment (movies, plays, theater, concerts, nightclubs, etc.)

____ Reduce (or eliminate) magazine subscriptions

____ Stop newspaper delivery

____ Stop junk mail

____ Stop answering the phone whenever it rings

____ Reduce your commute (if possible, walk or ride your bike to work)

____ Work where you live

____ Tell your family and friends you no longer do Christmas cards (or gifts, for that matter)

____ Take one suitcase if you vacation and only pack essential clothes

____ Take your vacation near or at home

____ Reduce your consumption to avoid luxury or designer items; favor products that are durable, easy to repair, and nonpolluting

____ Take steps to get out of debt

____ Keep only one credit card

____ Consolidate your bank accounts

____ Delegate busywork (e.g., yard work, house cleaning, tax preparation)

____ Simplify your eating habits to include whole, unprocessed foods

____ Buy groceries less often, in bulk

____ Make water your drink of choice

____ Pack your own lunch

____ Learn to say no

____ Stop trying to change people

____ Stop trying to please people—be yourself

____ Dispose of all personal possessions you don't really need

____ Do what you truly want for a living

Some of these changes can be done quickly; others involve a process. It may take a year or two, for example, to arrange your life so that you're doing something you truly enjoy for a living. To dispose of unnecessary possessions, put aside things you think you won't need for a year in a locked closet or storage compartment. At the end of the year, if you've not given them any thought throughout the entire time, let them go. Learning to say no or to stop always trying to please other people requires that you develop assertiveness skills, which you can acquire through classes, workshops, counseling, and books. Getting out of debt is a process that may be helped by consulting the book by Jerry Mundis, *How to Get Out of Debt, Stay Out of Debt, and Live Prosperously.*

I hope this chapter may have given you some ideas about how to reduce the complexity in your life. Living more simply has been important to my own personal well-being and may be important for you as well. Greater simplicity in your life will give you more time and ease to find peace of mind and appreciate the beauty of life. It will help you to make healing your problem with anxiety your first priority.

References and Further Reading

Elgin, Duane. 1993. *Voluntary Simplicity.* New York: William Morrow.

Mundis, Jerold. 1990. *How to Get Out of Debt, Stay Out of Debt, and Live Prosperously.* New York: Bantam Books.

St. James, Elaine. 1994. *Simplify Your Life.* New York: Hyperion.

3

Alternative Therapies

In recent years people suffering from anxiety have increasingly sought a variety of alternative therapies—approaches other than the two mainstream treatments offered by most professionals: cognitive-behavioral therapy and medication. The desire to explore alternative approaches reflects a general trend both in the mental health field as well as in medicine. Recent surveys have found that about 40 percent of the adult population in the United States seeks out the assistance of alternative health practitioners, often paying out of pocket, to address a variety of medical and health issues.

Reasons for the move to alternative therapies are varied. For people suffering from anxiety disorders, dissatisfaction with conventional treatments, particularly the side effects of prescription medications, often leads to an exploration of approaches such as herbs, acupuncture, yoga, or massage. There seems to be a desire to try natural approaches first before becoming dependent on medication. In addition, many people wish to take responsibility for their own recovery rather than relying on professionals who are often high priced, inadequately covered by managed care health plans, and sometimes not particularly empathic or understanding of their clients' needs. A large segment of the population seems to have decided that the time has come to take personal responsibility for their health and well-being, entrusting their doctors only with care in emergencies or severe illness.

How well do alternative therapies work? Are they effective in helping people to overcome anxiety disorders? Some alternative approaches—certain herbs and acupuncture, for example—appear to have direct, demonstrable effects on reducing anxiety symptoms or the depression that accompanies anxiety disorders in about 50 percent of cases. In my experience, however, such approaches are most helpful to persons whose anxiety and/or depression is in the *mild to moderate* range. "Mild to moderate" means your symptoms are a nuisance, probably an inconvenience, and may cause you a certain level of discomfort. However, they are not disabling. They don't prevent you from working, managing the routines of daily living, or maintaining relatively satisfying relationships with loved ones. And they do not cause you severe distress, a feeling of being frightened or overwhelmed, more than half of your waking hours. When anxiety (whether in the form of panic, phobias, or obsessive compulsive symptoms) interferes with your ability to function and causes you significant levels of distress, it may be said to fall in the *moderate to severe range*. Such anxiety may be helped by alternative approaches, but is best treated by a combination of well-administered cognitive-behavioral therapy and medication.

The primary value of alternative therapies is their ability to improve your *overall* level of health and well-being. Such approaches work to make you feel better *as a whole*, rather than relieving a specific problem such as panic attacks, obsessions or a fear of driving far from home. Their effect on anxiety symptoms is thus beneficial but *indirect*. Certainly if you feel better overall, you're less likely to be vulnerable to anxiety or depression symptoms. But you're also less likely to be bothered by *any other* stress-related symptoms, whether migraines, ulcers, low back pain, insomnia, or irritability. Wellness involves multiple levels of your total being. If you feel more healthy and well in general, you're not as likely to harbor the negative, fearful thoughts that instigate anxiety. You're also less likely to hold the bodily tension and breathing restriction that can aggravate anxiety. It's possible that even your brain neurotransmitters come into a better balance, improving your mood. In general, you feel more confident and content with yourself and your life. Alternative therapies work to help you feel better as a *whole person*. That's why they are often referred to as "holistic." As such, they can definitely have a beneficial effect on anxiety and depression—along with everything else.

This chapter offers a survey of alternative approaches that are currently popular with persons seeking help for anxiety (or depression) problems. These various approaches are divided into two sections:

1. *Herbs and Supplements*—These remedies help to restore and maintain your body's biochemical balance of neurotransmitters, hormones, enzymes, or nutrients. Certain herbs such as kava or valerian can directly reduce anxiety. Other supplements such as SAM-e, tryptophan, or DL-phenylalanine can help depression. Still others, particularly the B-vitamins and Vitamin C, improve your overall well-being by increasing your resilience to stress.

2. *Energy balance approaches*—These approaches, which include yoga, acupuncture, massage, and chiropractic improve well-being by releasing blocks to the flow of your body's vital energy or "life force." Such modalities also promote deep relaxation and increased mind-body integration.

There are many other approaches, often thought of as "alternative," which are not included in this chapter. Two of these, meditation and spirituality, are important enough to deserve separate chapters in their own right (see chapters 7 and 9). Physical exercise is also considered by some to be an "alternative therapy." However, it was a normal part of human life until replaced by the sedentary lifestyle that has affected and afflicted so many people in the last fifty years. The benefits of exercise for anxiety problems are discussed in detail in *The Anxiety & Phobia Workbook*.

There is no precise formula for determining which of the many alternative therapies might be helpful for you. In reading through this chapter, listen to your intuition in deciding which particular approaches you feel drawn to try. Some trial and error is probably inevitable in the process of exploring those methods that ultimately turn out to be most effective for your particular situation.

Herbs and Supplements

Herbs—plant-based medicines—have been an integral part of health care for thousands of years. In fact, about 25 percent of present-day prescription medications are still based on herbs. Pharmaceutical companies, however, are not very interested in herbs, because the plants from which they are derived cannot be patented and sold exclusively by any one company for profit.

Herbal treatments have been very popular in Europe and recently have gained increasing public interest in the United States. Most drug stores now offer an assortment of herbs that can treat conditions ranging from colds to poor memory.

Herbs tend to work more slowly and gently than prescription drugs. If you're used to the rapid and intense effects of a drug like Xanax, you need to be patient with the milder effect of a relaxing herb such as valerian or kava. The principal advantage of herbs is that they work naturally, in harmony with your body, rather than imposing a specific biochemical change, as in the case of drugs. Unlike medications, herbs generally have few or no side effects. Nor are they physically addictive, although you could become psychologically dependent on one that brings you consistent benefit.

Of the thousands of herbs available, this chapter examines a few that are relevant to people struggling with anxiety and/or depression. Those herbs that have a specific action on anxiety are discussed in the following section, "Relaxing Herbs," then several other herbs are described in the section "Other Helpful Herbs."

Apart from herbs, there are many other supplements that can be useful. The natural antidepressant SAM-e, for example, is for many people as effective as a prescription SSRI antidepressant, such as Prozac, yet it works within a few days (rather than weeks) with few or no side effects. People have used amino acids such as 5-hydroxy-tryptophan and DL-phenylalanine for many years to treat mild to moderate depression. After a ten-year absence, L-tryptophan has also become available again (by prescription) with potent effects in reducing both anxiety and insomnia. Glandular extracts and the hormone DHEA have helped many people with adrenal and other glandular weaknesses to feel more energy and aliveness. Finally, traditional vitamin supplements, particularly B-complex and vitamin C, can be very useful in supporting your nervous system and boosting your resilience to stress. Many of my clients have benefited from these supplements, and I hope you will try some of them for yourself.

Relaxing Herbs

Kava

Kava (or kava kava) is a natural tranquilizer that has become quite popular in the United States in recent years. Several clients of mine have testified that it's as potent a relaxer as Xanax. A member of the pepper tree family, kava is native to the South Pacific. Polynesians have used it for centuries in both ceremonial rituals and as a social relaxer. Small doses produce a sense of well-being, while large doses can produce lethargy, induce drowsiness, and reduce muscle tension.

In European countries such as Germany and Switzerland, kava has been approved for treatment of insomnia and anxiety. It appears that kava may tone down the activity of the limbic system, particularly the amygdala, which is a brain center associated with anxiety. Detailed neurophysiological effects of kava are not known at this time.

Kava's principal advantage over tranquilizers such as Xanax or Klonopin is that it's not addictive. It's also less likely to impair memory or aggravate depression in the way tranquilizers sometimes can. Research, mostly in Europe to date, indicates that it's an effective treatment for mild to moderate anxiety (not panic attacks), insomnia, headache and muscle tension, gastrointestinal spasm, and even urinary tract infections.

In buying kava, it is preferable to obtain a standardized extract with a specified percentage of *kavalactones*, the active ingredient. The percentage of kavalactones can vary from 30–70 percent. If you multiply the total number of milligrams of kava in each capsule or tablet by the percentage of kavalactones, you get the actual strength of the dose. For example, a 200 mg capsule with 70 percent kavalactones would actually be a 140 mg dose.

Most kava supplements at your health food store contain in the order of 50–70 mg kavalactones per capsule. Research in Europe has found that taking three or four doses of this strength daily may be as effective as a tranquilizer.

At present there is little hard data on the long-term effects of taking kava on a daily basis. In the Polynesian Islands, where residents use kava in high doses daily for long periods of time, skin discoloration sometimes occurs. Sometimes this progresses to scaling dermatitis, until the kava is discontinued. If you notice any of these effects, stop using kava immediately and do not resume without consulting a naturopath or informed physician. I would recommend at this time not to use kava on a *daily* basis for more than six months. On an intermittent basis, however, you can use it indefinitely.

In general, it's not a good idea to use kava in combination with tranquilizers such as Xanax or Klonopin. While not dangerous, such a combination can produce grogginess and even disorientation. Especially if you are taking a moderate to high dose of Xanax or Klonopin (more than 1.5 mg/day), refrain from using kava.

Kava should also not be taken if you have Parkinson's disease, or if you're pregnant or breast-feeding your baby. It should be used with caution before driving or operating machinery. For further information on kava, I recommend the book *Kava: Nature's Answer to Stress, Anxiety & Insomnia*, by Hyla Cass and Terrence McNally.

Valerian

Valerian is a herbal tranquilizer and sedative that is widely used in Europe. In recent years it has gained popularity in the United States. (Actually, this is a return of popularity, as it was in common use in the U.S. in the early part of the twentieth century.) Clinical studies, mostly in Europe, have found it to be as effective as tranquilizers in alleviating mild to moderate anxiety and insomnia. Yet it has fewer side effects and is nonaddictive. Valerian is also not as likely as prescription tranquilizers to impair memory and concentration or cause lethargy and drowsiness. (My personal impression is that valerian, while helpful, does not produce as strong a relaxing effect as tranquilizers such as Xanax and Klonopin.)

Valerian can be obtained at any health food store in three forms: capsules, liquid extract, or tea. In treating anxiety or insomnia, try each of these forms to see which you like best, following the instructions given on the bottle or package. Frequently you'll find valerian combined with other relaxing herbs such as passionflower, skullcap, hops, or chamomile. You may find these combinations to be more palatable and/or effective, so try them as well.

Valerian may take a week or so to reach its full effectiveness in treating anxiety or insomnia, so stay with it even if you don't get immediate results. As a general rule, I would not recommend using valerian on a *daily* basis for more than six months. You can use it two to three times per week, however, indefinitely.

Long experience in Europe indicates valerian is an especially safe herb. Still, there are occasional reports of "paradoxical" reactions of *increased* anxiety, restlessness, or heart palpitations, possibly due to allergy. Stop using valerian or any other herb if it causes such reactions.

St.-John's-wort

St.-John's-wort or *hypericum* has a long history of use. It was recommended by Hippocrates for anxiety more than two thousand years ago. Currently it is being used widely in Europe and the United States to treat symptoms of mild to moderate depression, as well as anxiety. In Germany it has outstripped even Prozac and accounts for over 50 percent of the antidepressant market. This fact alone testifies to its effectiveness.

Hypericum has a direct effect on relieving depression and appears to reduce anxiety as a secondary effect. European studies have found it to have antianxiety properties comparable to tranquilizers, although this finding has not yet been confirmed in the United States. Research has found evidence that hypericum enhances levels of all three neurotransmitters implicated in anxiety disorders: serotonin, norepinephrine, and dopamine. On this basis it might be seen as preferable to SSRI antidepressants, which only raise serotonin levels.

Hypericum, more commonly known as St.-John's-wort, is available in health food stores and many drug stores. Be sure to obtain brands that are standardized to contain 0.3 percent hypericin, the active ingredient. The standard dose is three 300 mg capsules per day.

When starting out, you may want to try two capsules per day to get used to the herb, then raise the dose to three capsules. If you find hypericum upsets your stomach, take each dose with a meal. In some studies, a double dose of 1800 mg/day has been found to be very effective, but I suggest you not exceed 900 mg/day except under the supervision of a qualified doctor.

It's important to keep in mind that hypericum takes four to six weeks to reach therapeutic effectiveness. If you're not seeing any benefit in the first two to three weeks, don't get discouraged and stop; you need to stick with it at least one month.

Hypericum has a very good safety record over the hundreds of years it has been used. For some persons, though, it can cause photosensitivity, an increased sensitivity to sunlight. If you are using hypericum and are in direct sunlight frequently, you may want to limit your exposure or use a sunscreen of SPF 30 or higher. Other side effects occasionally reported are stomach upset, dizziness, dry mouth, or mild allergic reactions. These reports are rare and, in general, side effects with hypericum are usually less than with SSRI and especially tricyclic antidepressants.

If you're already taking an SSRI or tricyclic antidepressant and want to switch to hypericum, it's best to wean off the prescription drug before starting the herb. In general, do not take an SSRI and hypericum together without your doctor's approval.

As far as I know, it is okay to take hypericum in conjunction with relaxing herbs such as kava or valerian. Also, I've not heard any problems with combining hypericum with tranquilizers such as Xanax and Klonopin. However, if you are taking an MAO-inhibitor antidepressant, such as Nardil or Parnate, do *not* take hypericum.

Hypericum is likely to be helpful if you are dealing with mild to moderate depression. It may also alleviate mild to moderate levels of anxiety after four to six weeks of use, although it is probably not effective in relieving panic attacks, obsessive compulsive disorder, or symptoms of post-traumatic stress disorder. If you are suffering from more severe anxiety symptoms, and have not obtained sufficient help from cognitive-behavioral therapy and other natural strategies, I recommend consulting with a qualified psychiatrist and considering a trial of an SSRI medication.

For further information on hypericum/St.-John's-wort, see the book *Hypericum & Depression*, by Harold Bloomfield.

Other Helpful Herbs

Passionflower

Passionflower is a good natural tranquilizer considered by many to be as effective as valerian. In higher doses it's often used to treat insomnia, as it relieves both nervous tension and relaxes muscles. It's available either in capsules or liquid extract at your health food store. Sometimes you'll find products that combine it with valerian or other relaxing herbs. Use it as directed on the bottle or package.

Gotu Kola

Gotu kola has been popular for thousands of years in India. It has a mildly relaxing effect and helps revitalize a weakened nervous system. It has also been found to help improve circulation, heighten memory function, and promote healing following childbirth. You can find it in most health food stores in capsules or extracts. I personally use gotu kola and find it to be beneficial.

Ginkgo Biloba

Derived from the ginkgo tree, ginkgo biloba can indirectly help reduce anxiety by improving concentration and mental clarity. It does this by increasing the flow of blood, oxygen, and nutrients to the brain. Studies have found that it can improve mental function in elderly people and also help tinnitus or "ringing in the ears." Available in 60 mg tablets, I recommend taking one to three 60 mg doses per day. If you're taking aspirin regularly, limit your use of ginkgo, since the combination can inhibit blood clotting.

Note: In using any of the herbs described above, be sure not to exceed the recommended dose. For further information on herbs, consult the books by Harold Bloomfield, Michael Tierra, or Earl Mindell in the bibliography or see a doctor (usually a holistic physician or naturopath) who is well-versed in the use of herbs.

SAM-e

Unlike the herbs just described, S-adenosyl-methionine (abbreviated SAM-e, pronounced "Sammy") is a substance that occurs naturally in the body. Widely popular in Europe for over a decade, it first became available in the U.S. in 1999. Extensive research done in Europe has found it to be equally effective in treating depression as prescription SSRI antidepressants. In Italy, in fact, it's more frequently prescribed for depression than Prozac. I have personally found SAM-e to be quite useful.

SAM-e appears to work by increasing serotonin and dopamine activity in the brain. While a healthy person manufactures enough of their own SAM-e, research has found that clinically depressed people are often deficient.

A major advantage of SAM-e is that it has almost no side effects. Since it naturally occurs in the body, adverse reactions are rare. Some people occasionally report nausea or queasiness when starting it, but this tends to go away after a few days. SAM-e also works very quickly. Unlike prescription antidepressants and St.-John's-wort, the benefits are usually felt within a few days of starting to take it.

In addition to helping with depression, SAM-e has been found useful in the treatment of osteoarthritis and fibromyalgia. It appears to restore and maintain healthy joint function by contributing to regeneration of cartilage. SAM-e also has potent antioxidant properties. It's used by the body to help synthesize glutathione, an important antioxidant involved in protecting cells from free-radical damage. Finally, it is beneficial to the liver and can assist in detoxifying the body from substances such as alcohol, drugs, and environmental toxins.

At the time of this writing, information on the use of SAM-e to treat anxiety is limited. Most available research has evaluated its effectiveness as an antidepressant. If it functions at all like the SSRIs, I would expect it to have antianxiety as well as antidepressant effects.

SAM-e is available in most health food stores and drugstores in 200 mg tablets. The recommended dose for depression is 800–1200 mg/day. Because it can cause nausea and GI disturbances for some people, start with 200 mg twice per day at first. After five days raise the dose to 200 mg four times per day. If you do not experience benefits after a week at this dose, you can raise the dose again to 1200 mg/day. If you're taking it primarily for arthritis or fibromyalgia, 800 mg/day is probably sufficient.

Persons with bipolar disorder (manic depression) should only take SAM-e under the supervision of a knowledgeable physician, as it can aggravate manic states.

For detailed information on SAM-e, see the book *Stop Depression Now* by Richard Brown, M.D.

Amino Acids

Amino acids are natural constituents of protein. For many years they have been used to treat both anxiety and mood disorders. Certain amino acids can have a similar effect as prescription antidepressants since they increase the amounts of particular neurotransmitters in the brain. While these amino acids may not be quite as potent as the prescription medications, they have the advantage of having fewer side effects. You may wish to talk to a qualified health care practitioner or see the book *The Way Up from Down* by Priscilla Slagle to expand on the information below.

Tryptophan

Tryptophan is a chemical precursor of serotonin. Taking supplemental tryptophan will increase serotonin levels in your brain, much as Prozac and other SSRI antidepressants do. However, tryptophan increases serotonin naturally by directly being converted into serotonin after it enters the brain. SSRI medications increase serotonin by blocking its reabsorption at nerve synapses. Tryptophan is available in two forms, 5-hydroxy tryptophan (5-HT) and L-tryptophan. Both forms help depression and anxiety by raising serotonin levels; however, L-tryptophan has a somewhat more sedative effect and works well as a sleep aid. L-tryptophan was recently reintroduced in the U.S. after a seven-year absence. A tainted batch of tryptophan caused a serious illness, eosinophilia myalgia, in 1989, and so the FDA banned it from over-the-counter sales. The L-tryptophan available today is safe and beneficial, although to my knowledge it is only available by prescription. As of this writing, 5-hydroxy tryptophan is available over the counter in health food stores. Consult your naturopathic or holistic physician if you wish to use tryptophan.

The recommended dose of L-tryptophan is 500–2,000 mg per day; 500 mg is effective as a mild relaxant, whereas 1,000–2,000 mg works as a sedative. For 5-HT, the recommended dose is 100–500 mg per day. The effect of tryptophan can be enhanced by taking it together with a carbohydrate snack, 50 mg vitamin B_6, and the amino acid taurine (500 mg). Avoid taking tryptophan with protein foods, as this causes other amino acids to compete with tryptophan to get into the brain.

Gamma Amino Butyric Acid

Gamma amino butyric acid (GABA) is actually a neurotransmitter that serves to reduce excessive nerve transmission in the brain. Supplemental GABA would be a potent tranquilizer except for the fact that only a very small percentage of what you take actually ever gets to the brain. Many people report they experience a mildly relaxing effect from doses of GABA in the 300–1,000 mg range. Various products containing GABA, alone or in combination with relaxing herbs, are available at your health food store. GABA is best taken on an empty stomach or in combination with a carbohydrate snack.

DL-Phenylalanine and Tyrosine

Used in the treatment of depression, DL-phenylalanine (DLPA) and tyrosine are chemical precursors of the neurotransmitter norepinephrine. Thus they work like tricyclic antidepressants such as imipramine (Tofranil), desipramine (Norpramin), or nortriptyline (Pamelor). They are less potent than prescription antidepressants but also have very few side effects. Doses range from 1,000–3,000 mg per day. Generally it is good to start with 500 mg and gradually increase the dose over a week. Try DLPA first and, if it has no effect, try tyrosine. Do not use DLPA or tyrosine if you are pregnant, have PKU (a disease requiring a phenylalanine-free diet), or are taking an MAO-inhibitor medication such as Nardil or Parnate. If you have high blood pressure, have a physician monitor your use of these amino acids. (See the book *The Way Up from Down*, by Priscilla Slagle, for more detailed information.)

Glandulars

Glandulars—concentrated forms of various animal glands—are frequently used to enhance the health of certain endocrine glands. For example, raw adrenal glandular extract is helpful in restoring optimal functioning of the adrenal glands, whose activity can be suppressed or exhausted in people who have been exposed to extreme or long-term stress. A number of my clients have found it to be useful. Symptoms of adrenal exhaustion include: 1) dizziness upon standing from a seated or prone position; 2) low stress-tolerance; 3) frequent fatigue or lethargy, 4) high allergic sensitivity, and/or 5) hypoglycemia. Other glandular supplements may be used to enhance the functioning of the thyroid, pituitary, thymus, or sex glands. I suggest you work with glandulars under the supervision of a nutritionally oriented physician or naturopath.

Hormones

Several types of hormones are now available at health food stores to supplement presumed deficiencies. Recently the two most popular entries to this category have been melatonin and dehydroepiandosterone (DHEA).

Melatonin is a hormone secreted at night by the pineal gland to signal the brain that it is time to go to sleep. Supplemental melatonin, in doses of 3 mg, have helped many people who have trouble getting to sleep. However, some persons report they get no benefit from melatonin and/or experience grogginess in the morning.

DHEA is a hormone manufactured by the adrenal cortex and is used in the synthesis of several other hormones in the body, including the sex hormones estrogen and testosterone. Many people report increased energy and sense of well-being, better ability to cope with stress, and improved mood and sleep after taking DHEA for a few weeks. I have personally found DHEA to be helpful. The standard recommended dose is 25 to 50 mg per day. Avoid taking higher doses, as some physicians believe that high doses can suppress the body's natural ability to make DHEA.

Vitamins

Vitamins play a critical role in regulating the thousands of metabolic reactions that occur every moment in your body. There has been controversy over the past two decades, however, regarding the need for taking vitamin supplements in addition to the vitamins naturally obtained in food. Even among nutritionists who generally advocate supplements, there is disagreement over what constitutes appropriate doses. The position offered here reflects both my personal experience as well as the experience of many of my clients.

Fifty years ago, the U.S. Food and Nutrition Board set up the RDA—the "recommended daily allowance"—as the standard amount of a vitamin needed by a healthy person. The amounts decided upon were the *minimum* amount of a vitamin needed to ward off diseases such as beriberi, rickets, scurvy, and night blindness. RDAs do not specify *optimal* amounts of vitamins needed to enhance and maximize health. Yet many physicians to this day argue that if you take a multivitamin at all, all you need is one containing the RDAs of vitamins A, B-complex, C, and E.

Such a recommendation underestimates the average person's supplementation need for several reasons. First, the standard diet eaten by a majority of persons in American society consists of large amounts of processed foods that are deficient or devoid of vitamins. Few persons eat the nutrient-rich, farm-fresh foods that our great grandparents enjoyed. Second, even those who are able to eat fresh whole grains, fruits, and vegetables may not get sufficient amounts of minerals. This is due to the widespread depletion of minerals in soils across the country that have been farmed for many decades. Third, the average person in modern society faces numerous special circumstances where the body's normal store of certain vitamins is rapidly depleted. If you're under stress, for example, you will rapidly deplete B vitamins, vitamin C, and calcium-magnesium. Smoking and drinking deplete certain B vitamins. Living in a polluted area will increase your need for antioxidant vitamins such as vitamin C, vitamin E, and selenium. Special conditions such as pregnancy, old age, or chronic degenerative diseases (such as arteriosclerosis, arthritis, or osteoporosis) can be benefited by high doses of certain vitamins.

For these reasons in particular, I recommend that you consider taking higher doses of supplements than provided by the RDAs. Some nutritionists have relabeled such doses ODAs—or "optimal daily allowance."

The following regimen of vitamin supplements is recommended for all anxiety disorders as well as any condition or illness accompanied by high stress.

1. Vitamin B-complex: 50 mg one or two times per day. B vitamins are necessary to maintain proper functioning of the nervous system. Taking all eleven of the B vitamins in a B-Complex at the suggested dose will increase your resiliency to stress.

2. Vitamin C (preferably with bioflavonoids): 2,000–4,000 mg per day. Vitamin C is well known for its ability to strengthen the immune system and promote healing from infection, disease, and injury. It is also important for the adrenal glands, whose proper functioning is necessary for your ability to cope with stress.

3. Calcium and magnesium in combination: 1,000–1,500 mg calcium to 500–1,000 mg magnesium (preferably chelated forms) per day. Calcium is involved in the process of nerve transmission. Its depletion can cause nerve cell overactivity, which may be one of the underlying causes of anxiety. Magnesium also plays an important role in nerve and muscle activity. Supplements with magnesium can help depression, dizziness, heart arrhythmias, muscle weakness, and PMS. Both calcium and magnesium work as natural tranquiliz-

ers when taken in the doses suggested above. It is good to take them together, as they work in tandem and balance each other.

4. Zinc: 30 mg per day. Zinc can have a calming effect on the nervous system. It also contributes to maintaining a healthy immune and reproductive system.

5. Chromium: 200 mcg per day. Chromium is necessary for proper utilization of blood glucose. It is especially important in stabilizing blood sugar levels in hypoglycemia.

6. Iron: take the dose recommended by your doctor if you have an iron deficiency. Occasionally iron deficiency is found to be an important contributing cause to panic attacks.

In taking vitamin supplements, please observe the following guidelines:

- Always take vitamins with meals. Digestive enzymes secreted in response to food will help digest vitamins.

- Taking B-complex or vitamin C in two or three doses throughout the day is preferable to a single large dose. The body can absorb only so much of a vitamin at a given time; it excretes what it doesn't use.

- Vitamins in capsule form are preferable to tablets, since they are easier to digest.

- Supplements obtained at health food stores are less likely to contain inferior quality fillers or binders, which can cause indigestion or allergic responses in some people.

Energy Balance Approaches

The idea of energy balance has its basis in the medical systems that have been utilized in the Far East for thousands of years. All of these systems assume that there is a subtle (nonphysical) energy that permeates and circulates throughout the body. Traditional Chinese medicine calls this "chi," eastern Indian medicine (ayurveda) calls it "prana," and Japanese healing traditions refer to it as "ki." The terms that best describe this energy in English would be "life force" or "vital energy." The difference in energy that you feel when you have the flu versus when you are healthy is an example of fluctuations in this type of energy.

In Chinese medicine, subtle energy is understood to be distributed throughout the body along channels called "meridians." In the Indian tradition these invisible channels—and the centers where the energy is concentrated—are called "nadi" and "chakras."

One of the most important functions of all of the energy-balance approaches is to harmonize and optimize the "flow" of subtle energy by releasing blocks to that flow. Blocked energy leads to tension, stress, and ultimately illness. In fact, Chinese and

Eastern Indian medicine trace all disease back to various types and degrees of blockage in the flow of vital energy. Regular practice of energy balance disciplines such as yoga or t'ai chi helps to release blocks to the natural flow of vitality. So does receiving treatments from healing arts that free up obstructions to subtle energy. This is particularly true for acupuncture, but also applies to various forms of massage and chiropractic treatment.

The invisible "energy body" (sometimes called "subtle body") that is the focus of Eastern medicine is, as you might expect, intimately related to the physical body. (It's thought to provide an energetic matrix or "template" for the physical body.) On a strictly physical level, energy balance practices help to relieve muscle tension, promote increased oxygenation of tissues and the brain, improve arterial circulation, promote elimination by the kidneys and colon, and stimulate increased production of hormones and neurotransmitters.

However, the fundamental purpose of the energy balance approaches is to promote mind-body integration–a harmonious interdependence and balance among the spiritual, mental, emotional, and physical aspects of your total being. "Wholeness" is equated with wellness. To the extent you function in an integrated, whole manner, you can experience the fullness of your being and genuine health. To the extent that you are out of touch with the wholeness of your being, you remain out of harmony with yourself and are subject to stress and "dis-ease," including anxiety.

Each of the modalities described below provides a pathway back to wholeness and integration. Any one of them can help promote inner peace and freedom from fear, as well as better health and well-being in general.

Yoga

The word yoga means to "yoke" or "unify." By definition, yoga is involved with promoting unity of mind, body, and spirit.

Although in the West yoga is usually thought of as a series of stretch exercises, it actually embraces a broad philosophy of life and an elaborate system for personal transformation. This system includes ethical precepts, a vegetarian diet, the familiar stretches or postures, specific practices for directing and controlling the breath, concentration practices, and deep meditation. It was originally laid out by the philosopher Pantanjali in the second century B.C. and is still practiced throughout the world today.

Yoga postures, by themselves, provide a very effective means to increase fitness, flexibility, and relaxation. They can be practiced alone or with a group. Many people, myself included, find that yoga simultaneously increases energy and vitality while calming the mind. Yoga may be compared to the cognitive-behavioral techniques of progressive muscle relaxation (PMR), in that it involves holding the body in certain flexed positions for a few moments and then relaxing. Both yoga and PMR lead to relaxation. However, I personally find yoga to be more effective than PMR in freeing up blocked energy. It seems to get energy moving up and down the spine and throughout the body in a way that doesn't happen as readily with PMR. Like vigorous exercise, yoga directly promotes mind-body integration. However, in many ways it is more specific. Each yoga posture reflects a mental attitude, whether that attitude is one of surrender, as in certain forward-bending poses, or of strengthening the will, as in a backward-bending pose. By emphasizing certain yoga postures and movements, you may be able to cultivate certain positive qualities or move through other negative, restrictive personality patterns. There is an entire school of "yoga therapy" that uses yoga as a methodology for addressing and working through personality issues.

If you are interested in learning yoga, the best place to start is with a class at a local health club or community college. If such classes are unavailable in your area, try working with a yoga video at home. The popular magazine *Yoga Journal* offers many excellent yoga videos. To supplement your practice you may want to look at books such as *Yoga for Health* by Richard Hittleman or *Light on Yoga* by B. Iyengar.

T'ai Chi

T'ai chi is an ancient form of movement and exercise intended to unite body and mind. It is said to have originated when a thirteenth-century Taoist monk in China watched a serpent and a crane in battle. As the crane attacked the snake, the snake would smoothly move its position, never allowing the crane to touch it. From this scene the monk developed thirteen moves which have been augmented down through the centuries. Presently, t'ai chi is practiced by millions of people in China and is popular throughout the rest of the world.

T'ai chi can best be described as a form of moving meditation. It consists of a series of movements that proceed slowly and gracefully, flowing one into another. These movements strengthen and ground the body while promoting the flow of "chi" or life force. Students of t'ai chi say that it teaches qualities of fluidity and grace—qualities that can extend to the way you live your entire life. Because the movements are done slowly, t'ai chi also teaches you how to slow down, both in your body and your mind. Like meditation, it helps you to achieve serenity, clarity, and concentration. Unlike meditation, however, it instills an ability to carry poise and concentration into movement.

Like yoga, t'ai chi helps you to work through blocks to the flow of your life energy, along with promoting physical benefits such as opening the joints (especially the knees), strengthening the spine and lower back, and massaging the internal organs. Because it's practiced with your entire body and with full presence of mind, t'ai chi is a very practical and effective way to foster mind-body integration.

You can find t'ai chi classes offered at some health clubs as well as some martial arts schools (though t'ai chi is generally not used as a form of self-defense). If classes are not available in your area, there are several excellent videos that teach the basic movements. Because it promotes the flow of "chi," t'ai chi is sometimes prescribed as an adjunct to acupuncture treatments.

Acupuncture

Acupuncture originated as a healing modality in China about three thousand years ago. Currently it's practiced in most advanced countries throughout the world. As with t'ai chi, it's based on the assumption that health is determined by the free and proper flow of *chi*, the vital or subtle energy that pervades all living things. Chi flows along channels in the body called meridians, each of which is linked to a specific organ. When the flow of energy is neither restricted nor excessive, the individual enjoys good health. If the energy flow is unbalanced in either direction, both physical and mental symptoms of distress or disease may result. For example, fear is understood to be due to blocked or excessive energy flow along the kidney meridian. Acupuncture treatments that aim to balance the kidney meridian (and other supporting meridians) can help to relieve fearfulness.

In an acupuncture treatment, the acupuncturist inserts thin needles at specific points in the body. Most people (myself included) feel only a slight prick or no pain at all from the procedure. Typically the needles are left in place for twenty to thirty minutes, after which it's common to feel very relaxed and rejuvenated. Repeated treatments (twice a week for a few weeks) are often needed to correct an ailment such as migraine headaches, allergies, or back pain. If you wish to utilize acupuncture to help anxiety, regular treatments on a weekly or biweekly basis for several months are advised. Often the acupuncturist will provide herbs in the form of teas or capsules to use at home to enhance the effects of the treatments. A few of my clients report that they have especially benefited from the use of Chinese herbs and continued to rely on them after finishing the acupuncture treatments.

For people who are uncomfortable with the use of needles, acupressure may be a viable alternative. Acupressure (and its cousin, Shiatsu) rely on the same principles as acupuncture; however, energy flow and balance along the meridians is promoted by manual pressure rather than needles. Acupressure is a simple and inexpensive form of energy balance practiced by many massage therapists. You can, in fact, utilize acupressure on your own. A number of self-acupressure books provide instructions for utilizing acupressure yourself.

Chiropractic

Most people think of chiropractic as a healing art that aims to relieve back pain induced by stress or injury. At a more basic level, though, chiropractic strives to promote health by optimizing the flow of nerve impulses up and down the spine and to other parts of the body. Because of the various stresses to which the spine is subject, individual vertebrae can move out of alignment. These misaligned vertebrae block the flow of nerve impulses between the brain and body, as well as between the spinal cord and various bodily organs. When nerve transmission to a specific organ is reduced or limited, that organ is likely to dysfunction, producing symptoms ranging from mild discomfort to illness. Misalignments of the spine may be caused by injury, but most frequently they are caused by stress. Muscles tightened under chronic stress tend to pull the vertebrae out of alignment. Even if the muscle tension is relieved through exercise or massage, the spinal vertebrae may not easily resume their normal configuration. Thus a chiropractor seeks to identify and correct vertebral misalignments in order to promote optimal nervous system function and thereby functional integrity of the body as a whole.

Chiropractic can be a helpful strategy for relieving chronic tension, whether or not accompanied by pain. An occasional visit to a chiropractor is likely to improve your overall experience of well-being. In locating a qualified chiropractor in your area, try to get a referral from a friend or relative. If you prefer not to receive direct manipulations to the spine, there are some chiropractors who practice a nonmanipulative form of adjustment sometimes referred to as "gentle chiropractic."

Massage

Therapeutic massage is a healing art designed to promote deep relaxation through skillful manipulation of muscles and soft body tissues. Professional massage therapists usually obtain 500–1,000 hours of formal training in anatomy, physiology, and various forms of bodywork including Swedish massage, deep tissue work, reflexology, acupressure, and Shiatsu.

Receiving a one-hour massage every week—or even twice per month—can promote deep relaxation by relieving chronic muscle tension that you may have been holding in your body for a long time. Massage can enhance and deepen the benefits you obtain from practicing progressive muscle relaxation (PMR). PMR tends to release acute, superficial tension in the outer muscles of your arms, legs, neck, and torso. Massage, particularly "deep tissue" massage, can undo chronic, long-standing tension held in the deeper muscles of the body. In addition to releasing muscle tension, massage can help cleanse your body of toxic accumulations by promoting lymphatic circulation and mobilizing a sluggish colon.

On a more psychological level, receiving a massage is a wonderful way to nurture yourself if you feel stressed. Massage can also provide a corrective emotional experience for survivors of abuse. If you grew up in a dysfunctional family where you either weren't touched or were touched inappropriately, massage can help you work through any painful feelings or resistance around being touched, increasing your ease with what is an innate need for all human beings.

There are several types of massage to choose from. Swedish massage, developed by Peter Ling in the 1800s, uses kneading, stroking, and shaking to induce the body to relax. This is the most common type of massage practiced. Deep tissue massage involves greater pressure on deeper muscles than Swedish massage and generally focuses on specific problem areas. Neuromuscular massage is a form of deep tissue massage that works with specific "trigger points" to release chronically tight muscles. Acupressure, while certainly relaxing, intentionally seeks to promote enhanced energy balance. Through firm pressure applied to specific points for three to ten seconds each, acupressure strives to release blocks to the flow of subtle energy through the acupuncture meridians.

If you'd like to read more about massage, I recommend *The Massage Book* by George Downing (1998).

The purpose of this chapter has been to offer a variety of alternative approaches for relieving anxiety that you're unlikely to find in most other books in the anxiety disorders field. Even though the chapter uses the word "alternative," none of these approaches is intended to *replace* cognitive-behavioral therapy. Cognitive-behavioral therapy is described at the beginning of chapter 1 and is very likely to help you no matter what type of anxiety difficulty you face. Some of the approaches in this chapter, such as certain herbs or acupuncture, for example, may be a suitable alternative to prescription medications if your anxiety symptoms are in the *mild to moderate* range of severity (inconvenient but not disabling). If you feel your anxiety problem is *severe*, however, I recommend you discuss the possibility of taking medication—in addition to obtaining cognitive-behavioral therapy—with a qualified psychiatrist or physician. As a general rule, do not combine relaxing herbs such as kava with prescription tranquilizers such as Xanax or Klonopin, and do not combine antidepressant supplements, such as SAM-e, St.-John's-wort, or 5-HT with prescription antidepressants (except under the supervision of a knowledgeable physician).

Any of the other modalities mentioned in this chapter, particularly energy balance approaches, combine well with any medication regime you might be taking. Please feel free to try them out whether your problem is mild or severe. Ultimately there is no conflict between so-called holistic or alternative approaches and traditional approaches such as the use of prescription medications. The real question to ask is, *What is the most compassionate thing you can do for yourself?* What works best for you to give you the most satisfying, fulfilling quality of life? Through a willingness to experiment with a number of approaches, and by trusting your own best intuition, you will arrive at the "right" combination of conventional and alternative approaches in your own case.

Record of Alternative Approaches Tried

Approach	Action Taken	Frequency per Week	Outcome (Results)
Herbs/Supplements 1. 2.			
Massage			
Yoga			
T'ai Chi			
Acupuncture			
Chiropractic			

1. Of the approaches you tried, which did you find most helpful?

2. Which of these approaches (if any) would you be willing to include in your life on a long-term basis?

What You Can Do Now

1. Having read through the chapter, you may have begun to get a sense about which alternative therapies you would like to try. I would recommend focusing on only one or two interventions at first—such as one herb and an energy balance approach, for example—so that you don't spread yourself too thin and can fully evaluate the effects of what you try. Use the worksheet on p. 46 to monitor the approaches you try and their outcome.

Herbs and Supplements

2. You may want to experiment with relaxing herbs such as kava, valerian, or passionflower to help relieve mild to moderate levels of anxiety. These herbs are available at most health food stores and drug stores. Be willing to try various forms (teas, capsules, tinctures) to see which you prefer. Avoid combining these herbs with benzodiazepine tranquilizers such as Xanax or Klonopin.
3. If mild to moderate depression is an issue, you may want to try SAM-e, St.-John's-wort, or 5-hydroxy-tryptophan to boost your serotonin level. It's best to try one of these supplements at a time so you can fully evaluate its effectiveness. St.-John's-wort *can* be combined with either SAM-e or 5-HT, however do not combine these supplements with an SSRI medication without consulting a knowledgeable physician.
4. Try the supplements recommended for anxiety and stress, especially B-complex, vitamin C, and calcium-magnesium, and evaluate how you feel.
5. You may want to explore whether amino acids can be helpful, specifically, GABA for anxiety and 5-hydroxy tryptophan, tyrosine, or DL-phenylalanine for depression. Consult the book by Priscilla Slagle (listed at the end of this chapter) or a physician experienced in the use of amino acid therapy for further information.
6. Consult with a holistic physician, naturopath, or qualified nutritionist before using glandulars or hormones (such as DHEA) on your own.

Energy Balance Approaches

7. Reread the section "Energy Balance Approaches." If you decide you'd like to learn yoga or t'ai chi, look for a class in your local area (often available through health clubs). If there are no classes, purchase an instructional video. (Good videos for yoga or t'ai chi can be found in the magazine *Yoga Journal*, available at 1-800-600-YOGA.)
8. If you would like to explore acupuncture, acupressure, therapeutic massage, or chiropractic, ask family or friends to recommend a qualified practitioner. If you need to go through the phone directory, ask practitioners you contact

about their education, training, and how many years they've been in practice. Only work with someone with whom you feel a good rapport. Massage and acupuncture are best done on a weekly basis at first.

9. For a comprehensive, encyclopedic resource covering over forty different alternative therapies, see the book *Alternative Medicine*, compiled by the Burton Goldberg Group, published by Future Medicine Publishing, Inc.

References and Further Reading

Herbs and Supplements

Bloomfield, Harold H., Mikael Nordfors, and Peter McWilliams. 1996. *Hypericum & Depression*. Santa Monica, Calif.: Prelude Press. (A good reference on St.-John's-wort.)

Bloomfield, Harold. 1998. *Healing Anxiety with Herbs*. New York: HarperCollins.

Brown, Richard. 1999. *Stop Depression Now: SAM-e*. New York: Putnam.

Cass, Hyla, and Terrence McNally. 1998. *Kava: Nature's Answer to Stress, Anxiety, & Insomnia*. Rocklin, Calif.: Prima Health.

Ley, Beth M. 1996. *DHEA: Unlocking the Secrets to the Fountain of Youth*. Newport Beach: BML Publications.

Mindell, Earl. 1979. *Vitamin Bible*. New York: Warner Books.

Murray, Michael. 1996. *Natural Alternatives to Prozac*. New York: William Morrow.

Sahelian, Ray. 1995. *Melatonin—Nature's Sleeping Pill*. Marina Del Rey, Calif.: Be Happier Press.

Slagle, Priscilla. 1987. *The Way Up from Down*. New York: Random House.

Energy Balance Approaches

Downing, George. 1998. *The Massage Book*. New York: Random House.

Hittleman, Richard. 1983. *Richard Hittleman's Yoga 28-Day Exercise Plan*. New York: Workman Publishing Co.

Hittleman, Richard. 1985. *Yoga for Health*. New York: Ballantine.

Iyengar, B. K. 1995. *Light on Yoga*. New York: Schocken Books.

McFarland, Stewart, and Mew Mong Tan. 1997. *Complete Book of T'ai Chi*. DK Publishing.

Mumford, Susan. 1995. *The Complete Guide to Massage*. New York: Plume/Penguin Books.

Pierce, Margaret, and Martin Pierce. 1996. *Yoga for Life*. Portland, Oregon: Rudra Press.

Yoshiro, Manaka, and Ian Urquhart. 1995. *The Layman's Guide to Acupuncture*. New York: Weatherhill.

4

Diet

Over the past twenty years the relationship between diet and mood has been well established. It's known that certain foods and substances tend to create additional stress and anxiety, while others promote a calmer and steadier mood. Certain natural substances have a directly calming effect, while others are known to have an antidepressant effect. You may not yet recognize connections between how you feel and what you eat. You may simply not notice that the amount of coffee or cola beverages you drink aggravates your anxiety level. You may be unaware that your anxiety and depression are aggravated by eating insufficient amounts of protein. Or you may be unaware of any connection between your consumption of white sugar and anxiety, depression, or premenstrual symptoms. I hope this chapter will clarify some of these connections and help you to make positive changes in the way you feel.

Your body depends on both an optimal quantity as well as quality of food. As for quantity, you need to balance the number of calories you consume with your level of energy expenditure. Sixty percent of adults in the United States are overweight due to a high caloric diet combined with a sedentary lifestyle. Most weight problems are resolved not by "fad diets" but simply by eating healthy foods in combination with sufficient exercise.

Just as important as quantity is the quality of what you eat. Taking care of your body means being willing to eat whole foods that are free of toxic, artificial substances. Your body also needs food that has sufficient energy to sustain its inner vitality rather than deplete it. The nutrient content of food is important, but so is its inherent "life force." Fresh raw vegetables and fruits are more compatible with health than their cooked, frozen, or canned counterparts: you will derive more energy from an apple than a bag of buttered popcorn. Finally, taking care of yourself means eating food of sufficient variety to meet the full range of your body's needs. This includes complex carbohydrates such as vegetables and whole grains; fats such as oils and nuts; and proteins such as poultry, fish, or soy products.

Guidelines for Improving Your Diet

The following is a series of guidelines for upgrading your diet. My suggestion is that you familiarize yourself with all of the guidelines but do not try to implement them all at once. Most people find it's easier to modify their diets gradually, making one or two basic changes at a time. (It took me about ten years to adopt all of the changes suggested below.)

As you read through these guidelines, be aware that the first three are most directly relevant to reducing your susceptibility to anxiety. The remaining guidelines are important, though, in enhancing your overall health and sense of well-being.

Minimize or Eliminate Caffeine

Of all the dietary factors that can aggravate anxiety and trigger panic attacks, caffeine is the most notorious. Several of my clients can trace their first panic attack to an excessive intake of caffeine. Many people find that they feel calmer and sleep better after they've reduced their caffeine consumption. Caffeine has a directly stimulating effect on several different systems in your body. It increases the level of the neurotransmitter norepinephrine in your brain, causing you to feel alert and awake. It also produces the very same physiological arousal response that is triggered when you are subjected to stress-induced sympathetic nervous system activity and a release of adrenaline.

Too much caffeine can keep you in a chronically tense, aroused condition, leaving you more vulnerable to generalized anxiety as well as panic attacks. Caffeine further contributes to stress by causing a depletion of vitamin B_1 (thiamine), which is one of the so-called antistress vitamins.

Caffeine is contained not only in coffee but in many types of tea, cola beverages, chocolate candy, cocoa, and over-the-counter drugs.

If you are prone either to generalized anxiety or panic attacks, I suggest that you reduce your total caffeine consumption to *less than 50 mg per day*. For example, one cup of percolated coffee or one diet cola beverage a day would be a maximum. For coffee lovers this may seem like a major sacrifice, but you may be surprised to find how much better you feel if you can wean yourself down to a single cup in the morning. The sacrifice may well be worth having fewer panic attacks or other anxiety symptoms. For those people who are very sensitive to caffeine, I would recommend eliminating it altogether.

Please note that there are tremendous individual differences in sensitivity to caffeine. As with any addictive drug, chronic caffeine consumption leads to increased tolerance and a potential for withdrawal symptoms. If you have been drinking five cups of coffee a day and abruptly cut down to one a day, you may have withdrawal reactions including fatigue, depression, and headaches. It's better to taper off gradually over a period of a month or two. Some people like to substitute decaffeinated coffee, which has about 4 mg of caffeine per cup, while others substitute herbal teas. At the opposite extreme of the sensitivity continuum are people who are made jittery by a single cola or cup of tea. Some of my clients have found that even small amounts of caffeine predispose them to panic or a sleepless night. It's important that you experiment to find out what *your own optimal* daily caffeine intake might be. For most people prone to anxiety or panic, this turns out to be less that 50 mg/day. Please refer to the *Caffeine Chart* that follows to determine your own level of caffeine intake.

In his book *Natural Health, Natural Medicine*, Andrew Weil, a well-known, holistic physician, recommends avoiding caffeine if you have any of the following: panic/anxiety, insomnia, migraine, cardiac arrhythmia, hypertension, gastrointestinal disorders, premenstrual syndrome, tension headaches, prostate trouble, or urinary disorder.

In addition to eliminating caffeine, it's important to eliminate stimulants that mimic the effects of caffeine. Ephedrine and pseudoephedrine, found in many over-the-counter cold remedies, can aggravate anxiety in sensitive persons.

Caffeine Chart

Caffeine content of coffee, tea, and cocoa (milligrams per 6-ounce cup)

Coffee, instant	60–70 mg
Coffee, percolated	90–110 mg
Coffee, drip	120–150 mg
Tea bag—five minute brew	50-60 mg
Tea bag—one minute brew	30–40 mg
Loose tea—five minute brew	40–50 mg
Cocoa	10–20 mg
Chocolate (dry, 1 oz)	5–10 mg
Decaffeinated Coffee	3–10 mg

Caffeine content of cola beverages (milligrams per 12-ounce can)

Coca-Cola	65 mg
Pepsi-Cola	43 mg
Dr Pepper	61 mg
Mountain Dew	50 mg

(Note: This table does not include caffeine present in over-the-counter medications such as NoDoz, Dexatrim, Anacin, Excedrin, or Midol.)

Reduce or Eliminate All Forms of Sugar

Our bodies are not equipped to process large amounts of sugar and, in fact, it was not until the twentieth century that most of us (other than the very wealthy) consumed large amounts of refined sugar. Today, the standard American diet includes white sugar in most beverages (coffee, tea, cola), sugar in cereal, sugar in salad dressings, sugar in processed meat, along with one or two desserts per day and perhaps a donut or a cookie on coffee breaks. This sugar may be disguised under a variety of names, including dextrose, sucrose, maltose, raw sugar, brown sugar, corn syrup, corn sweeteners, and high fructose. The average American consumes about *120 pounds* of sugar per year! The result of continually bombarding the body with this much sugar is the creation of a chronic disregulation in sugar metabolism. For some people this disregulation can lead to excessively high levels of blood sugar, or diabetes (whose prevalence has increased dramatically in this century). For an even larger number of individuals, the problem is just the opposite—periodic drops in blood sugar level *below* normal, a condition known as *hypoglycemia.*

The symptoms of hypoglycemia tend to appear when your blood sugar drops below 50–60 milligrams per milliliter—or when it drops very rapidly from a higher to a lower level. Typically this occurs about two to three hours after eating a meal. It can also occur *simply in response to stress,* since your body burns up sugar very rapidly under stress. The most common subjective symptoms of hypoglycemia are:

- Light-headedness
- Anxiety
- Trembling
- Feelings of unsteadiness or weakness
- Irritability
- Heart palpitations

These symptoms probably look familiar. All of them are symptoms that *can* accompany a panic attack. In fact, *for some people panic reactions may actually be caused by hypoglycemia.* Generally such people recover from panic simply by having something to eat. Their blood sugar rises and they feel better. (In fact, an informal, nonclinical way to diagnose hypoglycemia is to determine whether you have any of the above symptoms three or four hours after a meal, and whether they then go away as soon as you have something to eat.)

The majority of people with panic disorder or agoraphobia find that their panic reactions do *not* necessarily correlate with bouts of low blood sugar. Yet hypoglycemia can *aggravate* both generalized anxiety and panic attacks that have been caused for other reasons.

Hypoglycemia can be formally diagnosed through a clinical test called the "six-hour glucose tolerance test." After a twelve-hour fast you drink a highly concentrated sugar solution. Your blood sugar is then measured at half-hour intervals over a six-hour period. You will likely get a positive result on this test if you have a moderate to severe problem with hypoglycemia. Unfortunately, many *milder* cases of hypoglycemia are missed by the test. It's quite possible to have subjective symptoms of low blood sugar and test negative on a glucose tolerance test. Any of the following subjective symptoms are suggestive of hypoglycemia:

- You feel anxious, light-headed, weak, or irritable three or four hours after a meal (or in the middle of the night); these symptoms disappear within a few minutes of eating.

- You get a "high" feeling from consuming sugar and this changes to a depressed, irritable, or "spacey" feeling twenty to thirty minutes later.

- You experience anxiety, restlessness, or even palpitations and panic in the early morning hours, between 4:00 A.M. and 7:00 A.M. (Your blood sugar is lowest in the early morning because you have fasted all night.)

How do you deal with hypoglycemia? Fortunately, it's quite possible to overcome problems with low blood sugar by making several important dietary changes and taking certain supplements. If you suspect that you have hypoglycemia or have had it formally diagnosed, you may want to implement the following guidelines:

- Eliminate (as much as possible) all types of simple sugar from your diet. This includes foods that obviously contain white sugar or sucrose such as candy, ice cream, desserts, and soft drinks. It also includes subtler forms of sugar, such as honey, brown sugar, corn syrup, corn sweeteners, molasses, maltose, dextrose, and "high fructose." Be sure to read labels on any and all processed foods to detect these various forms of sugar.

- Substitute fruits (other than dried fruits, which are too concentrated in sugar) for sweets. Avoid fruit juices or dilute them 1:1 with water.

- Reduce or eliminate simple starches such as pasta, refined cereals, potato or corn chips, and white bread. Substitute instead "complex" carbohydrates such as whole grain breads and cereals, vegetables, and brown rice or other whole grains.

- Have a complex carbohydrate and protein snack (such as cheese and crackers or whole grain toast and tuna, for example) halfway between meals—around 10:30–11:00 A.M. and especially around 4:00–5:00 P.M. If you awaken early in the morning, you may also find that a small snack will help you to get back to sleep for a couple of hours. As an alternative to snacks between meals, you can try having four or five small meals per day no more than two or three hours apart. The point of either of these alternatives is to maintain a steadier blood sugar level.

- Take a vitamin B-complex: 25–50 mg of all eleven B vitamins once per day with meals (under stress, take two per day).
- Take vitamin C: 1,000 mg twice per day with meals.
- Organic trivalent chromium (often called "glucose tolerance factor"): 200 mcg per day. This is available at your local health-food store.

Vitamin B-complex as well as vitamin C help to increase your resiliency to stress, which can aggravate blood sugar swings. The B vitamins also help regulate the metabolic processes that convert carbohydrates to sugar in your body.

Trivalent chromium has a direct, stabilizing effect on your blood sugar level by facilitating the process by which insulin carries sugar to your cells.

If you're interested in exploring the subject of hypoglycemia in greater depth, you might want to read the following books: *Sugar Blues* by William Dufty, *Hypoglycemia: A Better Approach* by Paavo Airola, or *Low Blood Sugar and You* by Carlton Fredricks.

Minimize Eating Foods to Which You Are Allergic

An allergic reaction occurs when your body attempts to resist the intrusion of a foreign substance. For some people, certain foods affect the body like a foreign substance, not only causing classic allergic symptoms such as runny nose, mucus, and sneezing, but also a host of psychological or psychosomatic symptoms, including any of the following:

- Anxiety or panic
- Depression or mood swings
- Dizziness
- Irritability
- Insomnia
- Headaches
- Confusion and disorientation
- Fatigue

Such reactions occur in many individuals only when they eat an excessive amount of a particular food or a combination of offending foods, or if they have an excessively low resistance due to a cold or an infection. Other people are so highly sensitive that only a small amount of the wrong food can cause debilitating symptoms. Often the subtler, psychological symptoms have a delayed onset, making it difficult to connect them with the offending foods.

In our culture the two most common foods causing allergic reactions are milk or dairy products and wheat. It is casein in milk and gluten in wheat that tend to cause problems. Other foods that can be a source of allergic response include alcohol, chocolate, citrus fruits, corn, eggs, garlic, peanuts, yeast, shellfish, soy products, or tomatoes. One of the most telling signs of food allergy is addiction. You tend to crave and are addicted to the very foods to which you are allergic. While chocolate is the most flagrant example of this, you might also take pause if you find yourself tending to crave bread (wheat), corn chips (corn), dairy products, or another specific type of food. Many people go for years without recognizing that the very foods they crave the most have a subtle but toxic effect on their mood and well-being.

How can you find out whether food allergies are aggravating your problems with anxiety? As in the case of hypoglycemia, there are both formal tests you can obtain from a nutritionally oriented doctor as well as informal tests you can conduct on your own.

Among formal clinical tests for food allergies, the RAST test (Radio Allergo Sorbent Test) is probably the most reliable. This is a blood test which measures the presence of antibodies to a wide range of foods. Elevated levels of antibodies to specific foods in your blood suggest that you are allergic to those foods. Although expensive, the RAST test provides a detailed profile of all of the foods to which you're allergic and can be a very helpful diagnostic tool.

A less formal and expensive way to assess food allergies is to conduct your own "elimination" test. If you want to determine whether you are allergic to wheat, simply eliminate all products containing wheat from your diet for two weeks and notice whether you feel better. Then, at the end of the two weeks, suddenly eat a large amount of wheat and carefully monitor any symptoms which appear over the next twenty-four hours. After testing wheat, you might want to test milk and milk products. It's important to experiment with only one potentially allergic type of food at a time so that you don't confound your results.

Another way to test food allergies is to take your pulse after eating a meal. If it is elevated more than ten beats per minute above your normal rate, it's likely that you ate something you're allergic to.

The good news is that you probably do not have to permanently abstain from a food to which you are allergic. After a period of several months away from a food, it may be possible to eat it again occasionally without adverse effects. For example, instead of having bread at almost every meal, you'll find that you feel better having it only a couple times per week.

Food allergies can definitely be a contributing factor to excessive anxiety and mood swings for certain people. If you suspect this to be a problem, try experimenting with the elimination method and/or consult a qualified nutritionist or naturopathic doctor.

Reduce Saturated, Animal Fats and Increase Polyunsaturated or Monounsaturated, Vegetable-Based Fats

Saturated fats are the fats that come from animal sources: beef, poultry, bacon, butter, eggs, whole milk, and cheese.

Over the past fifty years it has been consistently documented that diets high in saturated, animal-based fats lead to increased risk of heart disease and stroke. High amounts of saturated fats consumed tend to end up as plaque deposits in your arteries, which over time accumulate to produce atherosclerosis. In fact, you may be surprised to know that saturated fat consumption correlates more highly with heart disease than even cholesterol intake. Beware of claims about low cholesterol in foods that are still high in saturated fats.

Still it is important to obtain at least 20 percent of your calories in fat. Up to half of this should be in the form of polyunsaturated or monounsaturated oils, which are derived from seeds, nuts, and vegetable sources. Be careful that vegetable oils such as sesame and safflower oil are fresh and not rancid. Keep oils refrigerated and discard them if they smell rancid or unpleasant. Rancid oils (and nuts) are full of oxidized molecules called "free radicals," which can damage DNA (potentially leading to cancer) or the interior walls of your arteries, (leading to atherosclerosis). Deep-fried foods are also a potent source of free radicals. (Antioxidant vitamins such as vitamin C, vitamin E, and selenium can help offset the effects of free radicals.)

Monounsaturated oils such as olive oil and canola oil are probably the safest to use. They tend to lower the "bad" type of cholesterol (LDL) without lowering the "good" kind (HDL). Buy them as "extra virgin" or cold-pressed. You may need to go to your local health food store, since brands available at the grocery store are often heated, which changes their molecular structure in unhealthy ways.

I would recommend that, in addition to vegetable-based oils, you obtain the remainder of your fat either from organic poultry or fresh seafood. Salmon contains a fat (omega-3 fatty acid) that has an especially beneficial impact on the body.

Eat Whole, Unprocessed Foods

Try to eat foods that are fresh and as close to their natural state as possible. As one person put it, "If it grows, eat it; otherwise don't." Whole foods include fresh fruits, fresh vegetables, whole grains, unrefined cereals, beans, nuts, seeds, sea vegetables, fresh fish, and free-range organic poultry. Foods are more than amalgamations of proteins, carbohydrates, fats, vitamins, and minerals. We derive nourishment not only from nutrients in food but from their energy fields—their "life force"—as well. The fresher and more whole a food is, the more life force it contains.

Food processing diminishes or destroys this life force in two ways. First, the food is *fragmented* at a cellular level. For example, in white flour the bran and germ of the wheat has been split off; what's left is only the pulp. In the process twenty different nutrients are removed. When the flour is subsequently "enriched," only four are put back in. Second, additives and preservatives are added to foods that are already partial or fragmented. These further reduce the life energy of the food and can be potentially toxic. Artificial colors and dyes, for example, can interact with and damage DNA. Some have been found to be toxic. Nitrites, added to many canned and processed meats, are not themselves carcinogenic but may easily react with protein breakdown by-products in the digestive tract to form highly carcinogenic compounds known as nitrosamines. Among artificial sweeteners, saccharin is known to be carcinogenic and aspartame (Nutrasweet) may be. There is some evidence that high amounts of aspartame may be linked to brain tumors in laboratory animals. People sensitive to aspartame may also experience symptoms such as headaches, nausea, dizziness, insomnia, or depression. Other additives to avoid include monosodium glutamate (MSG), BHA and BHT, and sulfites.

In short, you can do much to enhance your sense of well-being, as well as avoid potential hazards, by replacing processed foods with whole foods whenever possible.

Reduce Consumption of Commercial Beef, Pork, and Poultry

Red meat poses a number of health hazards. It is no accident that countries low in red meat consumption have lower rates of cardiovascular disease as well as cancer. As mentioned in the previous section, red meats are high in saturated fats. Frequent consumption of beef increases your risk of atherosclerosis, the main cause of heart attacks and strokes. Red meat, pork, and most commercially available forms of poultry are derived from animals that have been fed hormones to promote weight gain and growth. There are indications that these hormones stress the animals, and there is reason to believe that they may aggravate stress levels in meat consumers as well. One of the effects of feeding cows, pigs, and chickens hormones is that these hormones suppress the animal's immune systems, making them more susceptible to infectious disease. To solve this problem, the animals are given antibiotics. When you eat commercial beef, pork, or poultry, you may be ingesting antibiotic residues along with hormones. Finally, the conditions in which animals live prior to slaughter are often akin to torture. Is it any wonder that commercial beef and poultry don't taste as good as they did thirty to forty years ago? If you are interested in reading further about abuses of the meat industry and their impact both on your health and society at large, I recommend the book *Diet for a New America* by John Robbins.

Use Organic Foods When Possible

Organic foods are those fruits, vegetables, and grains that are grown with natural fertilizers and are not sprayed with pesticides or fungicides. Residues of these substances may be present in any fruit or vegetable not labeled organic. Meat and poultry in most places is likely to contain steroid and antibiotic residues unless it is labeled organic or, in the case of chicken, "free range." In response to consumer demand, some supermarkets have been offering produce guaranteed to be low or free of pesticide residues. Most health food stores also offer organic produce. I recommend you try to buy organic vegetables and fruits whenever possible. If they are unavailable in your area, you can minimize your exposure to harmful chemicals by observing the following guidelines:

- Wash all fruits and vegetables thoroughly before eating them.
- Remove the outer layers of head lettuce, cabbage, and other greens.
- If produce such as apples, cucumbers, or peppers have been waxed, peel them first (although this doesn't work well for peppers if you eat them raw).
- Avoid cooking with orange, lemon, or lime rind unless you obtain it from pesticide-free fruit.

Eat More Vegetables

Vegetables provide an excellent source of vitamins, minerals, and fiber. When fresh, they contribute life force to any meal. In an era where the standard diet is replete with sweets, soda pop, and snack foods, vegetables have become unpopular for many people. Yet this dislike is likely to have been acquired (most babies like vegetable baby foods) and can be unlearned. As you start to remove unhealthful foods from your diet, you may discover how tasty vegetables can be when they are fresh and properly prepared. Their natural flavors seem to come out best when they are lightly steamed.

It is a good idea to eat both raw and cooked vegetables on a daily basis. A salad consisting of different kinds of lettuce, cucumbers, radishes, carrots, onions, and tomatoes is a good accompaniment to lunch or dinner. Cooked broccoli, spinach, asparagus, string beans, or greens (such as kale, chard, or bok choy) go well with fish and rice for dinner. Cruciferous vegetables (cabbage, broccoli, kale, collards, mustard greens, brussels sprouts) are better eaten cooked than raw. These vegetables have several benefits, including protection against colon cancer, but also contain natural toxins that are broken down by cooking. My personal favorite is a mixture of carrots, potatoes, spinach, and broccoli with onions and ginger added for flavoring. If your energy is low, you will likely feel better after having such a mixture of lightly steamed vegetables, along with rice and tofu for balance.

Increase Fiber in Your Diet

Fiber consists of the indigestible parts of plants you eat. A certain amount in the diet is necessary for the proper functioning of your intestinal tract. If you're lacking fiber, you're likely to be prone to either digestive problems or constipation. Fiber can be found in grains, brans, fresh vegetables, and fruits. To increase your amount of fiber, you can try bran cereals or add bran to your favorite cereal. In general, try to eat ample amounts of fresh, raw vegetables and fruits. I suggest that you have some raw vegetables or a salad to accompany both lunch and dinner. Raw fruits are preferable between meals, since for many people it is difficult to digest fruit and proteins together. A certain amount of fiber is necessary, but too much (for example, a diet consisting solely of raw vegetables and whole grains) can stress the intestinal tract and cause bloating.

Chew Your Food

Apart from what you eat, the *way* you eat has an impact on the quality of your nutrition. If you eat too fast, or do not adequately chew your food, you will miss a lot of the nutrient content as well as cause yourself indigestion.

Digestion begins when you chew your food. If your food is not properly *predigested* in your mouth, much of it will not get adequately digested in your stomach. When this partially digested food passes on through your intestines, it is likely to putrefy and ferment causing bloating, cramps and gas. Moreover, you will get only a limited amount of the nutrition potentially available from your food, leading to the possibility of subtle forms of undernourishment.

To assure you get the full value of your food, give yourself time to eat and chew each mouthful of solid food at least fifteen to twenty times. If, after doing this, you still feel bloated or have problems with indigestion, I suggest you take digestive enzymes (available at health food stores) with or after each meal. If you properly digest your food, you should feel satisfied and comfortable after a meal rather than dull or lethargic.

Drink Six to Eight Glasses of Purified Water per Day

Why should you drink this amount of water? A primary reason is that water helps your kidneys. The main function of your kidneys is to filter out all kinds of toxic waste products of bodily metabolism as well as chemical and environmental pollutants from the outside. For your kidneys to operate properly, you need to drink plentiful amounts of water to help wash away waste products. You especially need to drink ample water if you live in a hot environment, eat a lot of protein, drink alcohol or coffee, take medications, or have urinary problems. The same is true if you are running a fever.

The purity of the water you drink is important. Most water purification plants focus primarily on disinfection, largely ignoring chemical contamination from industrial or agricultural wastes that find their way into ground water. Disinfection is often accomplished through chlorination, which poses additional hazards. Chlorine is a poisonous gas which can cause toxic by-products—trihalomethanes—which are known to cause cancer and birth defects. For all of these reasons, I strongly recommend you *avoid drinking tap water*.

You can instead buy bottled water or attach a water purification system to your tap. If you buy bottled water, demand a detailed analysis of its contents. Some bottled spring waters may come from sources that have been affected by contaminated ground water. The two types of water purification systems most in use are activated carbon filters and reverse osmosis systems. Both filter out chlorine and toxic organic molecules; however, reverse osmosis systems will also filter out toxic metals. The downside of reverse osmosis systems is that they waste a lot of water. Activated carbon filter systems require that you replace the filter periodically. Either system is a vast improvement over plain tap water, and certainly more convenient and cost-effective than continually purchasing bottled water.

Reduce Consumption of Milk and Milk Products

The dairy industry would like you to believe that milk is the healthiest and most nutritious of all drinks. Here are the facts:

- Lactose is part of the carbohydrate component of milk. Like many people, however, you may be *lactose intolerant*. Your stomach may not make the digestive enzyme lactase which is needed to digest milk sugar (lactose). As a result, when you drink milk, you may experience bloating, excess gas, and general intestinal distress.

- The butterfat in milk is the worst kind for your heart; it has a very high proportion of saturated fatty acids. Cheeses made from milk also have fifty to seventy percent butterfat content. If you must have milk or cheese, be sure to get the low-fat or nonfat variety.

- The protein in milk, known as casein, can produce an allergic response—most frequently in the form of mucus. It's common for milk and dairy products to aggravate chronic allergic conditions such as asthma, bronchitis, and sinusitis. Milk is also known to aggravate auto immune conditions, such as rheumatoid arthritis and lupus.

- Much of the commercial milk you drink contains residues of drugs and hormones used by the dairy industry to increase productivity of cows. Homogenization of milk removes bacteria but not the hormone residues. Raw milk from a certified dairy is likely to lack hormones, but it may contain bacteria.

In sum, I suggest you reduce your consumption of cow milk and milk-based products to a minimum. Cow milk is an ideal food for baby cows, but it wasn't intended for adult humans. Learn to enjoy (as I have) soy milk or rice milk, which are available in most health food stores.

Increase the Amount of Protein Relative to Carbohydrate You Eat

Until recently most nutritionists advocated eating a high amount of complex carbohydrates (e.g., whole grains, pastas, bread)—as much as 70 percent of total calories. The prevailing idea was that too much fat promoted cardiovascular disease and too much protein led to excessive acidity and toxicity in the body. The ideal diet was thought to consist of 15–20 percent fat, 15–20 percent protein, and the rest carbohydrates.

In the past few years, however, evidence has mounted against the idea of eating high quantities of carbohydrates. Carbohydrates are used by the body to produce sugar or glucose, the form of sugar the body and brain use for fuel. In order to transport glucose to the cells, your pancreas secretes insulin. Eating high levels of carbohydrates means your body produces higher levels of insulin, and too much insulin has an adverse effect on some of the body's most basic hormonal and neuroendocrine systems, especially those that produce prostaglandins and serotonin.

In short, eating high amounts of cereals, breads, pastas, or even grains (such as rice) or starchy vegetables (such as carrots, corn, and potatoes) can raise your insulin levels to the point that other basic systems are thrown out of balance. The answer is not to eliminate complex carbohydrates but to reduce them *proportionately* to the amounts of protein and fat you consume, *without increasing the total number of calories in your diet.* (By doing this, you will not end up eating a diet that is too high in fat or protein.) Instead, you will continue to eat fats and protein in moderation *while decreasing the amount of carbohydrate you have each meal relative to fat and protein.* The optimal ratio may be 30 percent protein, 30 percent fat, and 40 percent carbohydrate, with *vegetable* sources of protein and fat preferable to animal sources.

Considerable research supporting the value of reducing the proportion of carbohydrate relative to protein and fat is presented by Dr. Barry Sears in his book *The Zone.* Personally, after having eaten a mostly vegetarian diet, I've found that I have a higher level of energy and a greater sense of well-being since introducing more protein relative to carbohydrate in my diet. Other clients of mine have said that increasing protein relative to carbohydrate at each meal has had a favorable effect on both anxiety and depression. Anxiety and mood disorders often involve deficiencies in neurotransmitters, especially serotonin. The body has no way to make neurotransmitters (and serotonin in particular) without a steady supply of amino acids, which are derived from protein. Whether or not you agree with Dr. Sears' approach or choose to adopt a 40:30:30 diet, I highly recommend you have some protein (preferably in the form of fish, organic poultry, tofu, tempeh, or beans and grains) at every meal. On the other hand, aim not to exceed 30 percent protein—especially in the form of meat, chicken, or fish—as this may tend to make your body overly acidic.

What to Do When You Eat Out

The pressures and constraints of modern life require that many of us eat lunch or dinner outside of our homes. The problem is that most restaurant food, even at its best, provides too many calories, too much saturated fat, too much salt, and often food that has been cooked in stale or rancid oils. Much restaurant food is less fresh or "alive" than what you can obtain on your own. For the most part, eating in restaurants is not optimal for taking care of your health.

If you need to eat in restaurants often, I suggest the following guidelines:

- Avoid all fast food or "junk food" concessions.
- Whenever possible, eat out at natural food or health food restaurants that use whole, organic foods.
- If natural food restaurants are unavailable, go to high quality seafood restaurants and order fresh fish, preferably broiled without butter or oil. Accompany the fish with fresh vegetables, potatoes, or rice, and a green salad. On the salad, avoid creamy or dairy-based dressing.
- As a third choice, try a high-quality Chinese or Japanese restaurant, and have a meal consisting of rice, vegetables, and fresh fish or tofu (bean curd). In Chinese restaurants, be sure to ask the waitress to leave off MSG (monosodium glutamate), to which many people are allergic.
- As a general rule, when eating out have no more than one roll, one pat of butter, and minimize ordering cream-based soups such as clam chowder. Get your salad dressings on the side, using oil and vinegar or a low-fat Italian dressing. Stick with simple entrees such as chicken or whitefish without elaborate sauces or toppings. If possible, try to avoid high-fat desserts. Don't hesitate to ask your waitress for assistance in having food prepared according to your needs. Learn to enjoy the subtle tastes of simple foods. This becomes easy and desirable after a while when you omit rich, high fat, and sugary foods.

As you think back over the guidelines just described, keep in mind that it's neither necessary nor helpful to try to adopt them all at once. I recommend that you begin by reducing your caffeine and sugar consumption, which will have the most direct impact on reducing your vulnerability to stress and anxiety. Beyond that, go at your own pace in upgrading your diet. You are more likely to *maintain* a dietary change that you've decided you truly *want* to make.

Nutrition Questionnaire

The following questionnaire is designed to help you evaluate your eating habits and the quality of what you eat on a weekly basis. Fill it out today and then again every month to track positive changes you make in your diet.

1. Do you give yourself time to eat each meal? Are your meals leisurely and relaxed? How much time do you take for breakfast, lunch, and dinner?

2. Do you chew each mouthful of food thoroughly (i.e., at least fifteen times)?

3. Do you eat primarily whole, unprocessed foods (i.e., foods that have no artificial additives)? Make a list of whole foods you eat.

Examples of Whole Foods	Examples of Processed Foods
Fresh vegetables	Frozen or canned vegetables
Fresh fruits	Canned fruits
Whole grain breads	Vitamin-enriched breads
Brown rice, millet, and other grains	Brand name cereals
Whole grain cereals	Homogenized milk
Raw dairy and yogurt products	Meats bought in the average grocery store
Fish	Chips (potato or corn)
Organic poultry	TV dinners
Unsalted raw almonds or other nuts	

4. Are you within ten pounds of your ideal weight, given your age and frame size?

   Does your caloric intake exceed your energy expenditure?

5. Do you consume caffeine in the form of coffee (no. of cups per day ___), caffeinated tea (no. of cups per day ___), or cola beverages (no. of 12 oz cans ___ or 8 oz glasses ___ per day)?

6. Do you consume refined or unrefined sugars?

Sweet	No. per week
Teaspoon of sugar in coffee/tea	
Sugar on cereal	
Jelly on one piece of toast	
Sweet roll	
Donut	
Piece of pie	
Piece of cake	
Ice cream scoop	
Soft drinks with sugar	
Fruit juice with "high fructose"	
Candy bar	
Health food candy with honey	
Other honey-based sweet	
Cookies	

7. How many times per week do you eat meat (steak, roast beef, hamburger, ham, lamb, veal, pork chop)? ___

   How many times per week do you eat regular poultry? ___

   How many times per week do you eat organic poultry? ___

   How many times per week do you eat fish? ___

   White fish? ___ Shellfish (i.e., shrimp, prawns, crab, oysters, mussels, clams)? ___

   Small fish (i.e., sardines)? ___

8. How many times per week do you consume dairy products?

   Homogenized milk? ___ Yogurt? ___ Cheese? ___ Other? ___

   Pats of butter? ___ Ice cream? ___

   Creamy soups, sauces, casseroles, etc.? ___

9. How many eggs per week do you consume? ___

10. How many times per week do you eat fried foods (i.e., fried meats, fried potatoes, fried vegetables)? ___

11. How much fiber are you getting in your diet?

    Do you eat one raw vegetable and one cooked vegetable every day? ___

    No. per week ___

    Do you eat a whole grain food each day? No. per week ___

    Are you often constipated? No. of times per week ___

12. How many 8 oz glasses of purified or spring water do you consume per day (include water used to make coffee, tea)?

13. Do you have a salad every day? No. per week ___ What's in the salad?

14. Do you eat a balanced diet?

    Ideal

    Complex carbohydrates (fresh vegetables, whole grains)—50–60 percent

    Protein (fish, poultry, cheese, yogurt)—20–25 percent

    Fats (from animal-based foods, nuts, oils)—20–25 percent

15. Are there any foods that you especially crave (e.g., chocolate, bread, sweets, milk, cheese, etc.)? List them.

16. Do you try to buy organic produce only? About what percentage of your food is organic?

17. Do you put salt on your food? Yes ___ No ___

18. How many times per week do you eat in restaurants?

    No. of times per week ___ What kinds of restaurants? What do you eat?

19. How many alcoholic beverages do you have per week?

    No. per week ___ What kinds?

20. Do you take supplements? Which ones? What quantities per day?

This chapter has examined a variety of strategies for improving what you eat. I hope it has enabled you to begin making some connections between what you eat and the way you feel, if you haven't done so already. Following even a few (particularly the first three) of the guidelines suggested will help to reduce your susceptibility to anxiety. In working with this chapter, be willing to experiment at your own pace. What you eat does make a substantial difference in how you feel, yet each of us is unique. Only you can determine for yourself which of the numerous guidelines suggested in this chapter will be most beneficial in your particular case. Seek help from a holistic doctor, naturopath, or other qualified health professional if you need further guidance.

What You Can Do Now

1. Evaluate the amount of caffeine in your diet, using the *Caffeine Chart* in this chapter, and attempt to gradually reduce your intake to less than 50 mg per day. If you are especially sensitive, you may want to eliminate caffeine altogether, substituting decaf coffee (or herb teas) for regular coffee.

2. Reduce or stop smoking. In addition to significantly lessening your risk for cardiovascular disease and cancer, you will lower your susceptibility to panic attacks and anxiety.

3. Evaluate whether you experience the subjective symptoms of hypoglycemia—light-headedness, anxiety, depression, weakness, or shakiness—three or four hours after a meal (or in the early morning hours before rising) and whether they are quickly relieved by eating. You may want to follow this up with a formal six-hour glucose tolerance test. If you suspect that hypoglycemia is contributing to your problem with anxiety, strive to eliminate from your diet all forms of white sugar as well as brown sugar, honey, corn syrup, corn sweeteners, molasses, and high fructose. (Be careful also about aspartame, or Nutrasweet. There is some evidence of a link between this substance and panic disorder for certain people.) Most fresh, whole fruits (not dried) are fine if you're hypoglycemic, although fruit juices should be diluted with water. Observe the guidelines listed for dealing with hypoglycemia and consider taking the recommended supplements suggested in this chapter. You may want to consult a nutritionally oriented physician, naturopath, or qualified health practitioner to assist you in setting up an appropriate dietary and supplement regime.

4. Evaluate your susceptibility to food allergies. Take note of any types of food that you crave (paying attention particularly to wheat and dairy products) and try eliminating that food from your diet for two weeks. Then reintroduce the food and notice if you have any symptoms. If you suspect you have a problem with food allergies, consider getting a blood test from a holistic physician or naturopath.

5. Work with the remaining guidelines for improving your nutrition. Instituting even one or two of these guidelines is likely to increase your sense of well-being and resilience to anxiety and stress. In my experience, the guidelines recommending that you eat whole foods, chew your food well, and increase your intake of protein relative to carbohydrate are particularly important if you feel you are under considerable stress. *Avoid pushing yourself to radically change your diet all at once,* or you may end up rebelling against the idea of making any changes. Introduce one small change each week (or perhaps even each month) so that you gradually modify your dietary habits.

6. You are likely to find the books by Ballentine, Colbin, Haas, Sears, and Weil listed at the end of this chapter to be particularly helpful in providing more insight and knowledge about how to achieve a healthy diet. If you find yourself confused about what would be the most suitable diet, get help by consulting a holistic physician (M.D.) or naturopathic doctor (N.D.) in your area.

References and Further Reading

Airola, Paavo. 1977. *Hypoglycemia: A Better Approach*. Phoenix, Ariz.: Health Plus Publishers.

Balch, James, and Phyllis Balch. 1997. *Prescription for Nutritional Healing*. 2d ed. Garden City Park, N.Y.: Avery Publishing Group. (A comprehensive reference book.)

Ballentine, Rudolph. 1982. *Diet and Nutrition: A Holistic Approach*. Honesdale, Penn.: The Himalayan International Institute.

Colbin, Annemarie. 1996. *Food and Healing*. New York: Ballantine Books. (Excellent introductory book on nutrition.)

Dufty, William. 1993. *Sugar Blues*. New York: Warner Books. (Classic popular book on hypoglycemia.)

Haas, Elson M. 1992. *Staying Healthy with Nutrition*. Berkeley, Calif.: Celestial Arts. (A very thorough and comprehensive layperson's text on nutrition.)

Robbins, John. 1987. *Diet for a New America*. Walpole, N. H.: Stillpoint Publishing.

Sears, Barry. 1995. *The Zone*. New York: HarperCollins.

Tierra, Michael. 1998. *The Way of Herbs*. New York: Pocket Books. (Excellent reference on herbs.)

Weil, Andrew. 1995. *Natural Health, Natural Medicine*. New York: Houghton Mifflin.

———. 1995. *Spontaneous Healing*. New York: Fawcett Columbine. (Weil's informative and well-written books have spoken to great numbers of people exploring alternative approaches to health and wellness.)

Wurtman, Judith. 1988. *Managing Your Mind and Mood Through Food*. New York: Perennial Library.

5

Address Your Personality Issues

Three factors contribute to the development of an anxiety disorder: your *heredity*; your *personality*, which is influenced strongly by your upbringing and childhood experiences; and *cumulative stress*, the amount of stress you experience in your adult life. Your genes and your personality traits can *predispose* you toward a panic or phobic disorder, but actually developing that disorder is usually triggered either by one major stressor (such as the death of a loved one) or a series of life stresses over a period of time.

In this chapter I want to focus on personality traits I've observed frequently in people who struggle with anxiety. Taken together, this group of characteristics define what I call the *anxiety-prone personality*. Most people with anxiety difficulties display at least two or three of these traits, which include:

- excessive need for approval
- insecurity and overdependency
- overcontrol
- perfectionism
- overcautiousness
- "confinement phobia"

People prone to anxiety disorders also have plenty of positive traits, such as creativity, intuitive ability, emotional sensitivity, and amiability. Such traits often endear them to their relatives and friends. However, the purpose of this chapter is to focus on the more problematic personality traits that tend to aggravate anxiety.

Anxiety-prone personality characteristics tend to be associated with specific, deep-seated fears. Such "core fears" often have their origin in childhood or past trauma. They underlie most of the worries and phobias that come up for people with anxiety. The six traits described above are motivated by these core fears, which include: *fear of rejection; fear of abandonment; fear of losing control; fear of illness, injury, or death;* and the *fear of confinement.* Certainly there are other fears that can influence anxiety disorders, such as the fear of what is strange or unfamiliar, the fear of failure, or the fear of meaninglessness. Yet the five core fears just mentioned play the most central role in motivating anxiety-prone personality traits. These traits and the core fears tend to be associated in the following way:

Anxiety-Prone Trait	**Core Fear**
Excessive need for approval	Fear of rejection
Insecurity and overdependency	Fear of abandonment
Overcontrol	Fear of losing control
Perfectionism	Fear of rejection and losing control
Overcautiousness	Fear of illness, injury, death
Confinement phobia	Fear of being stuck, confined

Which of these characteristics fit you? If you've received therapy—particularly cognitive-behavioral therapy—for your anxiety disorder, were these issues addressed? Effective cognitive-behavioral treatment may help you deal with some of these issues *indirectly*. For example, changing self-talk and the underlying beliefs that cause social anxiety may help you to overcome your fear of rejection. Or taking time out to work on relaxation may enable you to let go of some of your overcontrol and perfectionism. Or, if you're agoraphobic and learn through exposure therapy to drive farther from home, you may begin to overcome feelings of insecurity and overdependency. Without a doubt, cognitive-behavioral therapy (CBT) can have a favorable impact on anxiety-prone personality traits and associated core fears. The question is whether it's enough. CBT tends to address primarily the *cognitive* aspects of your personality (i.e., your anxiety-provoking self-talk, attitudes, and beliefs). But there are also emotional factors that influence the traits and fears listed above. Insecurity and overdependency, for example, may be influenced by having not developed a strong sense of your own identity.

In this chapter, both cognitive and emotional aspects of the anxiety-prone personality will be considered, along with the all-important issue of self-worth.

There are six sections in what follows dealing with each of the six personality issues. Each section begins with a list of five questions to help you assess whether the particular trait applies to you. The remainder of the section describes the characteristic in more detail and then suggests strategies to help you overcome it.

The Excessive Need for Approval: Fear of Rejection

Answer true or false (circle one):

What others think of me is very important.	T	F
People won't like me if they see who I really am.	T	F
I want everyone to like me.	T	F
I should always be nice—not irritable or unpleasant.	T	F
My self-worth comes from caring for and helping others.	T	F

Being overly concerned with approval arises from an inner, emotional sense of being flawed or unworthy. The underlying fear is that others won't like you or will reject you. So you strive to go out of your way to please both strangers as well as those people you care about. In social situations, you feel vulnerable and always try hard to maintain a good impression. You may constantly be on guard about saying or doing something embarrassing. In intimate and family relationships, you go out of your way to take care of everyone else's needs at the expense of meeting your own. You may have a difficult time setting boundaries or saying "no." Since your self-esteem comes from pleasing others, you have a tendency to overextend yourself, often at your own expense.

An excessive need for approval often develops from having grown up with overly critical parents. If you were frequently criticized or punished, you probably learned to feel inadequate. Nothing you did was ever quite good enough. As a child you may have also learned to hide and discount your true impulses and needs so that you could live up to the image your parents wanted. If you were once anxious about your mother or father's approval, you may, as an adult, continue to be excessively concerned with getting others' approval. If you believed you had to go out of your way to receive your parents' acceptance, you may still try too hard to please others at the expense or your own feelings and needs. Apart from your parents, shame and a fear of rejection could have started with your experiences at school or with your peer group. If, for any reason, you were singled out by other children as being "different," "weird," "too short," "too smart," or whatever, you may have acquired a tendency to feel vulnerable or ashamed.

The long-term consequence of always accommodating and pleasing others at the expense of yourself is that you end up with a lot of withheld frustration and resentment. Such frustration and resentment can form the unconscious foundation for a lot of chronic tension and anxiety.

There is another kind of response to being overly concerned with approval (or fearing rejection). You tend to avoid closeness with other people in general. Instead of trying to please others to overcome your inner sense of shame, you simply withdraw from them. Believing you're unworthy to win others' acceptance anyway, you go your separate way. You find it hard to participate in groups or social situations because you're preoccupied with being criticized or embarrassed. You also find it difficult to risk getting close to someone unless you're certain of being liked. The end result of this pattern of avoidance may be social phobia—either specific social fears or a generalized anxiety about all kinds of social situations.

Thus, there are two ways the excessive need for approval or fear of rejection can manifest: overaccommodating others at your own expense, or avoiding social interaction and/or closeness. If you have both characteristics, don't feel bad. This is a common and surmountable problem.

Dealing with the Excessive Need for Approval

There are five basic strategies I rely on with clients who have problems with an excessive need for approval:

- Enhance self-worth and self-respect.
- Develop a realistic view of other people's approval.
- Develop assertiveness skills.
- Recognize and let go of codependency.
- Overcome social avoidance (social phobia), if applicable.

Enhance Self-Worth and Self-Respect

Many books have been written on the subject of self-esteem (see references at the end of the chapter). Briefly, self-esteem is about *how you relate to yourself*. Do you *like, respect, trust,* and *believe* in yourself? When you *like* yourself, you can live comfortably with both your personal strengths and weaknesses without undue self-criticism. You also acknowledge and take care of your own personal needs. When you *respect* yourself, you recognize your own dignity and value as a unique human being. You stand up for your basic rights. You ask for what you want and you can say "no" to what you don't want. *Self-trust* means you trust your body, feelings, and behavior. You feel consistent within yourself no matter what changes and challenges may occur in your outer environment. To *believe* in yourself means you feel you deserve to have the good things in life. You have goals toward which you're working and a personal sense of accomplishment about what you've done with your life.

A full discussion of how to develop self-esteem is outside the scope of this book. I've dealt with it in some detail in *The Anxiety & Phobia Workbook.*

Among the most important ways to develop self-esteem, I would include the following:

- *Make time to take care of your own basic needs.* These include the needs for security, attention, support, respect, nurturing, touch, intimacy, a sense of accomplishment, fun and play, self-expression, and creativity. You're willing to put your own needs on equal footing with the needs of others. You spend at least as much time taking care of yourself as you do on taking care of your house and car.

- *Make room in your life to develop a good support system.* Beyond your immediate family, you can develop a sense of community through building a circle of friends. There are many options for doing this, including support groups for women, men, persons dealing with anxiety disorders, survivors of various types of abuse or loss, and persons addressing addictions or codependency issues. If your town is too small to offer these kinds of groups, you can still build support and community through your local church, service organizations, or special interest groups. Feeling part of a community helps you to establish a stronger sense of your own self.

- *Find and express your own unique purpose in life.* An important means to building self-worth is to discover and express your unique purpose(s) in life. To know this purpose means to identify your own particular gifts and talents and then express them in a vocation or avocation. Your unique gift may be to inspire others, create music, provide leadership, counsel or teach. Or it may simply be to offer hospitality in your home or to beautify your backyard. The scale of what you do is not so important; rather it is your awareness of what you're here to do and your willingness to do it. In fact, as you get to know yourself, you'll find you *need* to do it. In many cases you may have to go back to school or obtain specific training to develop your particular skills and talents. Or you may need to find a job where your special capacity to work with or assist others can be fully realized. You know that you're expressing your life purpose when you feel inspiration and enthusiasm in the *process* of doing it. You are not doing it for some external goal; the process itself is intrinsically rewarding. Chapter 6 of this book examines how to identify and express your unique life purpose.

Develop a Realistic View of Other People's Approval

When people don't express approval toward you—or when they act rude or critical—how do you receive it? Do you tend to take it personally—to see it as further evidence of your own ineptness and lack or worth? Below are some common attitudes characteristic of people who place excessive emphasis on always being liked. These might be called "people-pleasing" attitudes. Following each is an alternative view which represents, in most cases, a more realistic outlook.

People-pleasing Attitude: "If someone isn't friendly to me, it's because there must be something wrong with me."
Alternative View: "People may be unable to express warmth or acceptance toward me for reasons having nothing to do with me. For example, their own problems, frustrations, or fatigue may get in the way of their being friendly and accepting."

People-pleasing Attitude: "Others' criticism only serves to underscore the fact that I really am unworthy."
Alternative View: "People who find fault with me may be projecting their own faults, which they can't admit to having, onto me. It's a human tendency to project unconscious flaws onto others."

People-pleasing Attitude: "I think I'm a nice person. Shouldn't everyone like me?"
Alternative View: "There will always be some people who just won't like me—no matter what I do. The process by which people are attracted to or repelled by others is often irrational."

People-pleasing Attitude: "Others' approval and acceptance of me is essential."
Alternative View: "It's not necessary to receive the approval of everyone I meet in order to live a happy and meaningful life—especially if I believe in and respect myself."

The next time you feel put off or rejected, take a moment to calm down and think about whether the person acting negatively is reacting to something you did, or if he or she might simply be upset about something that has little or nothing to do with you. Ask yourself whether you might be taking the other person's inconsiderate remarks or behavior too personally.

Develop Assertiveness Skills

Developing assertiveness begins with an awareness of your own needs—knowing what it is you want. Then you need to learn that it's okay to meet your needs without feeling selfish or fearing disapproval. You become assertive, finally, when *you know you have the right to ask for what you want.* You are conscious of your basic rights as a human being and *you are willing to exercise those rights.*

What are those basic rights? A partial list might include:

Personal Bill of Rights

1. I have the right to ask for what I want.
2. I have the right to say "no" to requests or demands I can't meet.
3. I have the right to express all of my feelings, positive or negative.
4. I have the right to change my mind.
5. I have the right to make mistakes and not have to be perfect.
6. I have the right to follow my own values and standards.
7. I have the right to say "no" to anything when I feel I am not ready, it is unsafe, or it violates my values.
8. I have the right to determine my own priorities.
9. I have the right *not* to be responsible for others' behavior, actions, feelings, or problems.
10. I have the right to expect honesty from others.
11. I have the right to be angry at someone I love.
12. I have the right to be uniquely myself.
13. I have the right to feel scared and say "I'm afraid."
14. I have the right to say "I don't know."
15. I have the right *not* to give excuses or reasons for my behavior.
16. I have the right to make decisions based on my feelings.
17. I have the right to my own needs for personal space and time.
18. I have the right to be playful and frivolous.
19. I have the right to be healthier than those around me.
20. I have the right to be in a environment.
21. I have the right to make friends and be comfortable around people.
22. I have the right to change and grow.
23. I have the right to have my needs and wants respected by others.
24. I have the right to be treated with dignity and respect.
25. I have the right to be happy.

I suggest you photocopy this list and post it in a conspicuous place. Take some time to read it through, giving thought to each particular right, on a daily basis for a few weeks.

To act assertively includes two things: you must be willing to ask for what you want *and* be willing to say "no" to what you do not want. The importance of learning to be assertive can best be appreciated when you consider the consequences of being unassertive, namely:

- People don't know what you want, so they may be indifferent to your needs or impose their own agenda.
- People take advantage of you (particularly when you can't set limits or say "no").
- You suffer stress from having your own needs going unmet.
- You end up resenting the people you want to love, because they aren't responsive to your unstated needs.

Becoming more assertive means you strike a balance between two extremes: passivity and aggressiveness.

Nonassertive or *passive* behavior involves yielding to someone else's preferences while discounting your own rights and needs. You don't express your feelings or let others know what you want. The result is that they remain ignorant of your feelings or wants (and thus can't fairly be blamed for not responding to them). Passive behavior also includes feeling guilty (as if you are imposing) when you do ask for what you want. If you give others the message that you're *not sure* you have the right to express your needs, they will tend to discount them. Anxiety-prone people are often passive because they are overly invested in being nice or pleasing to everybody. Or they may be afraid that the open expression of their needs will alienate a spouse or partner on whom they feel dependent.

Aggressive behavior, on the other hand, may involve communicating in a demanding, abrasive, or even hostile way with others. Aggressive people typically are insensitive to others' rights and feelings and will attempt to obtain what they want through coercion or intimidation. Aggressiveness succeeds by sheer force, creating enemies and conflict along the way. It often puts others on the defensive, leading them to withdraw or fight back rather than cooperate. For example, an aggressive way of telling someone you want a particular assignment at work would be to say: "That assignment has my name written on it. If you so much as look at the boss when she brings it up during the staff meeting, you're going to regret it."

Instead of being openly aggressive, many people are *passive-aggressive*. Rather than openly confronting an issue, you express angry, aggressive feelings in a covert fashion through passive resistance. You're angry at your boss, so you're perpetually late to work. You don't want to comply with your partner's request, so you procrastinate or "forget" about the request altogether. Instead of asking for or doing something about what you really want, you perpetually complain or moan about what is lacking. Passive-aggressive people seldom get what they want because they never get it across.

Their behavior tends to leave other people angry, confused, and resentful. A passive-aggressive way of asking for a particular assignment at work might be to point out how inappropriate someone *else* is for the job, or to say to a coworker, "If I got more interesting assignments, I might be able to get somewhere in this organization."

Assertive behavior, in contrast to the above-described styles, involves asking for what you want (or saying "no") in a simple, direct fashion that does not negate, attack, or manipulate anyone else. You communicate your feelings and needs honestly and directly while maintaining respect and consideration for others. You stand up for yourself and your rights without apologizing or feeling guilty. Others feel comfortable when you're assertive because they know where you stand. They respect you for your honesty and forthrightness. Instead of demanding or commanding, an assertive statement makes a simple, direct request, such as, "I would really like that assignment," or "I hope the boss decides to give that particular assignment to me."

Assertiveness is a skill you can learn. More detailed guidelines for cultivating assertive behavior can be found in the chapter "Asserting Yourself" in *The Anxiety & Phobia Workbook*, as well as in classic books on the subject such as *Your Perfect Right* by Robert Alberti and Michael Emmons or *Asserting Yourself* by Sharon and Gordon Bower. Even better, you may find a class on assertiveness at your local college or adult education center.

Let Go of Codependency

As previously defined, "codependent" behavior involves accommodating to others at the expense of your own needs and preferences. Your sense of self-worth depends on taking care of, pleasing, and sometimes trying to "save" or "reform" someone else (or many others).

Examine the following statements. Put a check next to those that apply:

___ If someone important to me expects me to do something, I should do it.

___ I should not ever be irritable or unpleasant.

___ I shouldn't do anything to make others angry at me.

___ I should keep people I love happy.

___ It's usually my fault if someone I care about is upset with me.

___ My self-esteem comes from helping others solve their problems.

___ I tend to overextend myself in taking care of others.

___ If necessary, I'll put my own values or needs aside in order to preserve my relationship with my significant other.

___ Giving to others is the most important way I have to feel good about myself.

___ Fear of someone else's anger has a lot of influence on what I say or do.

If you checked three or more statements, you probably need to address your own codependency.

The consequence of maintaining a codependent approach to life is a lot of silent resentment, frustration, and unmet personal needs. When these feelings and needs remain unconscious, they often resurface as anxiety—especially *chronic, generalized anxiety*. The long-term effects of codependency are enduring stress, fatigue, burnout, and eventually serious physical illness.

Recovering from codependency essentially involves learning to love and take care of yourself. It means giving at least equal time to your own needs alongside those of others. It means setting limits on how much you will do or tolerate, and learning to say "no" when appropriate. Working with the following list of affirmations can be a first step toward developing more self-respect and letting go of codependency. You might want to read through the list slowly (or listen to the list recorded on tape) once a day for a few weeks. Or you might pick one or two of the affirmations that are most relevant, write them in large print, and post them in a conspicuous place.

- I'm learning to take better care of myself.
- I recognize that my own needs are important.
- It's good for me to take time for myself.
- I'm finding a balance between my own needs and my concern for others.
- If I take good care of myself, I have more to offer others.
- It's okay to ask for what I want from others.
- I'm learning to accept myself just the way I am.
- It's okay to say "no" to others' demands when I need to.
- I don't have to be perfect to be accepted and loved.
- I can change myself, but I accept that I can't make another person change.
- I'm letting go of taking responsibility for other people's problems.
- I respect others enough to know that they can take responsibility for themselves.
- I'm letting go of guilt when I can't fulfill others' expectations.
- Compassion toward others is loving; feeling guilty about their feelings or reactions accomplishes nothing.
- I am learning to love myself more every day.

In order to deal with your own codependency issues, you may want to read some of the classic books on the subject, such as *Codependent No More* by Melody Beattie or *Women Who Love Too Much* by Robin Norwood. Also consider attending a local meeting of Codependents Anonymous, which offers a 12-step approach to overcoming codependent attitudes. When codependency is deep-seated, working with a skillful psychotherapist may be helpful.

In overcoming codependency, the bottom line is *to give yourself permission to take care of your own needs*. A principle that I've personally found helpful in this regard is expressed well by one of the affirmations above:

If I take good care of myself, I have more to offer others.

Overcome Social Avoidance (Social Phobia)

If fear of rejection has led you to distance yourself from people—especially groups—there are several specific things you can do. First and foremost, you need to build a sense of your own self-worth, as described above. In addition to this, cognitive-behavioral therapy offers three specific types of interventions:

- Social skills training
- Graded exposure to social situations
- Cognitive-behavioral group therapy

Social skills training may be appropriate if you feel at a loss about how to converse with people in small or large groups. You can gain proficiency in starting and maintaining conversations, drawing other people out, listening, maintaining good eye contact, and achieving self-disclosure through role-playing these skills with a family member or a therapist. You can also role-play more specific activities such as interviewing for a job, using small talk at a party, or asking someone out on a date. Once you gain confidence in such skills with a supportive friend or therapist, you can begin to try them out in real life.

Graded exposure to social situations involves setting up a series of specific activities that you commit to doing, either with the help of a therapist or on your own. The series of activities are arranged in a "hierarchy" from easiest to most difficult. A typical hierarchy might look like this:

Initiating Conversations

1. Call two stores to ask if something is in stock.
2. Call a counseling hotline and talk about yourself.
3. Attend a small meeting and say your name.
4. Attend a small meeting and make two comments.
5. Repeat 3 and 4 with a small group of friends.
6. Attend a social gathering and stay for twenty minutes.

7. Same as 6, but stay for an hour, responding when other people talk to you.
8. Same as 7, but you initiate at least two conversations.
9. Initiate conversations while waiting in line with people you don't know.
10. Walk up to someone in a shopping mall and make conversation.

You might also construct a hierarchy for one specific type of behavior, breaking it down into a series of steps. For example, in learning to ask someone out for a date, you might practice with people listed through a dating service before you try walking up to someone at a party. More detailed instructions for doing exposure in social situations can be found in the book *Dying of Embarrassment: Help for Social Anxiety and Social Phobia* (see references at the end of this chapter).

Cognitive-behavioral group therapy, if available in your area, is perhaps the optimal way to overcome social anxiety and a fear of participating in groups. In such a group you work on challenging and countering socially phobic thinking, (i.e., self-statements such as "I'll humiliate myself," "People will think I'm weird because I don't know what to say," or "What if they see me blush?") In addition, you practice speaking up, expressing your ideas, sustaining conversations, asking for what you want, responding to criticism, and engaging in other types of activities relevant to participating in groups. By continually practicing activities you previously avoided in a supportive group setting, you can learn to desensitize to them and gain confidence in yourself. If cognitive-behavioral group therapy is not available in your area, you can still do the work with a therapist experienced in working with social anxiety or social phobia. Then you can try out what you've learned in various group settings, beginning with situations you deem "easy" and progressing to more difficult ones. Learning to speak up or express your ideas, for example, can be practiced first in a class or workshop and ultimately at a toastmaster's meeting (or a similar training in public speaking).

Overcoming long-standing shyness or social anxiety takes work and sustained commitment on your part. You may find it somewhat easier under the guidance of a skilled cognitive-behavioral therapist who is familiar with social anxiety and social phobia. In some cases, medication can also be helpful. Current treatment strategies for more severe social anxiety combine therapy with an SSRI medication such as Paxil (or a benzodiazepine such as Klonopin). This combination of therapy and medication seems to be very effective for many people.

Insecurity and Overdependency: Fear of Abandonment

Answer true or false (circle one):

It's very hard for me to be alone.	T	F
I feel like nothing unless someone loves me.	T	F

It's very difficult for me if my partner or loved one(s) go away.	T	F
I fear I wouldn't be able to make it if something happened to my partner (or loved one).	T	F
I always feel at my best when someone is with me.	T	F

Insecurity and overdependency, along with a fear of being abandoned, are common issues for people with anxiety problems, especially those suffering from agoraphobia. When these traits are pronounced, you may have difficulty making decisions for yourself without a lot of reassurance or advice from others. You do not want to disagree with others close to you for fear of losing their support. You may lack confidence in yourself to take initiative to do things on your own apart from your significant other(s). Having a close relationship on which you depend may seem vital to your very survival. You fear that if you were to lose that relationship, you could not function or care for yourself.

The roots of insecurity and overdependency are many and varied. Most often they go back to early childhood. In my clinical experience, the most common childhood situations that foster such insecurity (and a fear of abandonment) include the following:

Significant Childhood Loss

If you were separated from a parent as a result of death or divorce, you may have been left feeling abandoned. You may have grown up with a sense of emptiness and insecurity inside that can be restimulated very intensely by losses of significant people in your adult life. As an adult, you may seek to overcome old feelings of abandonment by overdependence on a particular person or other addictions to food, drugs, work, or whatever works to cover the pain. You may feel frightened of venturing far from a safe person or place, as is common in agoraphobia. Or you may find it difficult to assert yourself for fear of alienating the person you most depend on.

Parental Abuse

Physical or sexual abuse are extreme forms of deprivation. They may leave you with a complex mix of feelings, including insecurity, dependency, inadequacy, lack of trust, guilt, and/or rage. Adults who were physically abused as children may feel like perpetual victims and have difficulty standing up for themselves. Survivors of abusive childhoods often, and understandably, have difficulty with intimate relationships in their adult lives. While less flagrant, constant verbal abuse can have equally damaging effects.

Parental Alcoholism or Drug Abuse

Much has been written in recent years on the effects of parental alcoholism on children. Chronic drinking or substance abuse creates a chaotic, unreliable family atmosphere in which it is difficult for a child to develop a basic sense of trust or security. The attendant denial of the problem, often by both parents, teaches the child to deny his or her own feelings and pain connected to the family situation. Many such children grow up not only insecure, but have low self-worth and a poor sense of personal identity. They are prone, in fact, to nearly all of the issues described in this chapter: excessive need for approval, excessive need to control, overcautiousness, overresponsibility, and perfectionism.

Parental Neglect

Some parents, because they are preoccupied with themselves, their work, or other concerns, simply fail to give their children adequate attention and nurturing. Children left to their own devices often grow up feeling very insecure, worthless, and/or lonely. As adults, they may have a tendency to discount or neglect their own needs. They easily become overdependent as adults, trying to recapture what they never received as children.

Parental Rejection

Even without physical, sexual, or verbal abuse, some parents impart a feeling to their children that they are unwanted. This profoundly damaging attitude teaches a child to grow up doubting his or her very right to exist. Such a person has a tendency toward self-rejection or self-sabotage. They fear both being abandoned and rejected by others. It remains possible for adults with such a past to overcome what their parents didn't give them through learning to love and care for themselves.

Parental Overprotectiveness

The child who is overprotected may never learn to trust the world outside of the immediate family and risk independence. As an adult, such a person may feel very insecure and afraid to venture far from a safe person or place. When you learn that the outside world is threatening, you automatically restrict your exploration and risk-taking. You grow up with a tendency to worry excessively and be overly concerned with safety. Through learning to acknowledge, assert, and care for their own needs, overprotected individuals can gain the confidence to make a life of their own and discover that the world is not such a dangerous place.

Addressing Insecurity, Overdependency, and the Fear of Abandonment

There are four basic approaches I utilize in working with clients' insecurity and overdependency:

- Develop self-worth
- Develop assertiveness
- Cultivate spirituality
- Face avoidances and fears

Self-Worth

Overcoming insecurity and overdependency requires that you develop a strong sense of self-worth (self-esteem). The same three paths to self-worth described in the previous section—"The Excessive Need for Approval"—are mentioned here again, but with a slightly different emphasis:

- *Taking care of your personal needs.* If you feel you didn't receive the love and support you needed as a small child, you may need to do some "reparenting" with yourself. By "reparenting," I mean playing the role of a good parent toward yourself. One way of doing this is to take time out each day to do something special or kind for yourself. In short, you put aside both work and household responsibilities and make time to nurture yourself.

  Building a loving relationship with yourself is really not much different from developing a close relationship with someone else; both require some time, energy, and commitment. Taking out regular "downtime," time devoted to rest and relaxation, is one way to do this. The following list describes a number of other simple activities that involve nurturing yourself. When outer life circumstances seem harsh, it is particularly important to make time for yourself without feeling guilty about being self-indulgent.

Self-Nurturing Activities

1. Take a warm bath.
2. Have breakfast in bed.
3. Take a sauna.
4. Get a massage.

5. Buy yourself a bouquet.
6. Take a bubble bath.
7. Go to a pet store and play with the animals.
8. Go for a scenic walk (this may involve driving to a park).
9. Visit a zoo.
10. Have a manicure or pedicure.
11. Stop and smell some flowers.
12. Take time to watch the sunrise or sunset.
13. If it's cold outdoors, sit by the fire indoors.
14. Relax with a good book, magazine, and/or soothing music.
15. Go rent a funny video.
16. Play your favorite music and dance to it by yourself.
17. Go to bed early.
18. Sleep outside under the stars.
19. Take a "mental health day" off from work.
20. Fix a special dinner just for yourself and eat by candlelight.
21. Sit and have a cup of your favorite herb tea.
22. Call a good friend—or several good friends.
23. Go out to a favorite restaurant.
24. Go to the beach (or lake, mountains, etc.).
25. Take a scenic drive.
26. Meditate.
27. Buy some new clothes.
28. Browse in a book or record store for as long as you want.
29. Buy yourself a cuddly stuffed animal and play with it (your inner child will thank you).
30. Write yourself an upbeat letter and mail it to yourself.
31. Ask a special person to nurture you (feed, cuddle, and/or read to you).
32. Buy yourself something special that you can afford.
33. Go see a good film or show.

34. Go to the park and feed the ducks, swing on the swings, and so on.
35. Visit a museum or other interesting place.
36. Give yourself more time than you need to accomplish whatever you're doing (let yourself dawdle).
37. Work on your favorite puzzle or puzzle book.
38. Sit in a hot tub or jacuzzi.
39. Record an affirmation tape.
40. Write out an ideal scenario concerning a goal, then visualize it.
41. Read an inspirational book.
42. Write a letter to an old friend.
43. Bake or cook something special.
44. Go window shopping.
45. Play with your pet.
46. Listen to a positive, motivational tape.
47. Write in a special diary about your accomplishments.
48. Apply fragrant lotion all over your body.
49. Exercise.
50. Sit and hold your favorite stuffed animal.

- *Developing a support system outside of your immediate family.* People who are insecure or overly dependent often rely exclusively on a partner or other family members to meet all of their emotional needs. They may even define themselves in terms of their relationship with this one person. This leaves them fearful about being separated from their loved one by time or space. If something were to happen to their special other, they couldn't conceive how their life would go on. They may have problems developing their own autonomous interests, goals, and pursuits because they organize their life around a special loved one.

  Does this description even partially fit you? If so, you can reduce your dependency on your immediate family by cultivating a circle of friends—a support system—outside of your family. Long-term friendships can provide a sense of stability and continuity to your life, no matter what is going on within your immediate family. Also, such friends provide insurance that you would not be left alone if something actually *did* happen to a close family member.

  You can build a support system through church, participation in community organizations, or by attending ongoing support groups for women, men, anxiety sufferers, codependents, addicts, abuse survivors, etc. Ask your local newspaper if they publish a listing of such groups.

- *Developing a stronger sense of personal identity.* If you are overly dependent on someone else (or fear being separated from them), you need to work on finding more of a life of your own. You're less likely to be vulnerable to insecurity and fears of abandonment if you've developed a strong sense of yourself. Having some kind of work where you feel useful is an important part of creating your own identity (being a homemaker is an acceptable option here). So is having interests and hobbies that allow you to express your own unique gifts and creativity. Chapter 6, "Find Your Unique Purpose," provides a questionnaire to help give your life an increased sense of meaning and direction. Discovering your own unique mission—the contribution that you can make to the world, however large or small—is an important aspect of developing a sense of personal identity. Once you find that mission or purpose, your life will gain a new inspiration and enthusiasm that reduces your dependency on others.

Develop Assertiveness

The ability to know your own rights, to ask directly for what you want and say "no" to what you don't want, are all aspects of assertiveness. As you become more secure in yourself and less dependent on others, you will naturally tend to act more assertively, because you respect and believe in yourself enough to do so. For further information, refer back to the discussion of assertiveness in the previous section of this chapter, "The Excessive Need for Approval."

Cultivate Spirituality

There is much healing and benefit to be obtained by cultivating your spiritual life. Developing a relationship with a Higher Power (God) may not cure a specific obsession or phobia, but it will provide you with the moral support, courage, and faith to follow through with all of the work involved in recovering from anxiety difficulties. It will certainly help you overcome the fear of abandonment or aloneness and increase your sense of inner security.

You may chooses to define "Higher Power" as a presence or reality that transcends your personal self and the human order of things. This reality has been called "God" in Western society and by many other names elsewhere. It can take the form of a specific being, such as Christ, or be as abstract as the "life force" in all things or the "eternal beingness" of the present moment. Each of us defines it in our own way. You may already have a well-developed understanding from your particular religious faith. Or you may not be interested at this time in seeking further understanding. The existence of your Higher Power cannot be rationalized or proved; it is something that is revealed in a personal way within your own experience. Developing a relationship with your

Higher Power requires effort and commitment. If you're willing to do your part, you will very likely receive inspiration and guidance that add to your sense of security.

Further discussion of various ways to approach and cultivate a relationship with a Higher Power are offered in three chapters of this book: "Letting Go," "Spirituality," and "Create Your Vision."

Face Avoidances and Fears

One of the best ways to overcome insecurity and overdependency is to directly confront whatever it is you avoid. If you're avoiding an external situation, such as flying, public speaking, driving on the expressway, or being home alone, then you need to do "incremental exposure." This is a process of *gradually* facing the situation you've avoided through a series of small, incremental steps, often with the help of a support person. Please see *The Anxiety & Phobia Workbook* for detailed information on how to undertake exposure.

If what you fear is more internal, such as your feelings of anger or sadness, traumatic memories from the past, or your own ability to succeed in life, you may want to seek out the help of a professional therapist to help you gradually accept and integrate disowned parts of yourself. In the context of psychotherapy, you can feel safe enough to address feelings, memories, or potentials within yourself that have been too painful or frightening to explore on your own. In general, people need to feel *safe* in order to have the courage to face what they've long avoided. Be willing to get support and assistance when you decide to confront your fears, whatever they may be. Ultimately, the fewer fears you live with, the more confident, safe and relaxed about life you will feel.

Overcontrol: Fear of Losing Control

Answer true or false (circle one):

I'm the only one who can solve my problems.	T	F
If I let someone get very close, I'm afraid of being controlled.	T	F
It's difficult for me to rely on others for help.	T	F
To feel "out of control" is one of the worst states I can imagine.	T	F
I like to keep my life and affairs very organized and structured.	T	F

In essence, the fear of losing control involves a difficulty with trust. It's difficult to let go and trust life, because life, by its very nature, is unpredictable and uncertain. So your response to this uncertainty is to be ever vigilant, tending to overmanipulate circumstances (or other people) without giving them time to unfold or respond in their natural sequence. Closely allied with the fear of losing control is perfectionism: a tendency to set excessively high standards as well as to be overly concerned with small flaws and mistakes. (See the section following this one on perfectionism.)

Often the fear of losing control has its origins in a traumatic personal history. Any traumatic experience that undermined your sense of life being stable and predictable—especially if it left you feeling frightened or powerless—might have instilled a fear of losing control. Having a parent suddenly leave or die during childhood, for example, could have left you feeling vulnerable, fearful of anything that might upset your basic sense of security and stability. Or if one of your parents abused alcohol, the resulting instability in your early family environment might have led you to respond with an excessive need to control. At the time, overcontrol might have seemed necessary to your very survival.

Any serious trauma—in childhood or adulthood—can lead you to respond with increased vigilance and distrust toward life. Survivors of severe trauma often develop highly controlled or controlling personalities. For them it may be the only way to maintain a semblance of stability when their whole world seems to have fallen apart.

Overcoming the excessive need for control takes time and persistence. You may find the following four strategies to be helpful:

Acceptance

Acceptance means learning to live a little more comfortably with the unpredictability of life—with the unexpected changes that occur daily on a small scale and, less often, on a large scale. It's inevitable that you'll encounter changes that you simply can't predict or control, whether in your environment, in the way others choose to behave, or in your own physical health. You may have resources to cope with these changes, but you're not always going to be prepared for them. Sometimes your personal life situation may seem relatively chaotic, disordered, or out of control. Developing acceptance means acquiring a willingness to take life as it comes. Rather than fearing those occasions when circumstances don't obey your expectations, you can learn to go with the change. Popular expressions for this are "go with the flow" and "take things in stride." In a word, acceptance implies *nonresistance*.

How do you cultivate greater acceptance? Letting go of perfectionism, as described in the next section, will provide a good start. A willingness to let go of unrealistic expectations can save you a lot of disappointment. Relaxation is also an important key. The more relaxed you remain, the less likely you are to be fearful and defensive when circumstances suddenly change and don't go your way. When you're relaxed, you slow down, and it's easier to go with rather than balk against the unexpected. Regular meditation practice can help you relax your need to control. You may find that chapter 7, "Meditation," offers some useful approaches to take life more in stride, learning to witness rather than react to the ups and downs of each day.

Finally, a sense of humor toward life can be quite helpful. Humor enables you to step back from those times when everything appears to be in disarray and get some perspective. If you can remain relaxed and laugh a little at situations that appear out of control, your response begins to change from "Oh my God!" to "Oh, well—that's the way it goes. Now what do I need to do?" Laughing at life's imperfections makes your journey through life a lot lighter.

Affirmations that can help you develop an attitude of acceptance include:

- I'm learning to take life as it comes.
- It's okay to let go and trust that things will work out.
- I can relax and tolerate a little disorder and ambiguity.
- I'm learning not to take myself or my life so seriously.

You may want to read those affirmations daily or write them in large print and post them around your house.

Cultivating Patience

People who have an overcontrolled approach to life's problems want to have them all figured out by tomorrow. Yet it's often true that difficult situations cannot be worked out immediately. All the pieces that contribute to a solution come together gradually over a period of time. Developing patience means you allow yourself to tolerate temporary muddles and ambiguity while you wait for all the necessary steps of the solution to unfold. As you develop more patience, you learn to let go and wait for a resolution to emerge. You begin to trust the process of life and stop micromanaging each step along the way.

Trusting That Most Problems Eventually Work Out

Developing trust that situations will work out goes along with cultivating patience. You may not see the solution to a particular difficulty easily or quickly. But if you always need to see in advance how something is going to work out, you can end up making yourself very anxious. There is an old saying, "Life is a river—you can't always see what's coming around the bend." Developing trust means believing that just about everything *eventually does work out*. Either you find a solution, or, if the problem can't be changed externally, you learn to alter your attitude toward it, so that coping becomes easier. When you look back over the problems you've encountered in your life, you'll find that in most, if not all cases, the problem eventually worked itself out.

Cultivating a Spiritual Approach to Life

Cultivating a spiritual approach to life can mean many things. In essence, it means believing in a Higher Power, Force, or Intelligence that transcends the world as you ordinarily perceive and know it. Very often it also implies having a personal relationship with that Power, Force, or Intelligence.

Developing your spirituality offers at least two ways to assuage the fear of losing control. First, it gives you the option to "turn over" any problem that seems insoluble, overwhelming, or just plain worrisome to the care of your Higher Power, however you choose to define that Power. This process is expressed in the third step of all 12-step programs as "[We] made a decision to turn our will and our lives over to the care of a Higher Power, as we understood that Power." This does *not* mean that you relinquish responsibility for handling the challenges that come up in life. It does mean believing in a higher resource ("higher" in the sense of being beyond your own capabilities) that can be of support and assistance when you've reached the point where a problem appears insoluble. Faith in such a resource allows you to let go of the idea that you have to fully control everything. Some of my clients find that they can practice approaching a phobic situation more easily by "turning over" their worry and anxiety to their Higher Power. See chapter 8, "Letting Go," for further discussion of the process of relinquishing fear to a Higher Power.

A second way that a spiritual view of life can reduce your need for control is in nurturing the belief that *there is a larger purpose in life beyond the overt appearance of what happens from day to day.* If you believe that there is no spiritual foundation to reality, then the unpredictable and unforeseen events of life can seem random and capricious. You can feel distressed because there is no explanation for why this bad event happened or that apparent unfair situation occurred. Most forms of spirituality offer an alternative view that the universe is not random. Events that may appear meaningless and brutal from a human perspective have some meaning or purpose in the broader scheme of things.

A popular phrase that expresses this idea is "Everything happens for some purpose." Often hindsight provides us with clearer vision. When you reflect deeply on some of the unforeseen mishaps in your life, you may see in retrospect how they served you—either in an obvious way or by promoting your growth as a human being. See the chapter "Spirituality" if you wish to explore further how spirituality can change your perception of life.

Perfectionism: Fear of Rejection and Losing Control

Answer true or false (circle one):

I'm not satisfied with less than the very best at my work or at school.	T	F

Achieving much in the world is important to me.	T	F
I should always be competent (I demand a lot of myself).	T	F
I have a low tolerance for mistakes, especially my own.	T	F
When things don't go exactly the way I planned, I get upset.	T	F

Perfectionism is a common trait among persons with anxiety difficulties. It is closely related to the fear of losing control, but also has associations with a low sense of self-worth and the fear of rejection.

Perfectionism can be defined as *the tendency to have expectations about yourself, others, and life that are unrealistically high*. When anything falls short, you become disappointed, frustrated, or critical. Perfectionism may also cause you to focus excessively on small flaws or mistakes in yourself or your accomplishments. In emphasizing what's wrong, you tend to discount and ignore what's right.

Perfectionism is a common cause of low self-esteem. It can cause you to be critical of every effort and convince you that nothing is ever good enough. It can also cause you to drive yourself to the point of chronic stress, exhaustion, and burnout. Every time perfectionism counsels you that you "should," "have to," or "must," you tend to push yourself forward out of anxiety, rather than from natural desire and inclination. The more perfectionistic you are, the more often you're likely to feel anxious.

Overcoming perfectionism requires a fundamental shift in your attitude toward yourself and how you approach life in general. The following seven guidelines are intended as a starting point for making such a shift.

Let Go of the Idea That Your Worth Is Determined By Your Achievements and Accomplishments

Outer accomplishment may be how society measures a person's "worth" or "social status." But are you willing to allow society to have the last word on your value as a person? Work on reinforcing the idea that your worth is a given. People ascribe inherent worth to pets and plants just by virtue of their existence. You as a human being have the same inherent worth. Be willing to recognize and affirm that you're lovable and acceptable as you are, apart from your outer accomplishments. If you need to measure yourself against any standard, try replacing society's definitions of value with the two values of learning to love others and growing in wisdom.

Recognize and Overcome Perfectionistic Thinking Styles

Perfectionism is expressed in the way you talk to yourself. Three types of thinking characteristic of a perfectionistic attitude are "should/must thinking," "all-or-nothing thinking," and "overgeneralization." Below are examples of self-statements associated with each thinking style and corresponding, more realistic counterstatements.

Perfectionistic Thinking Styles

Thinking Style	**Counterstatements**
Should/Must Thinking	
I should be able to do this right.	I'll do the best I can.
I must not make mistakes.	It's okay to make mistakes.
All-or-Nothing Thinking	
This is all wrong.	This is not *all* wrong. There are some parts of it that are okay and some that need attention.
I feel worthless.	Feeling worthless is just a feeling. I have many worthy traits and capabilities.
Overgeneralization	
I *always* foul things up.	It's simply untrue that I *always* foul things up. In this particular case, I'll go back and make the necessary corrections.
I'll *never* be able to do this.	If I take small steps and keep making an effort, over time I'll accomplish what I set out to do.

Spend one week noticing all the instances when you get involved in should/must thinking, all-or-nothing thinking, or overgeneralization. Keep a notebook with you so that you can write down instances of these thoughts as they occur. Examine what you're telling yourself at times when you feel particularly anxious or stressed. Pay special attention to your use of the words "should," "must," "have to," "always," "never," "all," or "none." After you've spent a week writing down your perfectionist self-statements, compose counterstatements for each one. In subsequent weeks, read over your list of counterstatements frequently to encourage yourself to cultivate a less perfectionist approach to life.

Stop Magnifying the Importance of Small Errors

One of the most problematic aspects of perfectionism is its mandate to focus on small flaws or errors. Perfectionists are prone to come down very hard on themselves for a single, minute mistake that has few or no immediate consequences, let alone any long-term effects. When you really think about it, how important is a mistake you make today going to be one month from now? Or one year from now? In 99.9 percent of cases, the mistake will be forgotten within a short period of time. There is no real learning without mistakes or setbacks. No great success was ever attained without many failures and mistakes along the way.

Focus on Positives

In dwelling on small errors or mistakes, perfectionists tend to discount their positive accomplishments. They selectively ignore anything positive they've done. A way to counter this tendency is to take inventory near the end of each day of positive things you've accomplished. Think about what ways, small or large, you've been helpful or pleasant to people during the day. Think of any small steps you've taken toward achieving your goals. What other things got done? What insights did you have?

Pay attention to whether you disqualify something positive with a "but"—for example, "I had a good practice session, *but* I became anxious near the end." Learn to leave off the "but" in your assessments of your attitudes and behavior.

Work on Goals That Are Realistic

Are your goals realistically attainable, or have you set them too high? Would you expect of anyone else the goals you set for yourself? Sometimes it's difficult to recognize the overly lofty nature of certain goals. It can be helpful to do a "reality check" with a friend or counselor to determine whether any particular goal is realistically attainable, or even reasonable to strive for. Are you expecting too much of yourself and the world? You may need to adjust some of your goals a bit in line with the limiting factors of time, energy, and resources. If your estimation of self-worth truly comes from within, rather than from what you achieve, you will be able to do this. Acceptance of personal limitations is the ultimate act of self-love.

Cultivate More Pleasure and Recreation in Your Life

Perfectionism has a tendency to make people rigid and self-denying. Your own human needs get sacrificed in favor of the pursuit of external goals. Ultimately this tendency can lead to a stifling of vitality and creativity. Pleasure—finding the enjoyment in life—reverses this trend.

The Sioux Indians have a wise saying: "The first thing people say after their death is—'Why was I so serious?'" Are you taking yourself too seriously and not allowing yourself time for fun, recreation, play, and rest? How can you make more time for leisure and pleasure? You can change by taking time every day to do at least one thing you enjoy.

Develop a Process Orientation

If you engage in sports, do you play to win or just to enjoy the activity of playing? In your life in general, are you "playing to win," channeling your energies into excelling at all costs, or are you enjoying the process of living day by day?

Most people find, especially as they get older, that to get the most enjoyment out of life, it works best to place value on the *process* of doing things—not just on the product or accomplishment. Popular cliches that express this idea include: "The journey is more important than the destination," and "Stop and smell the roses."

Overcautiousness: Fear of Illness, Injury, or Death

Answer true or false (circle one):

I'm reluctant to try new things, especially if they expose me to physical risk.	T	F
I often worry that minor bodily symptoms or ailments could be a serious illness.	T	F
The idea of death—my own or others—is very frightening to me.	T	F
I often worry about something terrible happening to a loved one.	T	F
I consider myself more cautious than adventurous.	T	F

Anxious people are often very cautious and avoid situations that carry even the slightest risk of injury. Or they may be hypervigilant about their health, fearing even the smallest bodily ailment to be a sign of severe disease. Fears of flying or driving freeways often relate to fears of injury or death, although they may also involve the fear of confinement. Excessive worry about the welfare of a loved one—what might happen to them while absent—is another form this issue can take.

Traumatic experiences in which you had a close brush with death or suffered injury or pain can predispose you to being overly cautious and fearful about any situation that might potentially cause a similar experience. It also happens frequently that the death of someone close to you can lead to increased sensitivity and fearfulness about death—for others or for yourself. Two different clients of mine, who each experienced the death of a parent from chronic illness, subsequently developed *hypochondriasis*—the fear that almost any minor ailment could be cancer or something terminal. Perhaps the fear of death can begin as early as birth, if the birth was difficult and there was a question about the newborn's survival.

Overcautiousness that arises from the fear of illness, injury, or death can severely limit your activities. You may perceive the world as a dangerous place and deny yourself access to much of what life can offer. An excessive need for safety can lead to boredom as well as restrict you from developing your full potential.

Accepting Mortality

The lesson for persons fearful of illness/injury/death is *to learn to fully accept the fact of human mortality*. In reality, there are no guarantees that adversity might not befall us—and the eventuality of our death is certain. Learning to accept these facts and take them in stride fosters your ability to make the most of your life. Attempting to ignore or run from them leaves you feeling vulnerable and unable to take even modest risks.

The best way to come to terms with your own mortality is not to dwell on it—or deny it. Simply *acknowledge* it and then go about living your life fully. Ultimately, the fear of injury or death is connected with a fear of not having fully lived your life. To die without having taken advantage of the opportunities your life offers is a dismal prospect. The more life-enhancing activities you engage in today—from small things such as going out to dinner to large things such as developing your creative gifts—the easier it becomes to accept the fact of death. Beyond this, you may also choose to assuage the fear of death by holding the view that your soul continues on after physical death (see the chapter "Spirituality"). Whether or not you believe in life after death, enjoying life in the here and now will help to make the fact of mortality more acceptable.

Learning to Take Risks

How do you deal with overcautiousness? How can you move out of your comfort zone and be willing to take more risks with your life? Working on your sense of self-worth, as previously described, is an important first step. Review the sections on self-worth in the parts of this chapter dealing with excessive need for approval, insecurity, and overdependency. Once you've gained some confidence in yourself, it's important to actually practice taking mild to moderate risks.

If you want to increase your risk-taking ability in general, make a list of risks you might consider taking in your life and then rank them from least to most difficult. Then proceed step by step up your list. If it helps to have a loved one accompany you in taking these risks, by all means include them. You can best increase your risk-taking ability by deliberately committing yourself to doing so and then following through, at your own pace, with whatever support you need. As you gain confidence with smaller risks, larger ones become more feasible.

The following examples pertain to physical risk:

1. Bicycling on level roads
2. Bicycling up and down hills
3. Ice skating
4. Roller skating or rollerblading
5. Riding a motor scooter on back roads
6. Snow skiing—beginner's slope
7. White-water rafting
8. Riding a motor scooter on busy roads
9. Snow skiing—intermediate slope
10. Jumping out of low-flying plane with a parachute

Hypochondriasis

A special problem sometimes associated with the fear of injury or death is hypochondriasis. This is a tendency to imagine that you have a serious illness and then persistently seek out medical authorities for reassurance. If you aren't fully satisfied with what one doctor says, you try going to another, obtaining a second, third, and fourth opinion in some cases. Hypochondriasis is a misdirected quest to create a sense of personal safety. It doesn't work: continually seeking reassurance will only add to anxiety. The most effective behavioral treatment (the same as is used with obsessive compulsive disorder) is response prevention—simply ceasing all your attempts to get reassurance and letting time pass to allow you to desensitize to the resulting anxiety. Working on building an inner sense of security, as previously described, is also very important. Using cognitive therapy in identifying and countering fearful thinking around your particular fear of illness will help. If you'd like more assistance, refer to my audio tape entitled "Fear of Illness" (available from the publisher of this book). Since hypochondriasis appears to have some relationship with obsessive compulsive disorder, SSRI medications are also often used in the treatment of more severe cases.

Confinement Phobia: Fear of Being Confined or Trapped

Answer true or false (circle one):

I get anxious in most situations where I have to stop and wait (for example, stoplights, standing in line at the grocery store).	T	F
I avoid or am afraid of traveling on public transportation—trains, buses, commercial jets.	T	F
It's uncomfortable for me to be in a closed-in place or in a crowd of people.	T	F
I often feel trapped by something in my life situation, such as my job, marriage, family responsibilities, health, or debt.	T	F
It's difficult for me to make a long-term commitment to someone or something.	T	F

The fear of confinement runs through a number of different phobias including: fear of flying, fear of elevators, fear of crowded public places, fear of small enclosed places (claustrophobia), and fear of being "stuck" anywhere (traffic, bridges, tunnels, or riding on public transportation). Of all of the types of fear, I believe that fear of confinement most frequently disguises an underlying fear of something else (what some psychologists would call a "displaced" fear).

Growing up in a dysfunctional family situation (for example, if your parents were physically or sexually abusive, or perhaps alcoholic) can instill a fear of being "unable to escape or get away." A child has no choice but to endure such mistreatment: it's easy to understand how a fear of being trapped might develop under such circumstances.

If the fear of confinement has its origin in childhood trauma (including birth trauma) where you literally were confined or trapped, you may benefit from seeking the assistance of a therapist skilled in treating post-traumatic stress difficulties. It may be necessary to recall the incident, fully express the feelings you had at the time, and then make a new decision—a reinterpretation—of the meaning of the incident so that you can let it go and be free to go on with your life. Techniques such as hypnotherapy and eye-movement desensitization and reprocessing (EMDR), as described in *The Anxiety & Phobia Workbook*, may help in this process.

In my experience with clients, fears of confinement are more frequently related to present circumstances than past. The fear may serve as a metaphor for some way in which you feel confined or trapped in your present life, whether in your job, your relationship with your partner, your economic constraints, your health limitations, or even your daily schedule. By addressing and freeing up the problem in your life, you suddenly find you can drive at rush hour or stand in line at the grocery store more easily. This is not to deny the importance of exposure therapy in overcoming situational phobias. Yet it may be necessary both to do exposure and address issues of interpersonal or existential confinement in your current life to ensure long-term recovery. If you happen to be dealing with a phobia where you have a problem with feeling trapped, you might ask yourself whether there is any broader sense in which you feel trapped by the circumstances of your current life.

Finally, the fear of confinement may arise simply from feeling trapped in your own body without the ability to easily move. When you are anxious, your muscles tighten up and your body naturally prepares for "fight or flight." However, if you're in a situation where it really is difficult to move (for example, the window seat on an airplane or next in line at a checkout counter), you may suddenly feel very stuck. There you are, in a sense "locked" within the tightening muscles of your abdomen, chest, shoulders, and neck with no way to actively channel the sympathetic nervous system arousal or adrenaline surging through your bloodstream. If the sensation grows strong enough, you may perceive it as entrapment—not just being stuck—*especially if you tell yourself you're "trapped."*

At this point you may escalate to a full-blown panic reaction with a strong urgency to run. Had you been able to move more easily in the first place, perhaps the perception and fear of entrapment would have never occurred.

In my experience, the most effective way to handle this situation is to *go with* your body's need to move, wherever possible. If you're standing in line at the checkout counter, put your bag down and leave the store for a minute, walk around, and then return. If you're stuck in traffic on the expressway, pull over to the shoulder if possible, get out and move about. If you're seated on an airplane, get up and walk to the bathroom and come back, repeating this several times if necessary. If you have to keep your seat belt fastened and can't leave your seat, shake your leg, wring a towel, write in your journal, but do *something* to channel the excess activation in your body. Keep telling yourself, "This restriction will be over in a while and I can get up and move again," or "There's nothing dangerous—I'll be able to move about soon," or "I may be restricted, but 'trapped' is a false perception." The better you become at perceiving the situation for what it is—*restriction and not entrapment*—the less anxiety you are likely to experience.

If fear of confinement is a problem, *you need to address the underlying issue.* Is your fear left over from a previous trauma? Is it a metaphor for some current restrictive situation in your life? Or is it simply your way of perceiving situations where your mobility is limited? Perhaps two or three of these possibilities are simultaneously true for you. When you understand the source of your fear, you can overcome it.

What You Can Do Now

1. As you've read through this chapter, I hope you've acquired a better idea of any personality issues that might be contributing to your problem with anxiety. Various strategies have been described for overcoming these issues. If you are highly self-motivated, you can probably utilize these strategies on your own. Simply making a commitment to do so is the most important first step. For

many persons, though, it is easiest to work through personality issues in the context of individual or group psychotherapy. In finding a good therapist, talk to friends who have had therapy or consult the Anxiety Disorders Association of America (at 301-231-9350) to locate a therapist who treats anxiety difficulties in your area. The ultimate criteria for evaluating therapy is your own gut feeling—do you feel comfortable with the therapy and do you feel you're truly receiving help? If you don't within the first few sessions, look for another therapist (or group). Apart from therapy, you can also deal with personality issues by participating in 12-step "anonymous" groups such as Phobics Anonymous, Emotions Anonymous, or Codependents Anonymous. Your local Alcoholics Anonymous organization may have a list of these other 12-step groups. See also *The Self-Help Sourcebook* for a list of several hundred national self-help organizations along with toll-free help lines (available from Self-Help Clearinghouse at 973-625-7101).

Use the following points to help you decide what your next step is. First determine which of the six personality traits and associated core fears described in this chapter apply to you, and then:

2. If excessive need for approval or fear of rejection is an issue, you likely need to work on self-esteem. See the chapter on self-esteem in *The Anxiety & Phobia Workbook* as well as the books by Bradshaw and Branden listed at the end of this chapter. If you feel you need to work on being more assertive, see the book by Alberti and Emmons in the references. You might also consider taking a class on assertiveness if one is available in your area. If you tend to be too much of a people pleaser at your own expense, you might want to read the books by Beattie or Norwood below, or consider getting involved with a Codependents Anonymous group in your area, if available. If you tend to avoid people, or have a problem with social anxiety, see the books by Zimbardo and Markway. You might also want to consider working with a therapist experienced in treating social phobia.

3. If insecurity, overdependency, and/or the fear of abandonment is an issue, it's important to work on self-esteem, either on your own or with a skilled therapist. Review the list, "Self-Nurturing Activities," and find at least one thing to do for yourself each day. Work on developing a better support system in your community if you feel overly dependent upon your significant other or family members. Finally, see chapter 6, "Find Your Unique Purpose," if you feel you need to give more attention to finding your niche in the world. If insecurity or the fear of abandonment are deep-seated and based on trauma from your past, you will likely benefit from working with a skilled psychotherapist.

4. If overcontrol is an issue for you, see chapter 8, "Letting Go", for further assistance.

5. Work on implementing the seven guidelines for overcoming perfectionism, if this is an issue for you. Also consult the book by Anthony and Swenson in the references.

6. Overcoming the fear of injury, illness, or death requires coming to terms with your own mortality and increasing your willingness to take risks. You may want to work with a counselor to assist you with this. If you tend to inflate the significance of minor body symptoms, you may want to purchase the tape, "Fear of Illness," available from New Harbinger at 1-800-748-6273.

7. When fears are deep-seated, they often have their origin in the past. If you feel you haven't received sufficient help for your anxiety or phobia from cognitive-behavioral therapy (including systematic exposure)—and especially if you had a traumatic childhood—you might want to consider working with a therapist who is skilled in addressing emotional issues left over from the past. There are, for example, therapists who specialize in working with people recovering from physical, sexual, or emotional abuse. Sometimes specific techniques such as hypnotherapy or eye movement desensitization and reprocessing (EMDR) can assist in this process (see *The Anxiety & Phobia Workbook*).

References and Further Reading

Alberti, Robert E., and Michael Emmons. 1995. *Your Perfect Right*. Revised edition. San Luis Obispo, Calif.: Impact Press.

Anthony, Martin, and Richard Swenson. 1998. *When Perfect Isn't Good Enough*. Oakland, Calif: New Harbinger Publications.

Bass, Ellen, and Laura Davis. 1994. *The Courage to Heal*. 3d ed. New York: Harper Collins. (incest, molestation)

Beattie, Melody. 1987. *Co-dependent No More*. San Francisco: Harper/Hazelden.

Bourne, Edmund J. 2000. *The Anxiety & Phobia Workbook*. 3rd ed. Oakland, Calif: New Harbinger Publications.

Bower, Sharon, and Gordon Bower. 1976. *Asserting Yourself*. Reading, Mass.: Addison-Wesley.

Bradshaw, John. 1988. *Healing the Shame That Binds You*. Deerfield Beach, Fla.: Health Communications, Inc.

———. 1990. *Homecoming: Reclaiming and Championing Your Inner Child*. New York: Bantam.

Branden, Nathaniel. 1969. *The Psychology of Self-Esteem*. New York: Nash.

Jeffers, Susan. 1987. *Feel the Fear and Do It Anyway*. San Diego, Calif.: Harcourt, Brace, Jovanovich.

Markway, Barbara, Cheryl Carmin, Alec Pollard, and Teresa Flynn. 1992. *Dying of Embarrassment: Help for Social Anxiety and Phobia*. Oakland, Calif.: New Harbinger Publications.

McKay, Matthew, and Patrick Fanning. 1992. *Self-Esteem*. 2d ed. Oakland, Calif.: New Harbinger Publications.

Miller, Alice. 1983. *The Drama of the Gifted Child*. New York: Basic Books. (emotional abuse)

Missildine, Hugh. 1963. *Your Inner Child of the Past*. New York: Simon & Schuster.

Norwood, Robin. 1985. *Women Who Love Too Much*. New York: Pocket Books.

Smith, Manuel J. 1975. *When I Say No, I Feel Guilty*. New York: Dial Press.

Whitfield, Charles. 1987. *Healing the Child Within*. Pompano Beach, Fla.: Health Communications.

Woititz, Janet. 1983. *Adult Children of Alcoholics*. Hollywood, Fla.: Health Communications.

Zimbardo, Philip. 1990. *Shyness: What It Is, What to Do About It*. Reading, Mass.: Addison-Wesley.

6

Find Your Unique Purpose

Among the many possible sources of anxiety, one that's common in contemporary society is a lack of personal meaning. The inability to find meaning in life usually reflects a degree of self-alienation. Such a condition results in a tendency to pursue satisfactions and stimulation on the outside rather than from within. Materialistic goals, a concern with appearances, and addictions may all be used to fill an inner emptiness which is often felt as an unsettled feeling or chronic anxiety. External solutions may work, but only temporarily—they provide a quick fix rather than a true healing.

To reestablish meaning in life is to rediscover your soul. An important step in this direction is to find your soul's own innate and natural expression of creativity. Your unique, innate creativity is itself not something you have to create. You came into the world with it, and it likely was evident when you were a child. Unfortunately, education, socialization, and the trauma of entering adulthood may have obscured the natural gifts and talents you brought into the world to express. If you've wandered too far away from your innermost wellspring of creativity, you've probably ended up, like many people, feeling too busy and too anxious. Rediscovering your unique creativity—what I'm referring to here as your unique life purpose—can go a long way toward healing self-alienation and thus anxiety. Life cannot be as empty or fearful when you experience it as purposeful and creative. Discovering your unique purpose (or purposes) will restore meaning to your life—and an increased willingness to look to yourself rather than the outside for the spark of life itself.

Defining "Life Purpose"

What is meant by the idea of "life purpose"? If you search inside yourself, you'll find it's something you need to do in order to feel whole, complete, and fulfilled in your life. It's uniquely your own—something that can't be duplicated. Only you can do it.

Your unique life purpose comes from within and has little or nothing to do with what your parents, partner, or friends might want you to do. It's something that expresses a particular talent, gift, skill, or desire that you hold most dear. In fulfilling it, you discover your own unique way to contribute to life.

Generally, your life purpose is something that goes beyond the limited needs of your own ego. It is "other-directed," having an impact on something or someone beyond just yourself. Your life purpose might involve raising a child, contributing to your community, or teaching something you've learned from your personal experience. When you're fulfilling your life purpose, your life takes on a new dimension of meaning beyond self-interest.

From a metaphysical standpoint, your life purpose is an important activity or service your soul came into this world to accomplish. The metaphysical idea of "life purpose" appears in various religious traditions. In Christianity it's referred to as a "calling," while in Hinduism it is spoken of as your "personal dharma." The assumption is that your life purpose, especially the gifts and talents on which it's based, is God-appointed. In some lofty sense, it was decided on and perhaps even planned out before you were born. You came into the world with your unique purpose as a potential. It's your choice and free will that determines whether you fulfill your particular purpose, as well as how you go about doing it. Yet the potential itself remains latent in your soul. As long as your life is focused solely on personal gratification of bodily and ego needs, you may continue to feel something is incomplete or missing. To the extent that you discover and begin to express your unique purpose, you are likely to feel a deep sense of rightness and direction in your life. To be aligned with your life purpose gives life a positive direction—not to may result in a sense of drifting, or keeping busy to avoid feeling empty. There is no longer as great a need to seek pleasure in outer material things, since you begin to feel an increasing inner satisfaction that you are "on course"—doing what you came here to do.

To align with your unique life purpose is an important step in healing yourself and becoming all you can be. It is to live more from the truth of your soul rather than from ego needs and goals. As such, you begin to be more in touch with the creative forces and guidance of Spirit.

It's important to realize that your life purpose may not necessarily be grand in scope. Size of impact is less important than *quality*. Your purpose may be about raising a family, contributing to a social or political cause, or sheltering injured or sick animals. Or, it might involve artistic pursuits, such as painting, playing an instrument, or writing poetry. Perhaps volunteering your services for a youth group or teaching a Sunday school class might fulfill your life purpose.

Often your life purpose does not become clear until you've worked through some of your personality issues, as was discussed in Chapter 5. Resolving unfinished business with your parents, taking care of your financial and security needs, overcoming social fears and learning to be assertive may all be part of the "groundwork" that needs to be done before you can fully express your life purpose. It's difficult for your creativity to fully blossom until you've freed up sufficient energy within yourself from personality and interpersonal conflicts. In fact, confronting and dealing with personality issues is also an important part of what you came here to do, along with expressing your unique creativity. In an important sense, a major part of your life purpose is to do the inner psychological work necessary to handle your personal needs and achieve a sense of identity and self-worth. (That's not to say that you can't begin to express your unique creativity while still addressing your personality issues.)

Discovering Your Own Life Purpose

If you currently feel out of touch with your life purpose, how do you go about discovering what it is? The questionnaire that follows is designed to stimulate your thinking in ways that can help you to formulate your own unique goals. Your answers to the questions may give you some insights into what it is that is most important for you to do with your life. Give yourself at least one full day to reflect on these questions and write out your answers. You may even want to ponder these questions for a week or a month. After you've arrived at the answers for yourself, practice visualizing what your life would look like if you were truly fulfilling your special purpose. I also recommend that you share your answers to these questions with a close personal friend or counselor and get that person's input and feedback. If realizing your purpose involves making a career change, it might be helpful to work with a career counselor. If it involves going back to school, you'll want to talk to an academic guidance counselor at the school you're considering (see the section of this chapter called "Implementing Your Life Purpose").

Life Purpose Questionnaire

1. Does the work I'm presently doing express what I truly want to be doing? If not, how can I begin to take steps toward discovering and doing work that would be more personally fulfilling?

2. Am I satisfied with the education I've obtained? Would I like to go back to school and increase my education and training? If so, how can I begin to move in that direction?

3. If I need to be doing my job for now, are there any hobbies or avocations that I've thought about developing?

4. Do I have creative outlets? Are there any areas of my life where I feel I can be creative? If not, what creative activities could I develop?

5. What kinds of interests or activities spark my enthusiasm? What do I naturally enjoy doing (alone, with friends, family, outdoors or indoors)?

6. What would I like to do with my life if I could do what I truly wanted? (Assume, for the purpose of this question, that money and the responsibilities of your current job and family are not a limitation.)

7. What would I like to accomplish with my life? What would I like to have accomplished by the time I reach seventy in order to feel that my life has been productive and meaningful?

8. In what way(s), however small, do I feel I could make the world a better place?

9. What are my most important values? What values give my life the greatest meaning? Some examples of values include:

Happy family life	Material success
Intimacy	Career achievement
Friendship	Creative expression
Good health	Personal growth
Peace of mind	Spiritual awareness
Serving others	Dedication to a social cause

10. Is there anything that I deeply value and yet feel I haven't fully experienced or realized in my life? What changes do I need to make—or what risks do I need to take—to more fully realize my most important values?

11. Do I have any special talents or skills that I haven't fully developed or expressed? What changes do I need to make—or what risks do I need to take—in order to develop and express my special talents and skills?

12. In the light of the above questions, I feel that my most important life purposes would include (list):

13. What obstacles exist to pursuing and realizing my life purposes?

14. What am I willing to commit to doing in the next month, year, and three years to eliminate the obstacles in Question 13 and move toward realizing my special purpose(s)?

    One month:

    One year:

    Three years:

Guidelines for Reflecting on Your Life Purpose

To assist you in thinking about the questions posed in the *Life Purpose Questionnaire*, you may find the following guidelines helpful:

1. Listen to what your heart tells you about what you would most love to do or be.

2. Be sure to separate your unique goals and objectives from those of your parents, spouse, friends, or others. Only you can know what your true mission is.

3. Your life purpose may or may not be your actual vocation. It could be a hobby, pastime, or avocation.
4. Notice negative self-talk that puts down the dreams or inner fantasies that your heart offers up. For example:

   "I can't do what I want and still make a living."

   "It's too late to go back and get the training."

   "It's too expensive."

   "It's impractical."

   "They won't approve."

   "I don't have the talent for it."

   "I don't have the time."

   "It's too much work—too difficult."

   "No one's going to be interested, anyway."

   Statements like these are often clues to showing you what your deepest purpose or "personal dream" actually might be.
5. Keep in mind the famous maxim: "God never gives us a vision without also giving us the capacity to make it come true."
6. Ask your own inner wisdom or Higher Power to help you discover and clarify what your life purpose might be. In your deepest self, you already know what your mission or purpose is.
7. Look for synchronicities. When you are moving toward or on the path of your life purpose, amazing coincidences will often happen to give you confirmation that you're on the right course.
8. Realize that fulfilling your life purpose may involve taking risks and giving up certain aspects of your life as you know it right now. Are you up to taking such risks? If not, how might you gain support to do so?

Visualize Your Life Purpose

After you have a good idea about the nature of your life purpose, write a scenario on a separate sheet of paper about what your life would look like if you were to fully realize this purpose (or purposes). You can design separate visualizations for each purpose or incorporate the realization of all of your life purposes into a single description. Be sure to make your scenario sufficiently detailed to include where you're living and working, who you're with, what activities make up your day, and what a typical day would look like. Once you've completed a detailed description, record it on tape, preferably in your own voice. You may want to record it after a few minutes of preliminary instructions to relax. Visualizing the fulfillment of your life purpose on a regular, consistent basis will go a long way toward helping you to actually realize your goal. (See Chapter 10, "Create Your Vision," for further discussion of this point.)

Implementing Your Life Purpose

Do the Necessary Research

If you're thinking about changing your occupation, you may want to work with a career counselor to help delineate new vocational options. If you already know what you want to do, consult the *Occupational Outlook Handbook* (1996) at your local library to find out about entry requirements and job prospects in your field of choice. If you want to take up a hobby in astronomy, gardening, or antique collecting, research existing information on the subject at the library or on the Internet if you have access. Talk to people who are already involved in the vocation or avocation that interests you.

Acquire the Necessary Skills and Training

Entering a new career generally requires retraining or retooling. If formal training is needed, is it available in your area? Can retraining be acquired by correspondence or apprenticing to someone already skilled in the field? Are you willing to make the time for retraining? Learning to do oil painting or play the piano will require a one or two year commitment to taking classes or working with a teacher. Many things you might do as a life purpose do not emerge spontaneously but require an intensive period of learning and/or training.

Persevere

Anything truly worth doing—and few things are likely to be more important to you than fulfilling your life purpose—will take time, effort, and discipline. Whether it's pursuing a new career or hobby, contributing to your larger community, or healing yourself from chronic illness—your unique life mission will require a consistent commitment and energy expenditure over time. The main reason why many noble projects fail is not for lack of inspiration or even skill, but lack of follow-through.

Watch for Negative Self-Talk

Continue to monitor yourself for negative attitudes or self-statements that interfere with your progress toward fulfilling your dream. Statements such as those mentioned under number 4 in the previous *Guidelines* section are notorious for interfering with the pursuit of anyone's creative purpose. Talk back to your inner critic or cynic with affirmative statements such as:

- "I accept and believe in myself."
- "I am a unique and creative person."
- "I have unique gifts that are mine to express."
- "I have the capability to realize my goals (or dream)."

Trust That the Universe Will Support You

Your unique creative purpose is something you came into the world to do. The sources of inspiration for it come from your own inner spiritual source—your Higher Power. So you can trust that, in pursuing your particular purpose, you will receive guidance and support from a place beyond your conscious self or ego. If you feel shaky about what you're doing, it's important to keep asking your Higher Power to assist you. If you are on course with your purpose, and ask with sincerity, help will be forthcoming.

Set Aside Time Each Day

The process of realizing your life purpose requires a time and energy commitment. To move it from the realm of ideas and inspiration into practical form will be helped by setting aside time each day to work on it. If you're at the beginning of the process, you need to make time to discover your purpose or do the necessary research to find out how to realize it. If you're at the stage of learning how to do it, this too requires a daily commitment until you have learned the requisite knowledge and skills.

Finally, actually expressing your purpose requires a regular commitment, time and effort. However, the work you'll be doing at this stage is work that you'll deeply enjoy.

Although this has been one of the shorter chapters in this book, don't underestimate its importance. If you've felt that your life doesn't have the meaning and sense of direction that you would like, spend some time with this chapter and consult the books listed in the references. Finding and expressing your unique creative gifts can go a long way toward healing your personal struggle with anxiety. It can help someone else, too. As Nelson Mandela once said: "You are a child of God; your playing small doesn't serve the world."

What You Can Do Now

1. Do you feel aware of your own unique life purpose or purposes? Use the *Life Purpose Questionnaire* to assist you in clarifying what you would most like to do with your life.

2. Review the section "Implementing Your Life Purpose." If you feel ready to begin taking action to express your unique purpose, what steps are you willing to take (for example, learning appropriate skills, talking to others involved in a particular vocation or hobby, making time in your schedule to develop a creative pursuit, etc.):

In the next month?

In the next year?

3. If you decide you want to change your line of work, you might do so by following these steps:

   Find a career counselor you respect (or take a course in exploring career options at a local college).

   Explore different options by:

   - Reading about different vocations in books such as *What Color Is Your Parachute?* and *The Occupational Outlook Handbook.*
   - Talking to people who hold positions in vocations to which you feel drawn.
   - Narrow down vocational options to one particular type of work (obtain whatever help you need to do this)—focus is extremely important in achieving goals.

   Obtain education or training for the line of work you've chosen.

   - Find out where training is available in your area (your local library is a good resource for doing your research).
   - Apply to appropriate schools or training programs.
   - Apply for an educational grant or loan if your education or training will require a full-time commitment.
   - Complete your education or training (if possible while maintaining your current job).

   Search for an entry-level position in your new career.

- Obtain resources that tell you where jobs are available (professional or trade newsletters, journals, alumni organizations, newspapers, and job hot lines are all good resources).
- Prepare a professional-looking résumé.
- Apply for jobs.
- Go for interviews.
- Begin you new career.

References and Further Reading

Bolles, Richard. 1997. *What Color Is Your Parachute?* Berkeley: Ten Speed Press.

Braham, Barbara J. 1991. *Finding Your Purpose.* Menlo Park, Calif.: Crisp Publications.

LeShan, Lawrence. 1989. *Cancer as a Turning Point.* New York: Dutton. (Although this book is written for persons dealing with cancer, it's relevant to anyone who wants to redesign their life to have greater meaning, purpose, and creativity. Case histories are inspiring and instructive.)

Occupational Outlook Handbook. 1996. Bureau of Labor Statistics. Washington D.C.: U.S. Government Printing Office.

Stephan, Naomi. 1989. *Finding Your Life Mission.* Walpole, New Hampshire: Stillpoint Publishing. (Many practical exercises for getting in touch with your unique purpose.)

7

Meditation

Meditation was conceived in ancient times as a methodology for transcending human suffering and reconnecting with the spiritual dimension of life. For thousands of years Eastern philosophy has taught that the origin of human suffering is in our automatic, conditioned thoughts and reactions (the term "automatic thoughts" used in cognitive therapy is very similar to this notion). Nothing in life is inherently bad except that *we think about it or react to it as such*. If we can step back and simply witness our reactive patterns, we are then able to free ourselves from suffering. According to the Eastern perspective, meditation is the method *par excellence* for achieving a state of freedom or "liberation" from the suffering we create in our minds. (Christian mystics have also practiced meditation down through the centuries.)

How does meditation help to achieve this freedom? In a word, you can say that it is by the enlargement or "expansion" of *awareness*. Awareness can be defined as a pure, *unconditioned* state of consciousness that we all can experience. It exists "behind" or prior to the conditioned patterns of thinking and emotional reactivity we've learned over a lifetime. This awareness is always available to us, but much of the time it's clouded by the incessant stream of mental chatter and/or emotional reactions that make up ordinary moment-to-moment experience. Only when we become very quiet and still, *willing to "just be" rather than striving to do anything*, can this uncluttered awareness that precedes our thoughts and feelings reemerge.

To expand or enlarge awareness is simply to allow yourself to settle into greater degrees of it. Awareness lies along a continuum—it's possible to enter into it by degrees. Our language, in fact, contains references to these varying degrees of awareness in the expressions "small-minded" vs. "large-minded." Another way of understanding degrees of awareness is by the concept of "depth." Greater awareness is associated with greater depth. Thinking that is associated with less awareness is called "shallow," that which is associated with greater awareness is called "deep." It's my observation that there is no limit to the potential enlargement or depth of awareness. As your awareness grows, it can continue to enlarge or deepen indefinitely. According to Eastern philosophy, your deepest inner awareness is a link or bridge to the experience of your Higher Power (God), that which has been spoken of in other contexts as "Universal Mind" (Spinoza, Hegel) or "Cosmic Consciousness" (Bucke). At a deep level, your individual awareness joins up—or flows into—a much larger awareness that has no limit, much as a drop of the ocean is continuous with the entire ocean. As you enlarge or deepen your personal awareness, you can begin to participate to a greater degree in a larger, more universal awareness. Remember that you don't have to do anything to enlarge your awareness; it is something that emerges naturally when you become still.

Meditation, then, is a very powerful method for enlarging or deepening your awareness. It enables you to set aside conditioned patterns of thinking and feeling long enough so that you can begin to experience the emergence of deeper levels of your own inborn awareness. Your deepest awareness is nothing to be afraid of because it's inherently beyond (or prior to) fear itself.

When you experience expanded awareness, you simply feel a deep sense of peace. Out of this place of inner peace can arise other nonconditioned states such as unconditional love, wisdom, deep insight, and joy. In itself, this state of peace is nothing you need to develop. It's always there, deep inside of you, and you can discover it if you can become still and quiet enough to *allow* it to emerge. The practice of meditation is the most straightforward way to do this.

Meditation practice allows you to expand your awareness to the point where it's *larger* than your fearful thoughts or emotional reactions. As soon as your awareness is larger than your fear, you are no longer swept up by the fear but able to *stand outside* of it—in your mind—and merely *witness* it. It's as though you're identified with a part of your mind that's larger than the part that's constricted by fearful thoughts. As you continue to practice meditation and enlarge your awareness, it becomes easier *on an ongoing basis* to observe the stream of thoughts and feelings that make up your experience. You are less prone to get "stuck" or lost in them.

You might be concerned that increasing your ability to observe your inner thoughts and feelings sounds like becoming internally divided rather than more connected with yourself. In fact, the opposite is true. It's your reactive thoughts and conditioned emotional patterns that tend to pull you away from your own center—to lead you away from your deeper inner self and into what has been popularly termed "mind trips" or "personal dramas." To practice meditation is to cultivate states of greater wholeness. As you deepen and enlarge your awareness, you begin to be in touch with more of yourself. Your reactive thoughts and feelings still occur, but you're not so strongly claimed by them. You are more free to truly enjoy your life because you don't get as stuck or lost in any particular state of fear, anger, guilt, shame, grief, and so on. Rather, you're able to acknowledge the reaction, allow it to move through, and let it go. Your inner consciousness becomes spacious enough so that you can observe a worried thought, then take action if it's reasonable or choose to let it go if it's unreasonable. You begin to experience a greater sense of wholeness because you are not as scattered and dispersed by your mind's endless cascade of reactive thoughts and feelings. While these thoughts and feelings still occur, your *relationship* to them is different. You become large enough to witness them rather than be carried away by them.

A final benefit of meditation practice is the development of compassion toward yourself. Just as you learn to become less reactive to mental, bodily, and circumstantial triggers of fear, you also learn to be less reactive (and thus less judgmental) toward yourself. Feelings of anger, shame, and self-reproach may arise if you don't like something you said, did, or what your body or brain is "doing to you." Yet you don't have to get stuck or lost in these feelings. Instead, you can witness them, allow them to pass, and cultivate an attitude of kindness and respect toward yourself. Human beings are actually compassionate by nature when they are able to rise above all the adverse mental/emotional conditioning acquired over a lifetime. Practicing meditation and moving into a stance of witnessing your own experience will help you to access this innate compassion within yourself.

Learning to Meditate

Learning to meditate is a process that involves at least four distinct stages:

- Right attitude
- Right technique
- Developing concentration
- Cultivating awareness

Right attitude is a mind-set or mental stance that you bring to meditation. Such an attitude takes time and commitment to develop. Fortunately, the practice of meditation itself helps you to learn right attitude. *Right technique* involves learning specific methods of sitting and focusing your awareness that facilitate meditation. *Developing concentration* involves practicing additional techniques to reduce the inevitable distractibility that all beginners (and sometimes veterans) of meditation confront. The culmination of these first three stages is "mindfulness." *Cultivating mindfulness* is the process of making a fundamental shift in your relationship with your own inner experience, as described in the preceding section. It is to develop an "inner observer" within yourself that enables you to bear witness rather than react to the ups and downs of everyday (and even moment-to-moment) existence.

Right Attitude

The attitude that you bring to the practice of meditation is critical. In fact, cultivating right attitude *is a part of the practice.* Your success and ability to persevere with meditation will in large part be determined by the way you approach it. The following eight aspects of right attitude are based on the writings of a prominent educator in the field of meditation, Jon Kabat-Zinn. Both of his books, *Full Catastrophe Living* (1990) and *Wherever You Go, There You Are* (1994), are highly recommended if you're serious about undertaking a regular meditation practice.

Beginner's Mind

To observe your immediate, ongoing experience without any judgments, preconceptions, or projections is often referred to as "beginner's mind." In essence, it is perceiving something with the freshness you would bring to it if you were seeing it for the very first time. It's seeing—and accepting—things as they actually are in the present moment, without the veil of your own assumptions and judgments about them. For example, next time you're in the presence of someone familiar, consider seeing them as much as possible as they actually are, apart from your feelings, thoughts, projections, or judgments. How would you see them if you were meeting them for the first time?

Nonstriving

Almost everything you do during your day is likely to be goal-directed. Meditation is one thing that is not. Although meditation takes effort to practice, it has no aim other than to "just be." When you sit down to meditate, it's best to clear your mind of any goals. You are not *trying* to relax, blank your mind, relieve stress, or reach enlightenment. You don't evaluate the quality of your meditation according to whether you reach such goals. The only intention you bring to meditation is simply to be—to observe your "here and now" experience as it is, perhaps using the repetition of a mantra or observing your breath to assist your focus. If you are tense, anxious, or in pain, you don't strive to get rid of these sensations; instead you simply observe and be with them as best you can. You let them remain simply as they are. In so doing, you cease resisting or struggling with them.

Acceptance

Acceptance is the opposite of striving. As you learn to simply be with whatever you experience in the moment, you cultivate acceptance. Acceptance does not mean that you have to like whatever comes up (such as tension or pain, for example), it simply means you're willing to be with it without trying to push it away. You may be familiar with the saying, "What you resist persists." As long as you resist or struggle with something, whether in meditation or life in general, you actually energize and magnify it. Acceptance allows the discomfort or problem to just be. While it may not go away, it becomes easier to deal with because you cease to struggle with and/or avoid it.

In life, acceptance does not mean that you resign yourself to the way things are and cease trying to change and grow. On the contrary, acceptance clears a space in your life to reflect clearly and act appropriately, since you remain unfettered by reacting to or struggling with the difficulty. Sometimes, of course, it's necessary to go through a range of emotional reactions first—such as fear, anger, or grief—in order to get to acceptance.

In meditation practice, acceptance develops as you learn to embrace each moment as it comes, without moving away from it. As you learn to do this, you discover that whatever was there for a given moment will soon change. More quickly, in fact, than if you tried to resist it.

Nonjudging

An important prerequisite for acceptance (as well as for beginner's mind) is nonjudging. When you pay attention to your ongoing experience through the day, you'll notice that you frequently judge things—both outer circumstances as well as your own moods and feelings. These judgments are based on your personal values and standards of what is "good" and "bad." If you doubt this, try taking just five minutes to notice how many things you judge during that short time interval. To practice meditation, it's important to learn not so much to stop judging but to gain some distance from the process. You can simply *observe* your inner judgments without reacting to them, least of all judging them! Instead you cultivate a suspension of any judgment, watching whatever comes up, including your own judging thoughts. You allow such thoughts to come and go, while continuing to observe your breathing or any other object you have selected as a focus for meditation.

Patience

Patience is a close cousin to acceptance and nonstriving. It means allowing things to unfold in their own natural time. It is letting your meditation practice be whatever it is without rushing it.

Patience is needed to make time to meditate for a half hour to an hour every day. Patience is also required to persist with your meditation practice through the days or weeks when nothing particularly interesting happens. To be patient is to stop hurrying. This often means going against the grain of a fast-paced society where rushing from one destination to another is the norm.

The patience you can bring to your meditation practice will help assure its success and permanence. Sitting in meditation regularly will help you develop patience, as it will help you cultivate all of the characteristics described in this section. The attitudes that help you develop a meditation practice are the very same attitudes that are deepened by the practice itself.

Letting Go

In India there is an efficient way to catch monkeys, recounted by Jon Kabat-Zinn. A hole is drilled in a coconut just large enough to accommodate a monkey's hand. The coconut is then secured to a tree by a wire. Then a banana is placed inside the coconut. The monkey comes, puts his hand in the coconut and grabs a hold of the banana. The hole is small enough so the monkey can put his open hand in but cannot pull his closed fist out. All the monkey needs to do to be free is to let go of the banana, yet most monkeys don't let go.

Our minds are often like the monkey. We grab on to a particular thought or emotional state—sometimes one that is actually painful—and then we don't let go. Cultivating the ability to let go is crucial to meditation practice, not to mention a less anxious life. When you hold on to any experience, whether pleasant or painful, you impede your ability to simply be present in the here and now without judgment or striving. Learning to let go of things is assisted by learning to accept them. Letting go is a natural consequence of a willingness to accept things as they are. If you find that, prior to meditation, you have a hard time letting go of some concern, you can actually use your meditation as a means to witness the thoughts and feelings you're creating around the concern—including the thought of "holding on" itself. *The more minutely you observe the specific thoughts and feelings you have created around a problem, the more quickly you'll be able to expand your awareness around that problem and let it go.* When the concern is intensely charged emotionally, it's probably best to release your feelings by talking or writing in a journal about them before you sit down to meditate. Cultivating all of the attitudes described in this section will help with letting go.

Trust

Another important attitude to bring to meditation is a basic trust in yourself. This means you honor your own instincts, reactions, and feelings, regardless of what any authority or other person may think or say. You refrain from judging what comes up in your experience and believe in the inherent goodness of your soul—your essential self. The practice of meditation is about becoming more fully your own self. Practicing mindfulness means you take responsibility for your own experience on a moment-to-moment basis. It's you who are responsible for your experience and no one else. To fully embrace that experience, you need to trust it. Trusting you own insights and wisdom helps you to develop compassion toward yourself as well as others.

Commitment and Self-Discipline

A strong commitment to work on yourself, along with the discipline to persevere and follow through with the process, is essential to establishing a meditation practice. While meditation is very simple in nature, it's not easy in practice. Learning to value and make time for "just being" on a regular basis requires a commitment in the midst of a society that is strongly oriented toward *doing*. Few of us have grown up with values that cherished nonstriving, and so learning to stop goal-directed activity, even for just thirty minutes per day, requires commitment and discipline. The commitment is similar to that which is required in athletic training. An athlete in training doesn't practice only when he or she just feels like it, when there is time enough to fit it in or other people to keep her company. The training requires the athlete to practice every day, regardless of how she feels or whether there is any immediate sense of accomplishment.

To establish a meditation practice, it's best to sit whether you feel like it or not—whether it's convenient or not—six or seven days per week, for at least two months. (If you find you're unable to sit that often at first, don't chastise yourself—just do your best.) At the end of this time, if you've truly practiced regularly, the process will likely be enough of a habit (and sufficiently self-reinforcing) to continue. The experience of meditation varies from session to session: sometimes it feels good, sometimes it seems ordinary, and other times you will find it difficult to meditate at all. Although the point is not to strive for anything, a long-term commitment to regular meditation practice will transform your life fundamentally. Without changing anything that might happen in your life, meditation will change your relationship to everything you experience, on a deep level. In my personal experience, the hard work involved in establishing and maintaining a meditation practice is worth it. There may be no conscious aim of meditation practice itself, but the benefits that naturally follow from developing your observing self are profound.

Right Technique: Guidelines for Practicing Meditation

There is a technique to proper meditation. Probably the most important aspect is to sit in the right fashion, which means sitting upright with your back straight either on the floor or in a chair. There seems to be a certain energetic alignment within the body that occurs from sitting up straight. It's not likely to happen when you're lying down, although lying down is fine for other forms of relaxation. It's also important to relax tight muscles before you meditate. In historic times, the main purpose of yoga postures was to relax and energetically balance the body prior to meditating. The guidelines that follow are intended to help make your meditation practice easier and more effective.

1. *Find a quiet environment.* Do what you can do to reduce external noises and distractions. If this is not completely possible, play a record or tape of soft, instrumental sounds, or sounds from nature. The sound of ocean waves also makes a good background.

2. *Reduce muscle tension.* If you're feeling tense, take some time (no more than ten minutes) to relax your muscles. Progressive muscle relaxation of the upper portion of the body—your head, neck, and shoulders—is often helpful (see Chapter 4). The following sequence of head and neck exercises may also be helpful (some progressive muscle relaxation in addition to this sequence is probably optimal).

    - Slowly touch your chin to your chest three times.
    - Bend your head back to stretch the back of your neck three times.
    - Bend your head over to your right shoulder three times.
    - Bend your head over to your left shoulder three times.

- Slowly rotate your head clockwise for three complete rotations.
- Slowly rotate your head counterclockwise for three complete rotations.

3. *Sit properly.*

   Eastern Style: Sit cross-legged on the floor with a cushion or pillow supporting your buttocks. Rest your hands on your thighs. Lean slightly forward so that some of your weight is supported by your thighs as well as your buttocks.

   Western Style (preferred by most Americans): Sit in a comfortable, straight-backed chair, with your feet on the floor and legs uncrossed, hands on your thighs (palms down or up, whichever you prefer).

   In either position, keep your back and neck *straight* without straining to do so. Do not assume a tight, inflexible posture. If you need to scratch or move, do so. In general, do not lie down or support your head; this will tend to promote sleep.

4. *Set aside twenty to thirty minutes for meditation* (beginners might wish to start out with ten minutes). You may wish to set a timer (within reach) or run a background tape that is twenty to thirty minutes long so that you'll know when you're done. If having a clock or watch available to look at makes you more comfortable, that's okay. After you have practiced twenty to thirty minutes per day for several weeks, you may wish to try longer periods of meditation up to an hour.

5. *Make it a regular practice to meditate every day.* Even if you meditate for only five minutes, it's important to do it every day. It's ideal if you can find a set time to practice meditating. Twice a day—upon rising in the morning and before retiring for the evening—is optimal; once per day is a minimum.

6. *Don't meditate on a full stomach.* Meditation is easier if you don't practice on a full stomach or when you're tired. If you are unable to meditate prior to a meal, wait at least a half hour after eating to do so.

7. *Select a focus for your attention.* The most common devices are your own breathing cycle or a mantra. The structured meditation exercises below use both of these techniques. Other common objects of meditation include pictures, repetitive music, or a candle flame.

Developing Concentration

As a preliminary to practicing meditation, it's helpful to work on developing your ability to concentrate or focus your mind. This will enable you to reduce the inevitable distractibility that occurs when you practice. Those forms of meditation that require continuous focus on a particular object are called "structured meditation." The two most common types—mantra and counting breaths—are described below. (See the book *How to Meditate* by Lawrence LeShan [1974] for more detailed information and exercises on structured meditation.)

Using a Mantra

1. Select a word or short phrase to focus on:
   - A Sanskrit mantra such as "Om Shanti," "Sri Ram," "So-Hum."
   - A word or phrase that has significance within your personal belief system, such as "Let go, let God," or "I am at peace."
2. Silently repeat this word or phrase, ideally on each exhalation.
3. As any thoughts, reactions, or distractions come to mind, just let them pass over and through you and gently bring your attention back to the repetitive word or phrase.
4. Continue this process for at least ten minutes.

Counting Breaths

1. As you sit quietly, focus on the inflow and outflow of your breath. Let yourself breathe slowly and evenly. Each time you breathe out, silently count the breath. You can count up to ten and start over again, or keep counting as high as you like.
2. Each time your focus wanders, bring it back to your breathing and counting. If you get caught in an internal monologue or fantasy, don't worry about it or judge yourself. Just relax and return to the count again.
3. When you lose track of the count, start over at one or at a round number like fifty or one hundred.
4. After practicing breath-counting meditation for a while, you may want to let go of the counting and just focus on the inflow and outflow of your breathing.
5. Continue this process for a minimum of ten minutes.

In doing structured meditation, it's important to concentrate on whatever you've chosen as your object of meditation—but *not to force or strain yourself to do so*. Proper meditation is a state of relaxed concentration. When thoughts, daydreams, or external stimuli distract you, attempt neither to hold on to them or to reject them too vigorously. Just allow them to come and go.

Mantra or breath-counting meditation exercises are useful when you first begin to practice meditation because they will help you develop your concentration. Some people, myself included, like to use them at the outset of each meditation session for five to ten minutes as a way to increase focus.

During any form of meditation it's generally helpful to close your eyes in order to reduce outside distractions. Some people, however, find they prefer to keep their eyes slightly open—just enough to see external objects indistinctly. This can reduce the tendency to be distracted by inner thoughts, feelings, and daydreams. Try this if you're having difficulty with distractibility.

You are unlikely to be aware of just how distractible your mind is until you first sit down to meditate. In India it's said that the untrained mind acts like a crazed or drunken monkey. Using structured meditation techniques will build your capacity to concentrate in the beginning. Later you may want to drop these forms and focus more directly on developing your observing self.

Cultivating Mindfulness

The basic instruction for meditation is simple—to gently pay attention to your breathing. You simply observe your breath as it flows in and out. You give your full attention to the feeling of your breath as it comes in and your full attention to the feeling of your breath as it goes out. You don't try to deepen your breath or do anything with it (unless you are using a breath-counting technique initially to help you focus). The idea is simply to observe the process of your breathing without force or effort, experiencing all the sensations, gross and subtle, associated with it.

The process of observing your own breathing cycle is simple, although it's not easy. After two or three minutes you're likely to find that your mind gets bored and wants to go on to do something else. Or your body will have had enough and want to shift your position or get up and do something. It's just at this point that the "work" of meditation begins. Instead of giving in to the impulse to do something else, you simply *observe* the impulse itself and then gently bring your attention back to your breathing, watching your breath from moment to moment.

The tendency to become distracted and stop observing your breath is inevitable. In five minutes it may happen ten or perhaps fifty times. It's *very important not to judge yourself* when you get distracted. Simply notice that you did and then gently bring your attention back to your breathing. If you don't like the fact that you're so distractible, simply notice your not liking it and then bring your focus back to your breath. If you're really enjoying how you feel, simply observe *that* and return to your inhalation and exhalation. Be aware that there is no such thing as a "good" meditation session or a "bad" one. Often you will notice that you feel "good" or "bad" about how a particular session went. Yet keep in mind that the whole point of meditation is to simply witness your experience in the present moment without striving to achieve anything or evaluating how well the experience went.

"Success" in meditation is just doing it. The more often you do it, the more quickly you will train your mind to be less reactive, more stable, and better able to observe. You will be training it to be able to take each moment as it comes, without valuing any one above any other. Working regularly with the resistance of your mind builds inner strength. Regular meditation practice will foster the development of the very attitudes that help facilitate the practice in the beginning: acceptance, patience, nonjudgment, letting go, and trust.

Meditation Exercises

The following five meditation exercises were inspired by Jon Kabat-Zinn, Jack Kornfield, and other teachers of meditation. They derive from basic practices that have been used by students of meditation for thousands of years. The exercises emphasize maintaining a focus on your breathing—continually bringing your attention back to your breath each time you become distracted. It's probably best to do them in sequence, spending a week or two on each exercise. Once you've gained some experience with meditation, you can incorporate aspects of all of the exercises into your daily practice. The walking meditation can be used by itself or as a break in the middle of a long period of sitting meditation.

Basic Meditation on the Breath

1. Sit in a comfortable yet upright position. Focus on your breathing as you breathe slowly from your abdomen for ten minutes. Let the sensations of inhaling and exhaling be the object of your focus.
2. If your mind wanders from the focus on your breath, let it do so without judging it. Then gently bring your attention back to your breath. Do this as many times as you need to during the course of your meditation. Attempt to concentrate on your breathing in a relaxed way, without forcing it.
3. If you find yourself getting frequently distracted, use the breath counting technique (counting on each exhale) described in the previous section of this chapter. When you feel you've relaxed enough to stay relatively well-focused on your breath, try dropping the count.
4. Begin practicing this exercise for ten minutes and gradually work up to thirty minutes. You may find it useful to set a timer or play a thirty-minute tape of meditative music so that you'll know when you're done.

Sensing Your Body During Meditation

1. Begin this exercise with focusing on your breath. Then extend your attention to include an awareness of your entire body. In particular, focus

on your arms and legs along with your breath. When your attention wanders, bring it back to focus on your arms and legs.

2. As in the preceding exercise, don't judge yourself when your mind wanders. Each time you find yourself distracted, gently bring your attention back to the focus on your arms, legs, and breathing. You may need to do this many times at first. With practice, your concentration should improve.

3. Start with practicing this exercise for ten minutes and work up to thirty minutes.

Witnessing Thoughts and Feelings

1. When you've become comfortable with the first two exercises above, let your awareness expand to include your thoughts and feelings.

2. Simply observe your thoughts and feelings as they come and go, just as you would watch cars going by or leaves floating down a river. Let each new thought or feeling be a new object to witness.

3. If you become "stuck" in feelings or reactions during this process, simply observe that and let it pass.

4. Note the impermanence of your thoughts and feelings. They tend to come and go quickly unless you prolong a particular one of them by "holding on" to it.

5. If certain thoughts keep coming back, let them do so. Just keep observing them doing this until they eventually move on.

6. If you notice particular feelings of restlessness, impatience, irritability, or "wanting to get through this," simply observe them without judgment and allow them to pass.

7. If feelings of fear, anxiety, anger, sadness, or depression arise, don't go into them. Just be with them, going back to your focus on breathing, until they pass. You'll find that staying with your breathing helps you to move through such feelings.

8. Any time you feel you're getting stuck in a thought or emotional reaction, just go back to a focus on your breathing and your arms and legs. If you find yourself particularly distracted, try counting your breaths from twenty down to one, one count on each exhale. Repeat this process until you feel more centered.

9. When you first begin to practice witnessing thoughts and feelings, begin with shorter periods of practice and then work up to thirty minutes per day.

Observing Whatever Comes into Awareness

Let yourself observe, without judgment, *whatever* passes through your awareness: thoughts, reactions, physical sensations of discomfort, impatience, restlessness, sleepiness, comfort, relaxation. Let each aspect of your experience arise and move on without giving any one aspect special attention. Whenever you get stuck in a particular thought or reaction, just go back to your breathing. Stay with your breathing as your principal focus. Practice acceptance and nonjudgment toward whatever occurs in your experience while you sit for thirty minutes each day.

Walking Meditation

1. In the privacy of your home, take five minutes to walk *slowly* with awareness. You can walk back and forth or in a loop.

2. Keep in mind as you walk that you're not trying to get anywhere; instead, you are being mindful of the process of walking itself.

3. Be fully present with each step that you take. Focus on the sensations you feel in your feet, ankles, calves, knees, and thighs as your legs move slowly through each step. Go as slowly as you wish in order to stay focused.

4. If your attention wanders into thoughts, reactions, or other distractions, allow it to do so without judgment. Then bring your focus back to the sensations in your legs and feet as you slowly walk.

5. Start practicing walking meditation for five minutes and work up to fifteen minutes.

Practicing any of these exercises regularly will help you establish a foundation for developing mindfulness as a way of life. Beginning a meditation practice is straightforward. Maintaining it takes additional commitment, as described in the following section.

One Month Meditation Practice Log

Keep track of your meditation practice for one month, describing and rating your level of relaxation for each practice session. You may want to make several copies of this log before using it for the first month.

Date	Time of Practice	Duration (Minutes)	Level of Relaxation 1–5	Comments on Session

Maintaining a Meditation Practice

The motivation, commitment, and self-discipline necessary to establish a meditation practice has already been touched on in the section on right attitude. Learning to meditate can be compared with learning a sport like baseball, racquetball, or golf. A considerable amount of time in training is necessary before you become proficient. This involves a commitment to keep sitting on those days when you don't feel like it or find it inconvenient to do. Setting aside a regular time to practice for thirty minutes to one hour each day makes this easier. The best times are generally first thing in the morning upon awakening or in the evening before you go to bed, provided you are not too tired. Other possible times would be before lunch or dinner. By setting aside a regular time, you "build in" a place in your life for meditation.

Besides your own personal commitment and self-discipline, there are several things that can greatly support your practice. Probably most supportive is to find a local class or group that meditates regularly. You may find such a class at a local hospital or college (adult education program) in your area. Or there may be a free-standing meditation group within driving distance. Programs in Transcendental Meditation, or "TM" (a specific form of meditation developed by Maharishi Mahesh Yogi), are offered in many areas. While TM teaches only mantra meditation, it's a good place to begin. Having the support of a group with whom you meditate regularly will assist your motivation at those times when it seems hard to keep up your daily practice.

In some areas you may be fortunate to be close to a teacher thoroughly grounded and skilled in the practice of meditation. If you are interested in finding a group or teacher in your area, you can write to:

Insight Meditation Society
1230 Pleasant Street
Barre, MA 01005-9701

or

Insight Meditation West
P.O. Box 909
Woodacre, CA 94973

The Insight Meditation Society offers meditation retreats in various places throughout the United States. A meditation retreat generally involves sitting in meditation for eight to twelve hours per day (with hourly breaks) for one to ten consecutive days, although a few go even longer. Doing a retreat is a powerful way to deepen your ongoing meditation practice. It is generally not recommended for beginners.

Finally, there are a number of excellent books that can support your practice. The two books mentioned by Jon Kabat-Zinn are a good place to start. Any of the books listed at the end of this chapter can also be helpful.

Meditation and Compassion

An important aspect of developing a capacity to observe your experience is to bring *compassion* into your observation. It may not be enough to learn merely to witness your reactive thoughts and feelings. Without cultivating compassion toward your reactivity, you may remain at war with it. To bring compassion and heart into your self-observation is to begin to make peace with yourself.

Many people, especially if they are perfectionistic, treat themselves as though they were a harsh drill sergeant disciplining a new recruit. If this seems hard to imagine, then watch yourself to see how much time you spend criticizing yourself, putting yourself down, or pushing and driving yourself to do what you don't really want to do. When you're not pushing or criticizing yourself, you may fall into a more passive stance of fear—or of being a victim. Out of fear, your mind constantly scares you with "What if this . . . What if that . . ." When you fall into a victim stance, you may depress yourself with "It's no use . . . It's hopeless . . . It's a lost cause . . ." As soon as you start to feel less depressed, your perfectionism may keep you on a treadmill with "I should . . . I must . . . I have to . . ." Notice how much you criticize, scare, depress, or push yourself, and you'll learn quite a bit about your own mind. Unfortunately, all of the cognitive therapy in the world is not going to help if you still basically dislike yourself.

Cultivating compassion in meditation is fundamental to changing your relationship with yourself. Compassion allows you to move away from judgment, criticism, and even contempt toward tolerance, acceptance, and love. Compassion depends on *accepting* yourself—and the rest of the world—*as it is*, an attitude that can be cultivated through meditation practice. Living with your limitations and embracing your humanness is something you can learn. Apart from this chapter, two later chapters in this book, "Letting Go" and "Learning to Love," provide some guidelines that may help you grow in your ability to accept and be more compassionate toward yourself. For a more in-depth statement about the role of compassion in meditation, see Jack Kornfield's book *A Path with Heart* (1993).

Medication and Meditation

Few, if any, books on meditation address the question of how prescription medications affect the experience of meditation. Some formal meditation training programs, such as Transcendental Meditation, request that beginners get off all nonessential prescription drugs before learning to meditate. My own observation, based on personal experience as well as the experience of clients, is that different medications affect different people in different ways.

Two generalizations, however, can be made:

1. Benzodiazepine medications such as Xanax, Ativan, or Klonopin seem to increase distractibility, making it more difficult to focus during meditation. It has been found that the benzodiazepines tend to increase beta wave activity in the

brain (rapid, nonsynchronous brain waves associated with thinking) and reduce the ability to enter into alpha brain-wave states (synchronous brain waves associated with relaxed states as in meditation). While it's certainly not impossible to meditate while taking a benzodiazepine medication, you may find it more difficult.

2. SSRI antidepressant medications (such as Prozac, Zoloft, Paxil, Luvox) do not seem to impede meditation for most people. There are a few people who report that meditation is more difficult while taking an SSRI medication. On the other hand, I've also heard reports that some people find it easier to meditate after taking SSRIs because they feel calmer and less subject to intrusive thoughts and feelings. In general, it seems the news regarding SSRIs and meditation is good: you can cultivate a meditation practice while taking an SSRI.

Unfortunately, I have no information on the effects of tricyclic antidepressants (such as imipramine or nortriptyline) or MAO-inhibitors on meditation. Nor do I with Buspar. It's possible to evaluate the effects of such medications if you stop the medication for a few days while meditating and then resume taking it. Please consult with your prescribing physician before you try this.

How Meditation Can Help Overcome Fear

Meditation practice helps you to develop your "inner observer." An important application of this is learning to *witness in detail* the *internal bodily and/or emotional* sensations that accompany negative feelings, particularly anxiety. Any negative feeling can be analyzed into two components: (1) internal sensations (or emotions) and (2) thoughts.

Unpleasant internal sensations include muscle tension, headache, fatigue, and indigestion, as well as vague aches and pains. Unpleasant emotions include states of fear, sadness, or anger that occur spontaneously without any thought. More complex feelings, including anxiety, consist of these basic sensations or emotions *combined with* mental interpretations or judgments about those sensations/emotions. For example, if you add the thought "What if I have a heart attack?" to the physical sensation of rapid heartbeat, you'll create a strong feeling of anxiety. If you add the thought "What will they think of me?" to a basic emotional state of fear, you create a more complex feeling of anxiety. If you can separate the basic sensations/emotions you experience from subsequent thoughts you have about them, more complex negative feelings simply don't arise. Anxiety will fade the moment you can separate out your immediate bodily sensations/emotions from any accompanying thoughts. As you develop your inner observer, you'll become more capable of doing just this.

The nature of fearful thoughts is to move you away from the present moment. When you add the thought "What if . . ." to an unpleasant inner sensation, you immediately begin to focus on future catastrophe rather than your present experience.

Anxiety is a mental "sleight of hand" that quickly takes you out of the immediacy of the present moment. As long as you allow your mind to distract you from the present moment, you may get stuck in what is only a possibility (the "what if" thought), not the concrete reality of what is actually happening here and now. *Anxiety will dissolve to the extent that you can clearly and simply observe what sensations you're experiencing in the present moment, without jumping ahead in your thoughts.*

So, it's possible to *learn to directly witness just the internal sensations/emotions* that accompany fear in the immediate moment apart from the negative mental interpretations and self-talk that add to it. The pioneer of behavioral approaches to handling anxiety, Claire Weekes (1978), made this distinction long ago. She referred to the internal body sensations as "first fear" and the accompanying fearful thoughts, which aggravate the situation, as "second fear." To the extent that you can learn to distinguish first and second fear as they occur, it becomes possible to eliminate the latter. In short, anxiety is an interweaving of unpleasant internal sensations and scary thoughts. If you can slow down enough—and stand back enough—to separate the two, anxiety will lose its grip on you.

Regular meditation practice is, in my opinion, the most powerful strategy available for distinguishing internal sensations from fearful thoughts. With practice, you can learn to witness your own internal sensations in the present moment so well that you actually see the point at which you begin to add negative fearful thoughts. When you reach this point, your negative, fearful thoughts are no longer *automatic*—they no longer happen outside your conscious awareness—and you're in a position to *choose* not to go with them. The final outcome of developing a strong inner observer is that you can actually achieve the goal Claire Weekes described—the ability to observe the sensations of first fear without moving on into the fearful thoughts.

What You Can Do Now

1. To begin a meditation practice, follow the guidelines in the sections "Right Technique" and "Developing Concentration" for two or three weeks. You may want to begin with ten-minute meditation periods and gradually increase the duration up to thirty minutes. Make a commitment to yourself to practice every day. Review the section on "Right Attitude" to help cultivate the proper attitudinal stance for meditating.

2. After two or three weeks—or when you feel you have gained some ability to maintain concentration—work with the exercises in the section "Cultivating Mindfulness." Stay with your daily practice of meditation, using your breath as a focus, indefinitely.

3. To support your practice, find a class or group that meditates regularly. If this is unavailable, I recommend you work with audiotapes relevant to meditation, which are available from the Insight Meditation Society (see p. 127 for

address). Also see the books on meditation listed in the references, especially those by Kabat-Zinn, Kornfield, and Goldstein.

References and Further Reading

Goldstein, Joseph, and Jack Kornfield. 1987. *Seeking the Heart of Wisdom: The Path of Insight Meditation.* Boston: Shambhala.

Harp, David. 1996. *The Three-Minute Meditator.* 3d ed. Oakland, Calif.: New Harbinger Publications.

LeShan, Lawrence. 1974. *How to Meditate.* New York: Bantam Books.

Levine, Stephen. 1979. *A Gradual Awakening.* Garden City, New York: Anchor/Doubleday.

Kabat-Zinn, Jon. 1990. *Full Catastrophe Living.* New York: Delta.

———. 1994. *Wherever You Go, There You Are.* New York: Hyperion.

Kornfield, Jack. 1993. *A Path with Heart.* New York: Bantam.

Weekes, Claire. 1978. *Hope and Help for Your Nerves.* New York: Bantam.

———. 1978. *Peace from Nervous Suffering.* New York: Bantam.

8

Letting Go

Most people are confronted at some time in their life with experiences that leave them feeling frightened, vulnerable, or powerless. Frequently these unpredictable events occur in childhood, such as the death or illness of a relative, the daily unpredictability of living with an alcoholic parent, or perhaps having to move frequently and change schools. In the process of trying to cope with such circumstances, it's common to acquire a strong need to maintain control, both of your environment and yourself. You become inclined to feel vulnerable and insecure if you don't seek to control everything you can. Such a need for control can take many forms. A common one is the incessant striving for perfection—the inability to tolerate mistakes or any behavior that falls short of unrealistically high standards. Another type of control is the tendency to deny or avoid uncomfortable feelings, particularly anger.

When years of seeking perfection is combined with a rigid need to discount unpleasant feelings, the end result may be panic attacks, phobias, and/or chronic anxiety. As life continues to serve up unpredictable changes—whether in the realm of job, income, health, or relationships—some of us attempt to tighten the reins of control further, with the consequence that anxiety and panic worsen.

An attitude of fundamental importance in overcoming anxiety is learning to let go. In this chapter I want to talk about two aspects of the letting-go process: 1) letting go in the face of everyday hassles and problems and 2) letting go in the face of a major life crisis.

Part 1: Letting Go in the Face of Daily Problems

How do you respond when your child misses the bus to school? The repairman doesn't complete the job? Your spouse unexpectedly goes on a business trip? The IRS says you underestimated your tax liability by $3,000? No one is immune from the almost daily twists of life that can keep us guessing what will happen next. The real question is: How do you respond to the ordinary ups and downs of living and maintain a semblance of equanimity? Someone may tell you to just "accept it" or "go with the flow"—but how do you do that? There are several approaches that can help.

Relaxation

Giving yourself ample time to relax is a most important key. Letting go of bodily tension helps to let go of emotional concerns. A relaxed mind cannot exist in a tense body. If you're already tense when your child runs through the living room with muddy shoes, you may suddenly find yourself a lot more tense—maybe even panicky. If, on the other hand, you've been pacing yourself through the day and have made time to take breaks and to breathe deeply, you'll likely handle the latest crisis more smoothly.

Staying relaxed throughout the day takes commitment, focus, and effort. Practicing muscle relaxation or meditation on a regular basis is a good start, but it may not be enough to offset an onslaught of stressors. It's important to make time for relaxation during the entire day. *Your ability to truly take time out to relax throughout your day*, giving yourself regular "minibreaks," such as five minutes of abdominal breathing, meditation, or just sitting quietly in your chair, every hour or two, will increase your resilience and ability to cope with whatever comes along. Granted, it's not easy to slow down and take time out for relaxation in a society that moves at a breakneck pace. Giving yourself time for breaks and downtime—even five minutes every two hours—is easy to overlook when you get busy. To make relaxation and downtime a priority in your daily life takes effort and commitment. Although often difficult at first, it can become a very self-reinforcing habit after a while. The more relaxed and centered you're able to remain throughout the day, the less defensive, controlling, and fearful you'll be when circumstances suddenly don't go your way. Relaxation enhances your *flexibility*, allowing you to move through almost any difficult situation—to let go and take a fresh perspective rather than struggle with painful feelings. See chapter 4 of *The Anxiety and Phobia Workbook* for more detailed guidelines on relaxation.

Humor

When your cat drags a dead mouse into the house you can either rage, panic, or laugh. Laughter is the opposite of control and closely associated with relaxation. Generally, the more perfectionistic and controlling your approach to life is, the easier it is to do anything but laugh. A sense of humor is one of the hard-won benefits of lowering perfectionistic standards. Humor is the ability to step back and get perspective when everything seems to be going out of control. It's a *choice in perception*—a choice to look at a certain situation as ridiculous or absurd as opposed to letting it become a major melodrama. When you've spent your life needing everything to be just so, it takes some intention to cultivate a sense of humor. An important first step is learning to relax the standards you impose on yourself—trying not to take yourself so seriously.

Laughter has a number of beneficial physiological effects. Research has shown that laughter reduces blood pressure and relieves muscle tension. It also stimulates the release of endorphins in the brain, leading to an overall sense of well-being. Laughter also activates the immune system by stimulating the production of white blood cells. In his well-known book, *Anatomy of an Illness* (1979), Norman Cousins recounts how a daily dose of laughter—from watching old Marx Brothers films and reruns of *Candid Camera*—helped him overcome a chronic degenerative disease. Humor certainly relieves fear and anxiety. You cannot perceive a situation as threatening (and thus anxiety-provoking) if you can find a way to laugh at it. Perhaps you can recall a situation that once made you anxious yet now, in retrospect, appears humorous.

How can you bring more humor into your life? Humor is something that can be cultivated. Find out what makes you laugh and then spend more time with it. Watching funny videos or TV shows is a good place to start. Or you may prefer reading collections of cartoons (such as Gary Larson, for example) and humor books. Some people enjoy going to comedy clubs to watch stand-up comedians. You can learn how to tell jokes by watching comedians in action. If you spend time around a friend or family member with a good sense of humor, it may tend to rub off. Finally, just smiling may be enough to trigger more positive, lighter thoughts and feelings. Whichever way you prefer, try making more time for laughter in your life. A little more laughter will go a long way to help you loosen up around daily hassles—rather than building them into major melodramas.

Patience

Patience is a close cousin of relaxation. I would define patience as a "nondriven" stance toward life, something that's only possible when you're relaxed. The stronger your tendency to push or drive yourself, the harder it is to be patient. As you learn to relax and pace yourself through life, it becomes easier to wait when something takes longer than you thought it would. A degree of striving is necessary to achieve any goal, but when striving becomes compulsive and driven, you lose the flexibility to handle temporary setbacks and obstacles. Developing your inner observing self through meditation (see chapter 7) is a wonderful way to cultivate patience. Awareness and mindfulness are the opposite of willful self-pushing; they help you maintain a present-centered focus rather than forcing you to try so hard to get somewhere. By staying mindfully in the present, you can be patient about delays and obstacles. The paradox is that the *less* you give energy to setbacks and obstacles, the more efficient and steady will be your progress toward your goals.

Return to Nature

One of the best ways to let go of your troubles in daily life is to put yourself in a park or woods. Reconnecting with nature can help you to get in touch with your body and soul in ways that can move you out beyond the confines of your worries and concerns. When you're stuck in a worry, you keep presenting the same issue to yourself over and over again. You're confined to a certain loop in your brain that keeps repeating like a broken record. From a position inside the loop it's hard to see your way out. The great outdoors provides you with a much larger context than the confines of your mind. It will often help you to move out of a closed mental circuit into a larger sense of communion with nature. There are few things more effective than taking a walk in a beautiful setting to loosen the grip of worry.

Creative Distraction

If nature is not immediately available (if you don't have time to commute to the nearest park, woods, river, lake, or beach), then the next easiest way to let go of mental overdrive is to find a creative distraction. Not all distractions work equally well. Some of us grew up with a parent or older sibling who told us, "Get your mind off of your problem"—and yet we weren't able to. In my experience, the distractions that work best are those which preoccupy body, heart, or soul (as opposed to the mind alone). It is hard to overcome the mind with the mind. As mentioned in the previous section, you need to shift to an activity or place that is larger than your mind in order to move outside your brain's tendency to loop. This can be something physical—your favorite exercise, team sport, gardening, or building project. Or it can be anything that sparks your enthusiasm. (Being moved or enthused is an activity of the soul.) Any distraction that engages body and/or soul is what I call a "creative" distraction. Examples might include:

- Your favorite hobby
- An uplifting book, video, or audio tape
- A stimulating conversation (in person or on the phone)
- Singing or playing a musical instrument
- Creative computer applications

As long as the distraction captures your enthusiasm, you'll more easily be able to let go of whatever might have preoccupied your mind.

Do Something for Someone Else

Mother Teresa once said her definition of "happiness" was finding a productive way to serve others. It's often true that a most effective way to let go of your own

Letting Go Worksheet

Keep track of the efforts you make to work on letting go by filling out this worksheet below once per week. Make 10 copies of the sheet before you start.

Approach	Action Taken	Outcome
Relaxation		
Humor/Laughter		
Patience		
Return to Nature		
Creative Distraction		
Do Something for Someone Else		

1. Of the approaches you tried, which did you find most effective in enabling you to let go?
2. Which of these approaches would you like to incorporate into your life on a more regular basis?

melodrama is to do something for someone else. Whether you listen to someone, write them a letter, pick up a gift, help someone with a task, or put in time volunteering your services, getting concerned about someone else's situation moves you out of a fixation on yourself. It also leaves you with a sense of satisfaction that you can be useful and helpful. Service to others is a most uplifting way to let go and move beyond your troubles. It is important, of course, to keep selfless concern and service in balance with caring for your own needs. Excessive devotion to others at a cost to yourself can become codependency or, as a friend of mine once put it, "idiot compassion."

Part 2: Letting Go in the Face of Crisis

There are situations in life where you may be confronted with something that goes far beyond the stress of everyday life and pushes you to the limit. You are suddenly faced with a crisis—perhaps a catastrophe—that doesn't respond easily or quickly to your efforts to cope. At such times you may feel frightened and up against a wall. You may despair that there doesn't seem much you can do to improve a very difficult circumstance. Examples of this type of crisis situation include: serious chronic illness, whether physical or mental; serious addiction to alcohol or drugs, where you've tried many times to stop but can't; catastrophic losses such as the loss of spouse or family to accident or disaster; loss of physical integrity due to accident or illness; sudden loss of financial resources; and so on.

When faced with this type of crisis, there are three choices you can make: 1) resignation or despair, which may lead to a sense of hopelessness; 2) continuing to struggle to control the situation on your own, which may work for a while but ultimately increases anxiety and frustration; or 3) asking for and accepting outside help in the form of support, additional knowledge, and guidance. How do these alternatives differ?

Resignation

Resignation usually involves making no further effort to resolve a challenging situation. After all your efforts on your own have failed, you decide that there's nothing further that can be done. Such a stance leads to despair and sometimes to suicide. Invariably it leads to depression.

Resignation tends to close you off from any outside help. If you're walking around with the attitude "what's the use," or "this is hopeless," you're certainly not likely to be open or willing to receive any help from others that might be available.

On occasion, resignation may develop *after* you've consistently sought help from others to no avail. Neither you nor anyone else seems to be able to offer much help for your difficulty. At this point you can choose to give way to resignation, or you can exercise a further option, to be discussed below.

Continuing to Struggle

This is the position where you believe that if you only exert enough effort, you'll be able to overcome your problem on your own. You may keep seeking ways to try to control a serious problem that stubbornly resists all of your efforts. As the struggle goes on for weeks or months, your anxiety and frustration levels can rise enormously. The problem with this position, just as with resignation, is that it closes you off to help from outside yourself. As long as you maintain the attitude "I'm the only one who can change (control) this," there is not much chance for other people to assist. Again, you may come to the point where you feel lost and bewildered about what to do.

Relying on Others

Relying on others means you let go of depending solely on yourself and have the humility and openness to ask for help—to seek out the support of family, friends, or professionals. In the case of a severe, chronic anxiety disorder, where might this help come from?

1. You may talk to a counselor and/or a therapist. Professional therapists can give you tools to manage anxiety and confront fears. They can provide empathy and unconditional acceptance that can help heal feelings of unworthiness. Finally, they can provide encouragement that empowers you to take action—to do the necessary work—to make changes in your life.

2. You can talk to others suffering from anxiety disorders, either individually or in a support group. Talking to others with anxiety can reassure you that you're not alone. Often it can give you new ideas and coping strategies to deal with your own situation (for example, hearing about someone else benefiting from medication). Also important, it can help you to stay on track with your own recovery process since you're acquainted with others who are working on getting better.

3. You can inform family and friends of your problem so they can have better understanding about it. This is especially important when you can't engage in activities you used to do effortlessly. If you're in a close, intimate relationship, you can strive to educate your partner in detail about the nature of your problem with anxiety so they can fully understand and support your recovery goals. This enables them to assist you in specific recovery tasks such as relaxation practice, graded exposure, or response prevention.

All of these sources of support together can help you to negotiate the process of recovery from a serious problem with anxiety. In fact, the combination of therapy, support groups, and family is often sufficient to help you move through nearly any major difficulty or crisis. *In some cases, however, even this is not enough.* All the help and resources available may be insufficient to heal the wound inflicted on your soul by the crisis situation or disability. After all therapy and support options have been exhausted, a problem may still not have improved enough to make life feel livable or worthwhile.

Turning to a Higher Power

When all else fails, it may be the moment to look to your Higher Power (God, Spirit) for help. While some persons may incorporate spiritual beliefs and practices throughout their healing journey, others begin to do so only when pushed to the limit. It may be only after a serious or life-threatening crisis that you first awaken to the spiritual dimension of life. Or perhaps it's after such a crisis that you move from a mere intellectual belief in God to a more personal experience of the presence of a Higher Power in your life. (A more complete discussion of spirituality is taken up in the following chapter.)

Turning to your Higher Power in no way diminishes the importance or necessity of relying on other sources of help. Practicing relaxation, exercise, and cognitive coping skills on a daily basis are all necessary. Having a good support system among family and friends is also vital to managing a difficult situation. However, a willingness to let go and trust in a Higher Power can add an entirely new dimension.

Deciding to ask for help from your Higher Power is a radical step because it involves relying on a resource you can neither see nor fully understand. When you turn to your Higher Power, you are not just looking for a consoling concept—a convenient idea to comfort you. Anyone who has uttered a sincere prayer for assistance from God knows it is more than simply a convenience. It is reaching out from your heart and soul for real assistance, assistance you've not been able to find to your satisfaction through everything else you have tried.

The nature of this decision to rely on a Higher Power is well summarized by the first three steps of the 12-step program of Alcoholics Anonymous:

Step 1: Recognizing that you are powerless to resolve your issues by your own efforts

Step 2: Coming to believe that there is a Higher Power that can help

Step 3: Turning your life and your will over to that Higher Power, as you understand it

This relinquishing of control—letting go to an Unseen Force—is an unusual and often difficult step for people in fear or anxiety. The more afraid you are, the more you may try to struggle to exert control. To relinquish control requires humility, trust, a willingness to tolerate uncertainty, and faith. Let's consider each of these qualities.

Humility

It's certainly humbling to turn over your sense of control to something like a Higher Power. Perhaps you've been attached to an image of yourself as being the master of your own life—always able to handle any situation on your own. Perhaps you view it as a sign of weakness that you've met a problem you cannot fully master by your own efforts. Or perhaps you feel others will regard you as weak for relying on an unseen, invisible source of help. It certainly goes against the value system of modern, Western society with its emphasis on individuality and self-determination. Particularly for men in American society, it's often difficult to give up the belief that they can surmount any obstacle by their own efforts.

It is humility that's needed first—humility to acknowledge and accept your ultimate powerlessness in the face of a severe and unrelenting crisis. The irony is that, once you embrace that humility and allow yourself to trust in a Higher Power, you may be surprised to feel a tremendous sense of relief. Suddenly you're delivered from the awesome task of relying solely on yourself. You no longer have to surmount what has seemed insurmountable on your own. The grim determination of self-will can give way to a gentler and more flexible attitude of accepting what gifts your Higher Power might have to offer.

Trust

If you are going to turn over—surrender—your sense of control and rely on a Higher Power, then such a Power needs to be fully trustworthy. Such a Power should have only your best interests in mind and be capable of offering support, strength, or guidance in the midst of your difficulties. Your ability to trust in a Higher Power thus depends in large part on what kind of concept you have of God.

What is your concept of a Higher Power? (Questions in the following chapter are designed to help you reflect on this.) To what extent is your present image of God a result of what you learned from your family, church, or minister as a child? Is this image one with which you feel comfortable? Some people were raised with mixed messages about the nature of God. They were taught that God can be both loving and wrathful—or both forgiving and judgmental. Certainly it would seem difficult to turn over your problems to such a God. To bare your soul to a potentially judgmental or wrathful God is an uncertain, even frightening prospect.

It's also possible that your feelings toward a Higher Power, the ultimate authority, might be colored by feelings you may have toward authority figures in general, particularly parents. If your parents were abusive, critical, or dominating, you might harbor unconscious feelings of fear or anger toward not only them but authority figures in general. And your fearful images of authority may, in turn, influence your perception and image of God. Certain traditional doctrines portraying God as wrathful or punitive can serve to reinforce such an image. So you may have grown up with mixed feelings toward the idea of Deity, feeling more comfortable with an agnostic or even atheistic worldview.

How is it possible to come to a "true" understanding of the nature of a Higher Power, free of negative projections based on false teachings or traumatic experiences in childhood? There is no easy answer to such a question. Each person needs to make his or her own search, facilitated by reading, talking to others, and, above all, asking Spirit directly for insight and clear understanding. Direct revelation of the nature of God through personal experience in prayer and meditation offers the most convincing answers. Speaking from my own experience in this regard, I have come into acquaintance with a Higher Power that is all-loving, forgiving, supportive, reliable, wholly nonjudgmental, and concerned for my and everyone else's highest good. Such a power seems to me eminently trustworthy. It's a great source of strength and security to know such a Power exists.

Tolerating Uncertainty

The need to control is born out of a desire to make life predictable, orderly, and in line with your expectations. Tolerating uncertainty can be challenging because it requires the precise opposite of this: living with a degree of chaos and unpredictability. However difficult it may be, there is a gift in chaos. It's at those times when a problem situation seems most uncertain or confusing that you are most likely to experience a shift in perception toward it. As long as you're stuck in your worry, you may tend to limit yourself from perceiving new approaches or solutions. Chaos and uncertainty can shake up a rigid mind-set to allow for a fresh perspective to emerge.

Tolerating uncertainty is something that can be *learned* through practice. You might want to start with something fairly small, such as leaving certain chores undone or not opening your mail for a day or two. Then work on postponing your worry about a more serious problem situation, using exercise, relaxation, or creative distractions to deal with the tension that may be left from not worrying. Assuming you've done what you realistically can, try to extend the period of not worrying about the problem as long as possible.

Once you've increased your capacity to tolerate uncertainty, it's easier to relinquish an intractable problem to the care of your Higher Power. A little faith will also help this process greatly.

Faith

Faith is the continual renewal, over time, of your trust in a Higher Power. It's the expectancy that your requests for assistance will receive a positive response. Faith often requires some degree of courage—the courage to continue believing in the possibility of assistance from your Higher Power no matter how "discouraging" the immediate situation appears. To have faith is to persevere in your conviction of the highest possible outcome no matter what obstacles may arise along the way.

Faith is not always easy to conjure up. It develops out of direct personal experience with relying on a Higher Power to provide support, peace of mind, understanding, or guidance. It may be challenged by circumstances where adversity reigns and prayers seem to go unanswered. In my own experience, however, faith is not blind. It tends to grow with time and experience in cultivating a relationship with your Higher Power.

It's something you can *learn* as you continue to practice letting go of those situations where help beyond your own means seems needed.

Keep in mind that reliance on a Higher Power does *not* mean relinquishing your responsibility for doing all you can to deal with a problem situation. Releasing your difficulty to a Higher Power in no way conflicts with developing self-responsibility. The two are on different levels. For example, working on overcoming anxiety means developing a variety of skills—abdominal breathing skills, relaxation skills, self-observation, use of constructive self-statements, exposure, accessing feelings, assertiveness, and so on. The capacity to let go and surrender to a Higher Power is of a different order. After you have made your best effort to work on your particular issues, you realize that there is an additional resource available. You learn to rely on assistance from your Higher Power *in conjunction with* your own best efforts. Specifically, you can ask for assistance from your Higher Power to help you with qualities of character—"soul qualities," if you will—that can help you in your journey toward recovery. These qualities include courage, faith, strength, perseverance, inspiration, and resourcefulness. Or you can simply leave your request open-ended: "May whatever I need come to me," "May whatever I need to know be revealed to me." None of this is in conflict with learning and practicing all of the important skills that can lead to mastery and self-reliance regarding the problem. There is a certain paradox here: relinquishing your problem to a Higher Power may actually support and enhance your own efforts to overcome it. This can be summed up in the maxim: "God helps those who help themselves."

Exercises for Letting Go

Release Meditation

The following exercise is intended to help you get in touch with your Higher Power and obtain assistance in dealing with any issue causing you worry or anxiety. Use the exercise only if it feels appropriate to you. (You may have your own methods of prayer and meditation that you find preferable.) Give yourself time to get relaxed and centered first before working with the affirmations and visualization.

1. Get comfortable in a seated position (or lie down, if you prefer). Spend at least five minutes using any technique you wish to get relaxed. You can do abdominal breathing, use progressive muscle relaxation, visualize going to a peaceful place, or meditate.

2. If you're not already aware of it, bring to mind the situation, person, or idea that worries you. Focus on this for several moments until you have it clearly in mind. If feelings of anxiety come up, allow yourself to feel them.

3. Affirm over and over, with as much conviction as you can,
   "I turn this over to my Higher Power (or God)."
   "I release this problem to my Higher Power (or God)."

   Simply repeat these statements slowly, calmly, and with feeling as many times as you wish until you begin to feel better. While doing this, it is good to bring to mind the following ideas about your Higher Power:

   - It is "all-knowing"—in other words, it has wisdom and intelligence that go beyond your conscious capacity to perceive solutions to problems.
   - In its greater wisdom, your Higher Power has a solution to whatever you're worried about.
   - Even though you can't see the solution to your worry right now, you can affirm faith that there is no problem that can't be resolved through the help of your Higher Power.
   - If your worry is focused on another person, remember that they too have a Higher Power that is looking out for their highest good.

4. If you are visually inclined, imagine that you're going to meet your Higher Power. You might see yourself in a garden or a beautiful setting of your choice, and then imagine that you see a figure—your Higher Power—approaching you. It may be indistinct at first and then grow clearer. You may notice that this figure exudes love and wisdom. It might be a wise old man or woman, a being of light, Jesus, the Supreme Being in your particular religion, or any other presence that adequately represents your Higher Power.

5. While in the presence of your Higher Power—whether you visualize it or not—simply find a way to ask for help. For example, you might say, "I ask for your help and guidance with __________." Keep repeating your request until you feel better.

   You may want to listen to see if your Higher Power has an immediate answer or an insight to offer you about your request. It's quite all right, though, simply to make your request and ask for help without getting an answer. The purpose of this process is to develop trust and belief in your Higher Power (what has traditionally been called "faith in God").

   The key to this part of the process is an attitude of genuine humility. By asking for help from your Higher Power, you relinquish some of your conscious control of the situation, and exercise a willingness to trust.

6. Optional: If it feels appropriate, visualize a beam of white light going to that place in your body that feels anxious or worried. Often this will be the solar plexus region (in the middle of your trunk right below the cen-

ter of your rib cage) or the "pit" of your stomach. Let that area be filled with light until the anxiety dissolves or fades away. Keep directing white light to that region until it completely settles down and is free of anxiety.

Give this entire process time. It may be necessary to persist with it for as long as a half hour to forty-five minutes in order to feel a genuine connection with your Higher Power and a deeply felt trust that the problem you're worried about can truly be resolved. If, after completing this process, your worry comes back the next day, simply repeat the exercise every day until you've released your worry. To many readers, this process will appear to be a variation on traditional prayer.

Release Prayer

(Prayer to Release a Problem)

You can use the following prayer at any time you wish to turn over a problem to the care of your Higher Power. This prayer is meant to serve as one example of a type of prayer that can be used to release a difficult situation to God. Feel free to use it as it is or as a basis for writing your own prayer for release.

Speak the prayer from your heart, and then repeat it daily until you feel you have received an answer.

Dear God,
I have done all I know to heal this problem—
And have tried every resource within my knowledge and power.
I now turn this over to your care.
I acknowledge my own inability
To will this difficulty away,
As its source lies deeper than my own conscious will.
I know, however, it is not beyond Your Power,
And that nothing is impossible through God.

So I ask that You help me to heal this situation.
Bring light into this darkness
And restore peace to my mind and heart.
I am grateful that You already know the way,
Even if I do not.
I now let go in trust and faith—
Knowing that it is through your perfect love and grace
That I may be restored to wholeness. Amen.

Spiritual Phrases

You can use any of the following spiritual phrases to help let go of anxiety or worry in the moment it arises. It's good to repeat a phrase several times over the course of two or three minutes. Try using your favorite phrase in combination with abdominal breathing, repeating the phrase each time you exhale. It's particularly powerful to sit quietly, close your eyes, and silently repeat a phrase on each exhale for several minutes.

Spirit (God) is with me.
I abide in God (or Spirit).
Let go—let God.
Grant me peace.
Grant me strength.
This too will pass.
The grace of God surrounds me.
God knows the way.
My Higher Power and I can handle this together.

Guided Meditation: Allowing Time for Healing

The following is a guided meditation I have used with clients who have been discouraged by a protracted illness or problem with anxiety. I suggest that you record it on tape, in your own voice or someone else's. Speak slowly and deliberately when making the recording. Then listen to the entire meditation while in a relaxed state, once per day. With repetition, this meditation should help you to let go of struggling with your illness and change the way you perceive it.

A Time to Heal

This is the time your body is taking to allow itself to fully rest and heal. It's futile to try to hurry your body. It has its own natural pace—which might involve an extended time of having to let go of your normal schedule of activities. Although it's hard to sit on the sidelines and wait, be assured that it's by taking this time out now that you can reemerge feeling healthy, more vital and strong.

You must have needed this time out to fully rest, or you wouldn't have had to reduce your activities for such an extended time. Getting angry or struggling with your condition serves no purpose. It certainly is frustrating to feel ill for an extended time, yet realize that this healing crisis is needed—it's a necessary step to ensure a longer and healthier life in the years ahead. Know that when your body and soul's need for rest and healing is complete, your healing crisis will be over and you can return to all the activities and goals that give your life meaning. Allow yourself to be patient now and trust that, even in the midst of feeling distressed, you are rebuilding your strength. Let yourself trust that you'll emerge from this time with a renewed feeling of good health—health that is built from the inside out—health that is built on a solid foundation because you've been required to slow down for a period of time.

So let yourself relax and cease struggling or fighting your body and soul's own natural wisdom. Remember to occupy your days with constructive activities. Patience is a great virtue and you can use this time as an opportunity to cultivate it. Patience is usually gained only at a price. You gain patience by learning to endure through difficult times. So recognize the present time as an opportunity to grow in two important ways: first, to give your body and soul a deep rest, so that you can regroup for the months and years ahead; and second, to learn patience—the willingness to wait and persevere through adversity. With patience, you can handle all the challenges life may bring with greater ease.

So right now . . . relax, let go, and realize that a Higher Wisdom is in charge of your life. Although you may feel frustrated or distressed, this Higher Wisdom knows what it's doing, and you can trust that you're going to be fine—that you'll emerge from this time a renewed and stronger person.

Remember to have faith that there is a purpose in everything and that nothing in life remains the same for long. In time this healing crisis will be over, and you can resume all the pursuits and goals that are important to you.

So allow yourself to breathe, relax, and trust. No matter how you feel physically, your healing process is moving forward at a deep level right now. You can trust that there is an end to this, that you will be healthy and strong again—and that in the future you will look back at this time as a necessary step in your life's course.

What You Can Do Now

1. Review "Part 1: Letting Go in the Face of Daily Problems." Of the various attitudes and approaches that can help with letting go—relaxation, humor, patience, returning to nature, creative distraction, helping others—which ones might you be willing to cultivate? What specifically can you do? Complete the *Letting Go Worksheet* for several weeks to clarify what works best for you.

2. If you feel discouraged or stuck in your problem with fear or anxiety, review the section "Turning to a Higher Power." Work with the "Release Meditation" or "Release Prayer" (or write your own) in order to ask your Higher Power for assistance. Use one of the spiritual phrases to address fear in the moment it

arises. Record and listen to the script "A Time to Heal" to up-level your attitude toward a protracted illness or disability.

3. To help develop greater faith, you might wish to keep a "faith journal." Every time you feel a prayer has been answered or you experience a small miracle in your daily life, write it down. Later, reading back over your journal entries will help to strengthen your belief in your Higher Power—not just as a concept but as an active presence in your life.

References and Further Reading

Cousins, Norman. 1979. *Anatomy of an Illness.* New York: Norton.

Jampolsky, Gerald. 1979. *Love Is Letting Go of Fear.* Berkeley, Calif.: Celestial Arts.

9

Spirituality

I believe that spirituality can offer much to help enlarge your view of life. Spirituality can offer answers to questions that may restore your faith in life and renew your optimism about your future, no matter what your current predicament might be. It can help develop the conviction (if you don't already have it) that you have a unique reason for being here—a unique purpose to serve—no matter how you might view yourself now. (See the chapter "Find Your Unique Purpose.") Even your struggle with anxiety can be understood as having a larger purpose—not simply as an accident of nature with which you have been arbitrarily afflicted.

For the purpose of this chapter, "spirituality" can be understood as distinct from religion. Different world religions have proposed various doctrines and belief systems about the nature of a Higher Power and humanity's relationship with it. Spirituality, on the other hand, refers to the *common experience* behind these various points of view—an experience involving an awareness of and relationship with "something" that transcends your personal self and the human order of things. This something has been referred to by many different names, the most common in our culture being "God."

This chapter explores a number of dimensions of spirituality. First, I will address how spirituality can help overcome anxiety and anxiety disorders. This section includes a description of personality and attitude changes—often brought about by an active spiritual life—that can help heal anxiety and fear. The section following that, "Exploring Your Own View of Spirituality," offers you the opportunity to explore some of your own ideas and personal experiences with spirituality. It may help you to clarify your ideas about the nature of your Higher Power and your relationship with such a Power. Finally, I will present my own personal understanding of spirituality, in the form of twelve assumptions that I believe are frequently associated with a spiritual view of life. You may find you agree or disagree with some of these ideas. If they help you to enlarge your view of life—and take a more compassionate view of your difficulties—they will have served their purpose.

How Spirituality Can Help Overcome Anxiety

Taking spirituality seriously does not imply doing away with cognitive-behavioral and biopsychiatric approaches to treating anxiety, panic attacks, and phobias. Cognitive-behavioral therapy is, without question, very effective in helping people to change catastrophic thoughts, which aggravate panic attacks and anticipatory anxiety. Exposure is very effective in helping people to confront and overcome many types of phobias. Medication is a critical part of treatment in many cases, helping people who are debilitated by panic attacks, agoraphobia, or OCD to be more responsive to cognitive-behavioral interventions. The current paradigm for treating anxiety disorders has provided a tremendous advance over the state of treatment prior to 1980. It will continue to be refined and improved into the foreseeable future.

I would like to suggest that spirituality, *in addition* to cognitive-behavioral therapy, has a special role to play in recovery from anxiety:

- It can increase your belief and hope that recovery is possible.
- It can provide a way to handle more severe and chronic anxiety disorders.
- It can lead to distinct changes in personality, attitude, and behavior that increase your ability to cope with an anxiety disorder.
- It can provide a more positive frame of reference for perceiving your difficulties with anxiety (and life in general). Instead of being an arbitrary hardship, your problem, however challenging, can be understood as an opportunity to grow and evolve as a human being.

The first three points are discussed in what follows. The fourth point is elaborated in considerable detail in the final section of this chapter.

Increased Hope in the Possibility of Recovery

Spirituality has always provided people with hope. The word "inspiration" literally means "in-spiriting." To be involved with some form of spirituality is to regularly experience inspiration, a sense of renewal or rejuvenation that can motivate you to persist in your efforts toward self-improvement. Spirituality doesn't take the place of doing the necessary footwork, which typically means learning concepts and skills and practicing them on a regular basis. However, it does provide the impetus to persist even when the journey gets difficult.

As anyone who has dealt with anxiety disorders knows, recovery is often fraught with setbacks. It's my impression and personal experience that working with spiritual practices such as prayer and meditation can be a very powerful way to sustain motivation in the face of these setbacks. Such practices provide ways to "keep the faith"—to keep moving forward toward your goal in spite of periods of discouragement. Sustaining faith in recovery, despite setbacks, is critical to overcoming any long-standing problem with anxiety.

Ways to Handle More Severe and Chronic Problems

Among the various anxiety disorders, some types of problems are easier to change than others. Panic disorder can often be relieved by effective cognitive-behavioral therapy, sometimes with and sometimes without medication. Specific phobias can often be remedied by systematic desensitization and graded exposure. Social phobia can be overcome by effective cognitive-behavioral group treatment. On the other hand, more severe cases of anxiety may show only moderate improvement in response to cognitive-behavioral treatment and/or medication. For example, severe post-traumatic stress disorder or severe OCD may improve only partially in response to the best available treatment. After years of good treatment and making your best effort with cognitive-behavioral approaches or medication, what do you do if you're still having some degree of difficulty? It is in this situation that I feel spirituality can have much to offer.

One thing you can do is to follow the path recommended in all of the 12-step programs—to "turn over" your problem to the care of your Higher Power. This does not mean relinquishing your responsibility for doing what you can to help yourself. It does imply that you're willing to admit that you cannot totally resolve the issue by your own will alone. Instead, you are open to receiving assistance, support, and guidance from a Higher Source. The previous chapter, "Letting Go," explores in more detail this approach of turning over a difficult problem to a Higher Power.

Another thing you can do is to visualize or affirm your ultimate recovery, despite any difficulties you currently face. This would seem to be an opposite approach to the one of letting go just described, yet it's actually complementary. The process of visualizing or affirming your healing can be empowered greatly by relying on a Higher Power to assist with the realization of your goal. The chapter "Create Your Vision" describes how it's possible to create a new experience of your life, no matter how restrictive or limiting your present condition might seem.

What are the possible outcomes of relying on spiritual resources to assist in recovery? From my own experience, I believe there are two possible outcomes—an actual miracle and/or an inner transformation:

1) A miracle may happen. The problem, no matter how resistant to conventional psychotherapeutic, medication, and self-help approaches—simply goes away. It is seemingly lifted, as a result not only of your own efforts but of something more—something beyond your own effort or understanding. This may not be a very frequent phenomenon, but it does sometimes happen. Traditional religion views such miracles as "grace" or "deliverance." This kind of thing happens, for example, in spontaneous, inexplicable remissions from terminal illness. It also happens in 12-step programs to people who felt completely defeated by their addictions prior to making a commitment to work the

steps. In my own experience I've seen it happen to a few persons with long-standing anxiety problems that did not respond to any conventional forms of treatment.

2) No miracle happens. Anxiety symptoms, whether in the form of panic, generalized anxiety, a particular phobia, an obsessive-compulsive problem—do not go away altogether in spite of good treatment and involvement with spirituality. However, you're able to make substantial *inner changes* in attitude that enable you to live so well with the problem that its intensity is significantly lessened. What once was a painful, seemingly insurmountable problem is now less painful—and thus less of a problem. You have developed sufficient inner peace, strength, and faith in life that you can accept your limitations with equanimity. Acceptance is not the same as resignation or fatalism. It means working with adversity as a way to deepen your relationship with your Higher Power and also to evolve as a human being. If your problem hasn't entirely gone away, despite your best efforts, you may conclude: "The lesson isn't over yet—there's more to learn by working with this limitation, either by way of healing it or accepting and transcending it (or both)."

Personality and Behavioral Changes Associated with Spirituality

Certain personality, attitudinal, and behavioral changes frequently occur in persons who have been involved with spirituality for a while. There is a field known as the "psychology of religion" which studies such changes. You would not (and probably cannot) deepen your involvement with spirituality out of a motive to "acquire" such personality changes. However, they are a natural consequence of making a long-term commitment to grow spiritually. I mention those here that I feel are particularly relevant to healing anxiety and anxiety disorders.

A Sense of Security and Safety

An abiding sense of inner security and safety can go a long way toward overcoming needless worry and the tendency to project potential catastrophe. Through developing a connection with your Higher Power, you can gain security through the conviction that you are not all alone in the universe, even at those times when you feel temporarily separated from other people. You feel increasingly safe as you come to believe that there is a source you can always turn to in times of difficulty. There is much security to be gained through the understanding that there is no problem or difficulty, however great, which cannot be resolved through the help of your Higher Power.

Peace of Mind

Peace of mind is the result of feeling a deep, abiding sense of security and safety. The more reliance and trust you develop in your Higher Power, the easier it becomes to deal with the inevitable challenges life brings without worry or fear. It's not that you give up your will to such a power; rather you learn that you can "let go" and turn to your Higher Power when you feel stuck with a problem in living and don't know how to proceed. Learning how to let go when solutions to problems aren't immediately apparent can help significantly to reduce worry and anxiety in your life (see the chapter on "Letting Go"). Peace of mind is what develops in the absence of such worry.

Ability to Gain Distance from Conditioned Emotional Reaction Patterns

Spiritual practices, particularly meditation, can help you to become more in touch with your unconditioned self. This is a deep, inner state of consciousness, beyond ego, that is always still and at peace no matter what melodramas you may be caught up with in your day-to-day life. Moving into your unconditioned self is like reaching a calm oasis beyond anything you might be anxious about. Such a state can be deliberately cultivated if you're willing to make the time for it.

Some ways to do so include meditation, quiet time devoted to inspirational reading, guided visualizations, inspirational music, or physical disciplines such as yoga or t'ai chi. See chapter 7 for a more in-depth discussion of meditation.

Relinquishing the Excessive Need to Control

Worry has to do with predicting unfavorable outcomes associated with situations you can't fully control. By worrying, you provide yourself with an illusion of control. If you worry about something enough, then you feel that somehow you're not at a total loss with it—you won't be caught off guard. If you were to stop worrying, you imagine that you would give up control. Spiritual growth, regardless of the tradition or approach you follow, encourages the cultivation of a willingness to surrender control. Without relinquishing self-responsibility, you learn to allow your Higher Power to have some influence in determining the outcome of situations you feel you can't control. I believe this is one of the most important aspects of spiritual growth that can contribute to reducing anxiety. Being able, at times, to turn over your worries to a Higher Power can relieve some of the burden you think you have to carry in order to solve your problems.

Increased Self-Worth

As you develop a relationship with a Higher Power, you come to recall that you did not actually create yourself. You remember that you are a part of the universe of creation as much as the birds, stars, and trees. If this is a benign and supportive universe we live in—and developing a relationship with your Higher Power will help you to believe that it is—then, in essence, you're good, lovable, and worthy of respect just by virtue of the fact that you're here. We treat our pets with respect and love just for being who they are, yet we often fail to do so with ourselves. However you behave—whatever choices you make—you are still inherently good and worthwhile. Your own judgments of yourself, however negative, do not ultimately count if you are a creation of the universe as much as everything else. As one person humorously put it: "God doesn't make junk." (It is, of course, a mistake to assume that this type of reasoning can be used to justify ignorant or unethical behavior. It's important to keep in mind the distinction between how a person behaves and what they are in essence.)

Relaxing Perfectionistic Standards of Achievement

If your essential worth is inborn, then basing self-worth on striving to meet external standards of perfection, standards prescribed by society (i.e., perfect career, perfect house, perfect figure, perfect children, and so on), is misplaced. Socially prescribed standards are relatively superficial, and striving for them does not provide ultimate satisfaction. While it is fine to do your best in life, it's also important to affirm your intrinsic worth—who you are, apart from outer accomplishments. When people are near death, it has been found that there are only two things that they invariably feel were important about their lives: 1) learning how to love others and 2) growing in wisdom. How would your view of yourself change if you evaluated yourself by these two standards?

Increased Capacity to Give and Receive Unconditional Love

A fundamental characteristic of your Higher Power is that it offers you an experience of unconditional love. This is a kind of love that differs from romantic love or even ordinary friendship. It entails an absolute caring for the welfare of another without any conditions. That is, no matter how another person appears or acts, you have compassion and care for them without judgment. As you develop a deeper connection with your Higher Power, you come to experience greater degrees of unconditional love in your life. You feel your heart opening more easily to people and their concerns. You feel freer of judgment toward them or of making comparisons among them. Unconditional love shows up both in your increased capacity to give love to others as well as to experience more of it coming into your life. You begin to experience less fear and more joy in your life as you help to inspire others to experience their own capacity for unconditional love. This kind of love also manifests itself through the experience of having everything you need in your life to get on with what you want to do. See the chapter "Love" for further discussion of this point.

Exploring Your Own View of Spirituality

The purpose of this section is to help you better understand your own ideas and experience with spirituality. By taking time to think about your answers to the questions posed in the exercises, you may gain clarity about: 1) your own personal concept of a

Higher Power or God and 2) what you might want to do, if anything, to deepen your commitment to spirituality.

What Is Your Concept of God?

One thousand years ago the medieval theologian St. Anselm argued that any concept of God is a contradiction, because God is infinite and anything that is truly infinite must be greater than any concept we can grasp. Humans nonetheless have attempted to comprehend the Divine in countless ways for thousands of years. Each of the major world religions proposes its own unique theology, attempting to answer questions both about what God is as well as the nature of our relationship as humans to God. In order to think or converse about a Higher Power at all, it seems necessary to have *some* concept about what God is, even if it's very approximate and incomplete.

A detailed excursion into the subject of theology is beyond the scope of this book. From the standpoint of overcoming fear, merely *having* a belief in a Higher Power is important. To embrace such a belief can give life a new dimension of meaning. You begin to trust that there is something beyond surface appearances—beyond your own little, everyday melodramas. When you have exhausted all your options and feel up against a wall in life, there is a higher resource you can turn to. You feel less alone in the universe. In short, *that* you believe in a Higher Power is more important than how you conceive of such a power.

Nevertheless, I am going to describe briefly some of the polarities that have traditionally influenced discussions about the nature of God. I do so in order to assist you in clarifying your own ideas about your Higher Power. If these distinctions help you to reflect on and clarify your own ideas about deity, they will have served their purpose.

Historically, deity has been conceptualized through four contrasting polarities. (A great deal of religious persecution has occurred and even wars waged around these differing views of God.)

- Theistic versus Nontheistic
- Personal versus Impersonal
- Monotheistic versus Polytheistic
- Immanent versus Transcendent

Let's consider each one:

Theistic versus Nontheistic

Theistic views of God use a personal name to refer to Divinity: God, Allah, Yahweh, Brahma, Heavenly Father, Lord, etc. The use of a name doesn't necessarily imply that God is like a person. Yet there is an implication that the Divine is in some respects a being, although perhaps not in any way we can understand the notion "being." If the

Divine were equated with a "being" in the usual sense, it would be difficult to see how it could be infinite or without limits. What kind of a being could be infinite?

Perhaps the most important implication of personal names such as God or Allah is the possibility of a personal experience and, in fact, a personal relationship with the Divine. It is the personal aspect of the Divine that permits us to have a personal encounter and intimate connection with a Higher Power. This can provide tremendous support, peace, and guidance in the face of difficult life circumstances. In short, theistic concepts point to the potential of a personal relationship with a Power greater than ourselves—not like a human relationship, but a relationship nonetheless.

In other contexts the words "Spirit," "Cosmic Consciousness," "Ground of Being," "the Absolute," "the Infinite," "Essence," or even "the Void" are used to refer to the Divine. These words seem to speak of a concept of deity having attributes that are nonpersonal, transpersonal, beyond something humans can personally relate to or even comprehend. If the Divine is truly infinite and beyond anything we can conceive, then nontheistic terms would seem very appropriate. Such terms are capable of more fully encompassing everything that the Divine might be. God's personal aspect (which we refer to by a personal name) is probably the most important characteristic of deity to us humans. Yet it's unlikely to fully contain all that Divinity is. Words like "Spirit," "Essence," and "the Absolute" are more open-ended—they leave more room for a deity of infinite proportions.

Personal versus Impersonal

This polarity echoes the previous one. You can have a personal relationship with your Higher Power, and yet the full compass of Deity likely goes beyond your relationship with it. Deity may reveal itself to you in a highly personal way, and yet Deity itself, in its mysterious and intrinsic nature, may be impersonal or transpersonal.

Monotheistic versus Polytheistic

Ancient peoples such as the ancient Egyptians, Greeks, Romans, and Celts worshipped a pantheon of deities. There were gods of love, war, the sea, earth, the underworld, knowledge, the bounty of nature, and on and on. Some people even attributed deities to every local mountain, hill, and sacred place. "Sub-deity" beings (for lack of a better word) such as elves, fairies, rock spirits, and tree spirits abounded throughout many traditions. In addition to Jesus and Mary, Catholics have worshipped archangels, angels, and saints. Hindus have worshipped Shiva, Vishnu, and a host of other deities.

All of these polytheistic notions conceive of the Divine as a plurality. Often these pluralistic concepts coexist with a monotheistic one. The Greeks placed Zeus above the other gods; Native Americans place the Great Spirit above the spirits of the wind, earth, fire, and directions. Catholics place God and Christ above the archangels and angels. Hindus place Brahma above all other deities.

In recent years there has been a resurgence of interest in polytheistic approaches to the Divine. For example, there has been a revival of interest in the pantheon of Celtic deities among people who want to celebrate the spirituality of the earth and view God as present in all aspects of nature. Other people have sought to revive an interest in angels and archangels. At least a dozen recent books have explored the various types and functions of angels.

Some people give these polytheistic notions precedence; others see them as coexisting with a monotheistic view of Deity. Such popular expressions as "It all goes back to the Source," or "We're all one" convey this idea of relating the many spirits to the One Spirit.

Immanent versus Transcendent

This polarity is related to the previous one. If you believe somehow that there is a spiritual force in every rock, tree, and mountain (that deity is immanent in nature) then you may perceive the Divine as a multiplicity that "inspires" every physical thing in creation. The philosopher Spinoza conceived of the world in this way. So did most Native Americans. A well-known spiritually based community in Scotland, called Findhorn, revived this form of animism in recent times by claiming to actually communicate with the spirits of individual plants, as well as archetypal spirits that oversee an entire plant or animal species, what they called *devas*.

The transcendent view of the Divine, on the other hand, is reflected in the Buddhist notion that the ultimate transcends everything that exists and everything we can conceive that exists. Nirvana, or the Great Formless Reality, lies beyond all manifest creation, and beyond even the potential or archetypal forms of what might exist. Christianity leans toward a transcendent view of God, maintaining that God is totally beyond the natural and human order of things. And yet it allows for the immanence of God in believing that the Holy Spirit is able to enter into human awareness and inspire us.

Where do you stand on these contrasting views of Deity?

In my own attempts to reckon with the nature of the Divine, I've thought a lot about these dichotomies. After some years I've come to two conclusions:

1. In some way, both sides of each polarity are true.

2. The seeming contradictions between the polarities are only seeming. We humans find it hard to conceive of our world except in terms of dualities. However, on the level at which the Divine exists, there are no dualities—the Divine itself is beyond duality.

A useful metaphor that has helped me to resolve some of the seeming contradictions is the notion of a *holographic universe*, intimated by the late physicist David Bohm. According to Bohm, all of the separate things we perceive in the physical world constitute what he calls the "explicate order." However, these various things are all enfolded into one another in a way that renders them "all one." The level on which this happens is beyond our perception and construction of a three-dimensional universe. Bohm refers to this level as the "implicate order." Bohm's ideas are not philosophical speculations but constructs that help to explain the phenomena of modern quantum physics. Though not yet fully substantiated, there is actually some empirical evidence to support Bohm's view that the universe is organized holographically. (Bohm prefers to describe the universe as a "holomovement," since viewing it as a hologram is artificially static.) A popular explanation of Bohm's ideas, making them available to the public, can be found in Michael Talbot's book *The Holographic Universe* (1992).

If everything that exists is organized like a hologram, the implications are remarkable to the point of defying comprehension. One of the most fundamental aspects of a holographic image is that every part contains the information about the whole. If the entire universe is organized holographically, that means everything, including you, me, and the neighbor's cat, implicitly contains the whole. We're all enfolded through the implicate order back into one. In a sense, we're all emanations or permutations of one singular reality.

If you believe this, it doesn't really matter whether you want to emphasize polytheistic vs. monotheistic or immanent vs. transcendent views of the Divine. Such dualities are humanly constructed distinctions. In a holographic universe they don't exist. The many aren't really distinct from the One, because each of the many is simply another permutation of the Whole. Spirit is both immanent and transcendent since, ultimately, the distinction doesn't exist. So you can let go, and enjoy whatever construct of the Divine makes you most comfortable. All of the distinctions can be understood as different facets of the same crystal—different views of the same elephant.

What Is Your Concept of and Relationship with a Higher Power?

Reflect on the following questions. Write your responses in the spaces provided or on a separate sheet of paper.

1. What does the idea of God or a Higher Power mean to you personally?

2. Describe the attributes defining your notion of God, Spirit, or a Higher Power. When you think about the nature of God, what ideas and images come to mind? Is God personal or impersonal? Close or distant? Inside or outside?

3. Do you experience a personal, conscious connection with your Higher Power? How have you experienced this connection?

4. What obstacles do you feel interfere with your acceptance and/or experience of a Higher Power?

5. What would you hope to gain by developing and/or deepening your connection with a Higher Power?

What Personal Experiences Speak to You of the Presence of the Divine?

If you feel you already have a personal relationship with your Higher Power or God, how do you experience it? As you think back over your life, perhaps you can recall times when you felt inspired, moved, or uplifted beyond your everyday awareness. These are moments when you felt touched by something larger than yourself or believed there might be more to life than meets the eye.

Personal Spiritual Experiences

Write your responses to the following questions in the spaces provided or on a separate sheet of paper.

1. What situations, places, persons, activities, or events give you a feeling of inspiration? A feeling of wonder or awe?

2. Which of the following experiences do you consider to be "spiritual"? Write down an example of an inspiring experience you had in each case.

   Natural beauty
   (A place or occasion in nature that filled you with awe or wonder)

   Deep insight
   (A sudden recognition of something you knew to be true)

   Creative inspiration
   (Something creative you felt genuinely inspired to do)

Expressions of love received or given
(Indicate when and with whom)

3. The following experiences are commonly thought to be spiritual. Describe any of your own personal experiences that apply.

   Receiving answers to prayers

   Synchronicities (uncanny coincidences)

   Guidance

   Miracles or healing?

4. Mystical or visionary experiences—describe instances where you experienced any of the following:

   Feeling supported by a loving presence

   A sudden feeling of peace in the midst of turmoil

   A sense of the oneness of everything—or of yourself being one with or part of everything

   Experiencing an infusion of light that led to a feeling of peace, bliss, or joy

   Witnessing a spiritual being or presence (i.e., angels, Jesus, or other figures within your particular spiritual tradition)

Other (any other experience you consider to be a direct manifestation of your Higher Power i.e. spiritual conversion, near-death experiences, out-of-the-body experiences, or other non-ordinary states of consciousness)

How Can You Deepen Your Connection with Your Higher Power?

Cultivating a relationship with your Higher Power is in some ways similar to developing a relationship with another person. The more time and energy you give to it, the closer and deeper the relationship becomes. If you're willing to give such a relationship high priority, it will develop into an important part of your everyday life.

Among the many ways to spend time cultivating spirituality, five most common and widely practiced methods include:

Prayer—a way of actively communicating with your Higher Power, usually in the form of a request. Sometimes you may ask for a particular quality such as strength, peace, or clarity. Other times you may ask for your Higher Power simply to be present in a particular situation. Or you may relinquish a problem to God without asking for anything in particular.

Meditation—a practice of becoming quiet to the point that you get in touch with a deeper part of your inner being, one that is nonreactive, beyond conditioning, and ultimately in tune with your Higher Power. Meditation is a way to learn to disidentify with self-limiting emotions and thoughts so that you can witness rather than react to them. For thousands of years, meditation has been a way to "still the mind" and directly access the "kingdom of heaven within." (See the earlier chapter, "Meditation.")

Reading spiritual literature—reading uplifting spiritual books (or listening to tapes) is a wonderful way to move away from worry or a negative mind-set. You can choose from traditional sacred books such as the Bible or a wide range of contemporary books. A list of my personal favorites can be found in appendix 3.

Spiritual fellowship—remembering the sacred in the presence of others is a common and powerful way to renew your connection with God. This can happen through church attendance, spiritual classes and workshops, or sacred rituals (see below).

Compassionate service—serving others out of a genuine motive to help. This can be volunteer work or just simple acts of kindness to others in day-to-day life.

There are many other ways of cultivating a relationship with your Higher Power that have developed out of specific religious traditions and affiliations. Some of the most common ones include:

- Twelve-step work—attending twelve-step groups and working the steps to overcome specific addictions

- Listening to sacred music—classical or modern
- Sacred singing or chanting (e.g., joining a church choir)
- Sacred dance (e.g., Sufi dancing)
- Guided visualizations
- Working with spiritual affirmations (see the chapter "Create Your Vision")
- Attending classes or workshops on religious topics

All of these activities may contribute to strengthening and deepening your relationship with your Higher Power. If you're ready to make a commitment to cultivating a deeper relationship with your Higher Power, complete the following exercise.

My Spiritual Practices

Reflect on the following questions and write your responses in the spaces provided or on a separate sheet of paper.

1. Do you pray? How often? With what effect? Do you believe your prayers have been heard or answered?

2. Do you meditate? How often? For how long? With what effect?

3. Do you read religious or inspirational teachings? How often? With what effect? What teachings have influenced you the most?

4. Do you engage in any other spiritual practices (e.g., chanting, rituals, singing, dancing, vision quests, etc.)? How often? With what effect?

5. Are you involved with a church, center, or other spiritually based group of people? How often are you in contact with this group? What do you get out of it?

In the space on the next page (or on a separate piece of paper), write a statement of commitment to yourself. Which of the above activities would you be willing, in the next month, to give more of your time?

Everyday Uplifts

If Spirit is truly everywhere and ever present, it can be found in many ordinary activities of daily life, provided you are open and aware. Any of the following common activities may help you to connect with spirituality. Each provides a way to move into a place larger than your worries and personal dramas.

1. Take a walk outdoors—rain or shine. Experiencing the open space of outdoors, beyond the four walls of work or home, can provide an immediate uplift (especially if away from concrete and cars).

2. Walk near water. Whether waves, ripples, or rapids, there is something quite soothing to the soul in a natural body of water.

3. Get up to watch the sunrise (or wait to watch the sunset). The magnificence of a sky full of colors is well known for its ability to inspire.

4. Visit an art museum. Exploring the inner world of great artists can touch aspects of your soul otherwise unknown.

5. Listen to great classical music. The best-known works of Bach, Mozart, Beethoven, and Brahms are particularly inspiring.

6. Visit historic sites. Looking backward in time may give you an entirely new perspective on the present.

7. Watch a great movie. The best movies have the capacity to move you to a higher plane of consciousness. Many of the greatest films have won "best picture" Oscars or were nominated for the same. This is a good idea for an uplift during inclement weather.

8. Read a short, inspirational statement. Your local bookstore is full of pocket-sized books that offer daily meditations or affirmations.

9. Play with a pet. The unconditional love of an animal can help you to remember that capacity within yourself.
10. Hug your children. Children remind you to love at those times when you least expect to.
11. Make something with your hands. Creativity is the soul's expression in material form. Whether a model airplane, a garden, a pie, or a painting, a creative project is an excellent way to move into a larger space within yourself.
12. Perform an act of kindness. Helping someone else overcomes self-absorption. When done from the heart, it will inevitably lighten your soul.

Twelve Ideas Regarding Spirituality: A Personal View

The purpose of this chapter is to invite you to enlarge your view of life by exploring your ideas and experiences regarding spirituality. You may, of course, already have a well-defined understanding of spirituality—or you may still be searching to know more. In either case, *by embracing a spiritual view of life, you can reframe the way you perceive your own difficulties with fear or anxiety*. Spirituality can offer insights both into the meaning of your problem with anxiety as well as how to go about healing it.

If you are still exploring what spirituality means, I offer the following twelve ideas to stimulate your thinking. These ideas are not taken from any one source, tradition, or creed, but are based on my own personal experience. They have been useful points of departure for discussion with a number of my clients. You may or may not agree with them. As you read through the ideas, give consideration to those that fit or make sense to you and feel free to discard those that do not. Each of us has a basic philosophy about life, which we have to formulate for ourselves.

Some of these ideas may stimulate questions that you may want to discuss with a significant other, a trusted friend, or even a minister, priest, or rabbi. All of these ideas can lead to a more optimistic and tolerant view of life. They have done this for me personally. As you adopt any of these ideas that fit for you, you may find your attitude about your condition—as well as life in general—becoming a little more positive and less burdensome.

1. *Life is a school. The primary meaning and purpose of life is that it is a "classroom" for growth in consciousness.*

   Most people tend to define their life's meaning in terms of those people, activities, self-images, or objects to which they attach the greatest value. Whatever you value most in life—whether family, another individual, work, a particular role or self-image, your health, or material possessions—these things are probably what define your life's meaning. If you lost what you valued the most, your life might seem to lose its meaning. Think for a moment about what you value most highly in your life and what gives you the greatest satisfaction and comfort. Then imagine what your life would be like if these things were all suddenly taken away.

The truth, of course, is that everything you value most *will* eventually pass away. Nothing that you cherish lasts forever. Yet if everything you value must someday cease to be, what is the *ultimate* meaning of life? And as long as you assume that there is nothing more to existence than your present life—what there is right now—then there doesn't seem to be *any* ultimate meaning. You end up saying (along with Jean-Paul Sartre and other existentialists) that the only meaning life has is what you make of it in the present moment. Apart from this, life appears to have no meaning in and of itself. Since everything, including life itself, eventually passes away, how can there be any ultimate point to any of it?

Most forms of spirituality, traditional and modern, move beyond this existential predicament. Most of them make some kind of assumption that human life is not all there is. Something of us persists beyond human life, and so life comes to be seen as a temporary sojourn—not the final destination. Life comes to be understood as a preparation or training ground for something else that cannot be fully understood or revealed while you're alive.

It is this particular interpretation of life's "ultimate" meaning that I found to be most valid and helpful. If the final meaning of life is that it is a classroom or school for growth in consciousness—for the development of wisdom and the capacity to love—then the fact that everything passes away takes on an entirely new meaning. The tasks and challenges that come up in life, and your response to them, do not have eternal repercussions. Nor do they have no meaning at all. They are more like lessons in a school, lessons to which you apply yourself, and which you try to master as best you can. Each lesson is repeated until it's mastered. As you master old lessons, new ones are put before you. This "earth school" is thus a place where you learn and grow; it's not your final dwelling place. Eventually it's time to leave this classroom and move on.

2. ***Adversity and difficult situations are lessons designed for your growth—they are not random, capricious acts of fate. In the larger scheme of things, everything happens for a purpose.***

   If you accept the idea that life is a classroom, then the adversity and difficulties that come into your life may be viewed as part of the curriculum—as lessons for growth. This is a very different point of view from one that sees life's misfortunes as random quirks of fate. The latter perspective leads to a sense of victimization. You can end up feeling powerless in a capricious world that appears to be completely inequitable in its treatment of people, some of whom have such good luck, while others have misfortune heaped upon them.

   The view proposed here is that the difficulties of life are lessons to promote growth in wisdom, compassion, love, and other positive qualities (some religious traditions refer to "tests," although I prefer the notion of "lessons").

The greater the difficulty, the greater the potential for learning and growth. If you accept this idea, then the next question you may ask is, who established the curriculum or "assigns" your life lessons? Many of us may ask this question in one form or another when a given life challenge seems particularly difficult. We tend to protest and even rail against some of the misfortunes and limitations we're faced with. The question arises: "How could a loving God permit this?"

There is no easy answer to this question. None of us can fully understand how our life lessons are administered and assigned, though different spiritual traditions have different views on this matter (Eastern traditions speak of "karma," while Judeo-Christian traditions speak of "tests" and "temptations"). Each of us has to struggle with the challenges life brings without fully understanding why. What does seem apparent is that growth could not occur if the lessons were always easy. If the purpose of life is for us to grow in wisdom, consciousness, and compassion, then at least some of the lessons need to be difficult. This may not be an altogether consoling view, but it at least makes some sense out of the difficult situations that occur in life.

Given this view, you can stop asking, "Why did this happen to me?" and instead ask the more constructive questions: "What is this meant to teach me? How can I learn from this?" You might take whatever worry or concern is bothering you most in your life at this time and try asking the latter two questions instead of the first.

3. ***Your personal limitations and flaws are the "grist" you have to work with for your inner growth. Sometimes you can heal and overcome them with modest effort. In other cases, they may stay with you for a long time in order to push you to evolve and develop to your fullest potential. You are not "wrong" or in any way to blame because of your limitations.***

   Think for a moment about some of your own personal limitations—the ones you find most difficult to live with. If you're dealing with an anxiety disorder, think about your condition. You may ask why anyone should have to deal with a difficult condition such as panic disorder, agoraphobia, social phobia, or an obsessive-compulsive disorder even for a few months, let alone a longer time. Hopefully you have utilized all of the best treatments—including medication, if necessary—and have experienced a significant and genuine recovery. In many cases, a full recovery from an anxiety disorder is certainly possible. Suppose, however, that you have received all the best treatments, worked very hard for one or two years, and have experienced *some* improvement—yet you're still dealing with your condition to a degree. Is that a reason for you to think of yourself as a failure? A reason to think that you are somehow less skillful or persistent than those people who overcame their condition quickly?

   If you've worked hard on overcoming your condition, but are still troubled by it, perhaps there is some significant growth experience to find in the process of having to work with your difficulty for a long time. It all depends upon the lesson you happen to be learning. Having a difficult condition that is easily dispensed within a short time would certainly help develop your confidence in your own self-mastery—an important lesson in itself. Yet it wouldn't necessarily develop qualities of compassion or patience. It often seems that only through having to struggle with our own infirmities for a time can we learn fully how to feel compassion or have patience with others' difficulties.

As a second example, suppose that your lesson is to learn how to let go of the excessive need for control—even more, to learn how to let go and allow your Higher Power or God to have an impact on your life. One way (not the only way) this might be learned is to have to deal with a difficult situation in which all your efforts to control just don't work. The ability to let go of control is often fostered by those very difficulties in life that are most challenging. Some conditions and situations are so challenging that they *compel* us to let go. There is no other alternative. To struggle or fight against the condition only creates more distress and suffering. It is often at the exact moment when you fully let go of your worry or stop struggling that you may experience some kind of response or relief from your Higher Power. To let go and trust in your Higher Power should not be thought of as foregoing responsibility for your life. Rather, it involves doing all you can to help yourself first, while at the same time turning things over to another source of assistance.

In sum, it's a mistake to fault yourself for having any intractable condition, no matter how disabling or how long you've had it. It is there to foster and deepen certain qualities of your inner self. *How you respond to it and what you learn from it is what's important—not the condition itself.*

4. ***Your life has a creative purpose and mission. There is something creative that is yours to develop and offer.***

Your life is not a random sequence of accidental events—it follows a plan. This plan is created from a level that none of us can fully understand. Part of this plan consists of the lessons for growth in consciousness that were described in the preceding three sections.

Another very important aspect of the plan is your creative endowments, talents, or "gifts." Each of us has at least one personal form of creativity that can give our life meaning and purpose. The development and full expression of your creative talents and gifts is your "life purpose" or "life mission" spoken of in chapter 6 of this book.

Your life purpose is something that you feel you *need* to do in order to feel whole, complete, and fulfilled in your life. It's uniquely your own—something that can't be duplicated. Only you can do it. It comes from within, and has nothing to do with what your parents, partner, or friends might want you to do. Generally it moves you beyond yourself and has an impact on something or someone else.

Your purpose or mission can be a vocation or avocation—its scope can extend to the entire world or to just one other person. Examples would include: raising a family, mastering a musical instrument, volunteering your services to help youth or the elderly, writing poems, speaking eloquently before groups, or tending the garden in your backyard.

Until you develop and express your creative gifts, your life will seem incomplete. You will feel more anxiety because you're not making time to do what you truly want to do, what you were in fact born to do. See the chapter "Finding Your Unique Purpose" for further discussion of these ideas and guidelines for discovering your own special purpose.

5. *A Higher Source of support and guidance is always available.*

This idea is at the basis of much of this chapter. Fear and anxiety are based on the perception that you are separate and alone—or else on the anticipation of rejection or loss that might eventually result in being separate and alone. The truth is that you're not alone. Even at those times when you might find it difficult to turn to other human beings for support, there remains another source of support that can always be called on. Your Higher Power is not merely an abstract entity that created and sustains the universe. It is a force, power, or presence with which you can enter into a personal relationship. This relationship is as personal as any you could have with another human being.

In this personal relationship, you can experience both *support* and *guidance*. Support often appears in the form of inspiration or enthusiasm that can help lift and sustain you at times of low motivation and discouragement. Guidance can come in the form of clear insights and intuitions that provide discrimination and direction about what you need to do. Frequently this type of inspired insight or realization is wiser than anything you might have figured out with your rational mind.

You may experience a dilemma about this. If you think of inspiration and intuition originating in your own subconscious mind, how do they come then from a Higher Power—from something seemingly separate from you? Certainly from the perspective of the conscious mind, everything does seem separate—you perceive yourself as separate from others, the world, and most likely from a Higher Power. There is another level, though, that the conscious mind can't comprehend, where all things are joined. Eastern philosophy refers to this as "the One in which all things reside." The modern physicist David Bohm speaks of the "implicate order" in which everything is connected. In the Bible (New Testament) this idea is expressed in the statement: "The Kingdom of Heaven is within you."

To receive support and guidance from your Higher Power, you simply need to ask. Nothing more is necessary. While this might seem easy enough, it may not be in practice if you believe that you're supposed to figure out and handle everything entirely on your own. Or it may not be easy if you feel that it's irrational, weak, or in some other way beneath your dignity to rely on an invisible power for support. To trust and rely on your Higher Power, it takes a certain willingness to let go of control as well as a certain humility (it's often humbling to come to the realization that you can't handle something completely on your own). The ability to let go and trust is something that can be learned. Often the life lessons that are the hardest—the ones that push you to your absolute limit—tend to be the ones that have the most to teach about letting go.

As you increasingly learn to allow your Higher Power (Spirit) to assist in your life, you can grow in trusting that it is sometimes appropriate to relinquish control. Chapter 8, "Letting Go," explores this point further.

6. ***Contact with your Higher Power is directly available within your personal experience.***

   You can discover a personal relationship with your Higher Power within your own immediate experience. It is a two-way relationship—you can receive support, guidance, inspiration, peace of mind, inner strength, hope, and many other gifts from your Higher Power; you can also communicate your needs to Spirit through prayer, and directly communicate feelings of gratitude and reverence. Such a relationship can deepen and grow to the extent that you choose to give it attention and time.

   There are numerous ways in which your Higher Power can manifest itself in your personal experience. Feelings of awe in the presence of nature, a deep insight that seems to come out of nowhere, synchronicities (uncanny coincidences), a sudden feeling of support in times of turmoil, and small miracles are some of the more common types of spiritual experience. See the exercise called *Spiritual Experiences* earlier in this chapter to explore your own experiences with spirituality.

7. ***Requests sincerely asked of your Higher Power are answered.***

   This idea is really an extension of the previous point about your Higher Power being a source of support and guidance. The point is emphasized to underscore the fact that your Higher Power's support and guidance is not only bestowed on you—you can deliberately ask for it. The famous quote of Jesus, "Ask and you shall receive," is true regardless of the particular spiritual tradition or orientation you follow.

   It is the assumption of all religious approaches that incorporate prayer that prayer will be answered. Perhaps you have had experiences of your prayers being answered. It often seems that the degree of earnestness of your request has something to do with how readily the prayer receives a response. A common example is when you feel overwhelmed with some situation and you almost literally cry out for help to your Higher Power. In many cases, something about the situation improves or shifts, often within a short time.

   There is actually scientific research that confirms the efficacy of prayer. Several well-controlled empirical studies of prayer are reported in the book *Recovering the Soul: A Scientific and Spiritual Search* by Larry Dossey (1989).

In sum, there is both anecdotal and research support for the idea that prayer is effective. This doesn't mean that whatever you pray for will come true. There are some qualifications that, I've discovered in my experience, need to be kept in mind: 1) the request needs to be made with genuine earnestness and sincerity, 2) the "answer" or response to prayer may not come immediately—it may take days, weeks, or months, 3) the answer may not come all at once—instead, only a step in the direction of the answer may come (for example, if you're praying for healing from chronic pain, the answer may come in the form of a strong intuition to visit a particular doctor or healing practitioner). Prayer can be answered in many ways, and sometimes the answer may not be what you expected. It's not possible to know in advance how a particular prayer will be answered (that is where faith comes in). What can be trusted is that there will be an answer, and that the answer will serve your highest good.

8. ***What you truly ask for or intend from the deepest level of yourself—from your heart—will tend to come to you.***

   One of the most powerful things that can foster positive change and healing is a sincerely held intention. With clients, and in my own experience, I have observed how the power of intention can promote miraculous consequences. What you believe in and commit to with your whole heart tends to come true. When the intention is for your own highest good—and when it doesn't conflict with anyone else's highest good—it is most likely to become manifest.

   A deeply held intention shifts and focuses your own consciousness. It also appears to have ramifications on events in the world apart from you. Events in the outer world will tend to align with your most deeply held intention. Goethe summed this up in his famous remark:

> Concerning all acts of initiative or creation,
> there is one elementary truth;
> the ignorance of which kills countless ideas and splendid plans.
>
> The moment one definitely commits oneself,
> then Providence moves too.
>
> All sorts of things occur to help one
> that would never otherwise have occurred.
>
> A whole stream of events issue from the decision,
> raising in one's favor
> all manner of unforeseen incidents and assistance,
> which no person could have dreamt
> would have come their way.

A positive belief in your ability to recover from anxiety will not only help your mood and perception of your situation—it will actually help draw to you the healing you seek. The idea that you can actually create a positive reality in accord with your beliefs is explored in detail in the chapter "Create Your Vision."

9. ***Each of us is an individualized expression of Spirit.***

   There is an aspect of your innermost being that is connected with and is an extension of All Being. This aspect has been referred to as the "Self" (or "Atman") in Eastern philosophy. Many people in the West have called it the "soul." Transpersonal psychology refers to it as the "Higher Self." The Higher Self is understood as an individualized or personalized aspect of Universal Spirit that is at the very center of your being. In short, each of us, at our core, is an individualized expression of the One Spirit that exists in all things. Each of us is a drop in the ocean that is God.

   It's important to add that your conscious, ego self or personality is not a direct extension of God. It can be disturbing to hear people say they are "ultimately one with God" and then imagine they are talking about their personal ego. (Many would call that blasphemous.) Your *conscious self* (personality) is instead a complex series of concepts, memories, habits, and images that you have created over a lifetime. *Who you think you are* is something you've learned and created—it's not who you *essentially* are. The part of you that is connected with God is mostly unconscious and tends to emerge only in moments of heightened awareness or deep meditation. The "I" that can observe "me" or reflect on "who I am" lies closer to that inner core of being that is a part of Spirit.

10. ***Evil is not a separate force but a misuse of one's creative power.***

    When you're separated or alienated from your innermost being, what you create—in your mind as well as in your physical reality—is not likely to be in complete harmony or to completely fulfill you. Such creations are out of step with your essence and therefore the essence of all things. To the extent that you are out of alignment with your true self, you may create self-limiting situations in your life. Since no one is perfect, this happens, to varying degrees, to everyone. Life for everyone is a mix of affirmation and restriction, light and dark, or what we label "good" and "evil." Without these polarities, life would not allow for learning. There is no way to learn what light really is without darkness—or what love and beauty truly are without fear and ugliness. A life without polarities or contrasts would not offer much opportunity to grow. If life truly is a school, polarities are likely to be a necessary part of it.

    "Evil" is not an inherent force separate from and against God. (If this were so, God could not be infinite, as something else would exist outside of and independent of God.) It is instead a misuse of our creative power when we make choices that are not in step with our innermost self—our soul. This leads to outcomes that are contrary to our highest good, which is the same as our well-being, happiness, and fulfillment. If we choose to do our *highest* good, we are naturally fulfilled—there can be no disappointment in the outcome. All other choices outside of this may bring relative degrees of satisfaction and/or suffering, either of which lasts only for a while. We are not punished by an angry God for our mistakes; instead, we reap negative consequences—sooner or later—as a result of our own actions that are out of step with our Higher Self (and thus the universe). To err is simply not to be true to your own deepest self.

"Evil" is a relative term—it is a matter of degree. Eating food that is not healthful may be out of alignment with your true self, but would not usually be called evil. Neither would unintentionally causing an accident that hurts someone else. Actions labeled evil (for example, serious crimes) are usually deliberate and grossly out of alignment with the perpetrator's innermost being or soul. If, as has been said, "we are all one," or "joined at the highest level," to willfully do harm to another is to harm oneself, and all of Being. In the Bible, Christ says: "Even as you do it unto the least of them, you do it unto Me." In time one will eventually reap the fruits of one's actions. In Eastern philosophy this is spoken of as "karma." In the Bible it is said, "As you sow, so shall you reap." Although God is not wrathful or punitive, there is a law of conservation in the universe whereby each of us will, sooner or later, absorb the effects of our actions, for better or for worse.

We "should" therefore want to do what is our highest good—what we can intuitively discern to be our highest good—*not* because we should do it in any *moral* sense, but because our highest good is always what we truly *want* in our deepest, innermost self anyway. If there is any ethical imperative, it is to do what our innermost being or soul truly wants. As Shakespeare put it: "This above all—to thine own self be true." When you're in doubt about how to do that, the operative question is, *"What is the most loving thing I can do, both for myself and others?"*

11. ***Love is stronger than fear. Pure, unconditional love emanates from your Higher Power and is at the very center of your being and all beings. All fears can be understood as different forms of separation—separation from others, ourselves, and God—separation from the love that unites all things.***

Love is stronger than fear because it goes deeper. Consciously love is the experience of feeling your heart go out toward unity with someone or something other than yourself. On a deeper level, love is the "ground state" or essential foundation of the entire universe. This is a view that is common both to Eastern and Western religions. Love isn't something we either possess or don't possess, because it literally *defines* what we are at our core and in essence. Fear may go deep, but never as deep as love, because fear only arises when we feel separate from the ground state that unifies us with everything else.

Most of the anxiety you experience may be related to specific fears of abandonment, rejection and humiliation, loss of control, confinement, injury, or death. Fear can take on any of these forms, based on your conditioning and past experience. Yet none of these fears could ever arise if you did not experience separation. The existence of fear always points to a degree of separation—separation of your conscious mind from your innermost being, separation from others, and/or separation from God. If it's true that in essence all of us are united as one, then every fear we feel—no matter how much we believe it—is, in fact, just an illusion. If we could perceive things the way they truly are, there would be no reason to have any more fear.

Love and fear constitute perhaps the most profound duality in human existence. Yet the former can always overcome the latter.

12. ***Death is not an end but a transition. Our essential nature or soul survives physical death. (To fear death as "the end" is simply an illusion.)***

This basic idea is shared by all of the world's religions. They all assume that an individual's soul continues to exist after physical death, although they differ somewhat in their conceptions about the nature of the afterlife.

Actual evidence for this view has emerged in the past fifteen years from the widespread research on "near-death experiences." As you most likely already know, near-death experiences are based on reports of what people experienced between the time when their vital signs indicated imminent or clinical death and when they were subsequently revived. These reports all share several things, such as passing through a tunnel, meeting a being of light that radiates love and understanding, witnessing a scene-by-scene review of one's entire life, and sometimes meeting relatives who've already died. A smaller number of these reports describe otherworldly scenes and locales. Though the thousands of such reports that have been collected worldwide don't "prove" that consciousness survives death, they certainly make a strong case in that direction. Further evidence that near-death survivors get a peek into an afterlife comes from the fact that many of them lose their fear of death and become more deeply spiritual following their experience.

Does fear of death come up for you or underlie other fears you might have about illness or injury? If so, I would suggest that you read the literature on near-death experiences and come to your own conclusions about life after death. The book *Life After Life* (1976) by Raymond Moody is a good start, but I would especially recommend the book *Heading Toward Omega* by Kenneth Ring (1985).

Your Personal Spiritual Belief System

Allow the preceding twelve spiritual ideas to be a springboard for reflecting on your own spiritual beliefs and convictions.

Of these twelve ideas, which ones do you find helpful? Are there any with which you disagree? How would believing these ideas change your view of your anxiety condition? Your view of life in general? You may wish to discuss some of these ideas with a significant other, a trusted friend, or a minister, priest, or rabbi.

The twelve ideas are briefly restated below:

Write your opinion of each belief in the space provided or on a separate piece of paper.

Twelve Ideas Associated with Spirituality

1. Much of what we experience in life consists of lessons for our spiritual progress. Life can be understood as a "school" for spiritual growth.

2. Adversity and difficult situations in life are not random acts of fate—they are part of a larger purpose.

3. Personal limitations (including physical or mental disabilities) are not "bad luck" but challenges to be used for personal and spiritual growth.

4. Each individual's life has a creative purpose and mission.

5. A Higher Source of support and guidance is always available to us.

6. Contact with your Higher Power is directly available within your personal experience.

7. Requests sincerely asked of your Higher Power are answered.

8. Our beliefs and expectations create our reality in life. You will attract to yourself what you truly want.

9. Each of us (our souls, not our minds or egos) is an individualized expression of the Universal Spirit (God).

10. Evil is not a separate force in the universe but a misuse of human beings' creative power.

11. Love is stronger than—and can overcome—any fear.

12. Death is not the end of our existence. Some aspect of each of us (our soul) survives and continues on after physical death.

What You Can Do Now

1. Go back through the chapter and work through those exercises that are personally meaningful to you.
2. Make a commitment to add one spiritual activity or practice (for example, prayer or inspirational reading) to your daily routine starting this week.
3. Make your own list of inspirational books to read, drawing from your own religious tradition, from the list which follows, or from appendix 3. Read one book each month.

References and Further Reading

Chopra, Deepak. 1994. *The Seven Spiritual Laws of Success.* San Rafael, Calif.: New World Library.

Dossey, Larry. 1989. *Recovering the Soul: A Scientific and Spiritual Search.* New York: Bantam.

Moody, Raymond. 1976. *Life After Life.* New York: Bantam.

Norwood, Robin. 1994. *Why Me, Why This, Why Now.* New York: Carol Southern Books.

Peck, Scott. 1978. *The Road Less Traveled.* New York: Simon & Schuster.

———. 1993. *Further Along the Road Less Traveled.* New York: Simon & Schuster.

Ring, Kenneth. 1985. *Heading Toward Omega.* New York: William Morrow.

Rodegast, Pat. 1985. *Emmanuel's Book.* New York: Bantam.

———. 1989. *Emmanuel's Book, II.* New York: Bantam.

Talbot, Michael. 1992. *The Holographic Universe.* New York: HarperCollins.

Walsch, Neale. 1996. *Conversations with God (Book I).* New York: Putnam.

Williamson, Marianne. 1994. *Illuminata.* New York: Random House.

Zukav, Gary. 1990. *The Seat of the Soul.* New York: Fireside Books.

10

Create Your Vision

Human beings are endowed with free will. You are free to choose experiences of freedom or restriction, abundance or lack, joy or misery—according to the most cherished thoughts and beliefs you hold. Your life will tend to reflect those thoughts and beliefs you hold in mind and give energy to. What you believe in, for good or ill, does tend to come to you: "It is done unto you as you believe."

When you don't like the way your life is going, it's most important to examine self-limiting beliefs and attitudes that might be contributing to your circumstances. Then you can resolve to make a new choice—to think differently and more constructively. Free will is an awesome responsibility, but it also implies that you always have the power to *recreate* your life and circumstances, in accord with the way you think and believe.

How to Create Your Goal

The first step in creating something you want is to truly believe that you can do so. That means you need to work on setting aside any fears, doubts, feelings of resignation, or hopelessness you may have about the possibility of attaining what you seek. You need to stop focusing on problems and refocus your attention and energy on *creating what you want instead* of your problems. This requires an open mind, as well as courage and tenacity. If you've derived a sense of identity from having your problem—or being victimized by it—you need to be willing to give up that identity. If you are in considerable distress over the problem, you need the courage to look past your distress and pain and focus primarily on what you'd rather have in your life. Finally, since the process of creating a goal usually takes time, you need tenacity to keep visioning and revisioning the goal that you seek, no matter what setbacks and discouragement arise along the way.

In order to have the courage and tenacity to keep affirming your goal, you need to be willing at least to *entertain* the idea that what you believe in will actually come to pass. That is, you need to be open-minded about the basic principle, "It is done unto you as you believe." If you regard this idea as a naive, "pie-in-the-sky" viewpoint, then you may get easily discouraged when what you visualize or affirm does not immediately come about. (I've developed a theory of how creating your reality might actually work, which is presented in appendix 4. It's fairly abstract and philosophical, so read it only if you're interested.)

I must admit that when I first encountered the idea that beliefs can create reality, I was skeptical. If this notion were true, why did so many people have unfulfilled dreams and unanswered prayers? If overcoming adversity were simply a matter of choosing to believe differently, why didn't more people "choose" their way out of their predicaments in life? If a new belief could actually pay the rent or put food on the table, this certainly wasn't immediately obvious or evident to me. Three things have subsequently led me to lose my skepticism, and to actually give some credence to the idea that what happens in your life reflects your beliefs. The first and most important was that when I put the idea to the test, it actually worked for me. Many times in my life I have chosen to visualize and affirm a goal that, on the face of it, seemed unlikely or impossible. Yet if I continued my visualization long enough, the goal did in fact manifest, quite to my surprise. This has happened often enough that I've come to believe that there really *is* something to it.

Second, I've found that "creating your reality" is not a pie-in-the-sky notion or a form of "magical thinking" because you *still have to do all the footwork*. Entertaining a visualization of prosperity is not going to pay the rent or put food on the table unless you also take action, such as going out and looking for a job. What it might do, however, is make your job search easier by encouraging a confluence of events that bring you in touch with persons or situations that lead to the "right job." Envisioning your recovery *by itself* will not lead to healing your anxiety disorder. You still need to make a conscientious effort to change your self-talk, practice relaxation and exercise, use *in vivo* exposure, or improve assertiveness, as the case may be. However, sincere visualizations and affirmations of your goal may "attract" you to the right therapist, medication, or other supportive resources in ways that you would not have foreseen or even attempted to foresee otherwise. If you affirm healing *in conjunction with doing all the necessary footwork*, outside circumstances tend to conspire to promote your achieving a high degree of recovery.

Finally, I have come to realize that when you choose to create a positive goal, it may not manifest in quite the way or form you expected. There may be some modifications in your goal along the way to bringing it into reality. For example, you may visualize the goal of a loving relationship, but instead of attracting a new partner you wind up with a child to nurture and care for. Or you may affirm 100 percent recovery from a particular anxiety disorder, and the result is that you attain 80 percent recovery yet also acquire a whole new attitude and greater peace of mind to bring to handling the residual 20 percent of symptoms that remain. It's important not to be too attached to the exact form in which a goal manifests. Just be clear that your goal is attainable in its essence or *spirit*, if not in the *form* you originally conceived it. If you want more peace in your life, you can create it—in time.

Really trusting the idea that it's possible to create what you believe is the most liberating realization I've gained along the path to my own recovery. In essence, it means there is no adversity in life that cannot be overcome. You do not have to be a victim of any circumstance, no matter how difficult it *appears*, because you can create an altogether new circumstance. The power of mind and spirit always exceeds the power of *any* adverse situation. Just knowing that has given me a tremendous sense of hope and optimism. I hope it will for you, too.

With all this in mind, I ask you now to consider the following seven-step process for creating your goals. You can use these steps for visualizing or affirming your recovery from anxiety—or for any other goal you seek. These steps have worked well for me and for many of my clients. Be sure to see the sections following these steps on how to develop visualizations and affirmations as well as clearing resistance and self-limiting beliefs. These sections will assist you with steps two and three. For further assistance beyond this chapter in creating your goals, I highly recommend the book *Creative Visualization* by Shakti Gawain (1995). Twenty years after its original publication, it's still the clearest, most articulate, and most practical description of the creative process I know of.

Steps for Creating Your Goal

1. ***Set your goal.***

   Decide what it is you would like to change or realize in your life. Most likely this will be overcoming your problem with anxiety. However, your goal can be on any level—physical, emotional, mental, or spiritual. You might want a new job, a new or better relationship, clarity about making an important decision, or peace of mind. To illustrate how the process of creation works, let's suppose you want to overcome a condition of chronic anxiety or fear and achieve a state of wholeness and health.

2. ***Develop a visualization or affirmation of your goal (or both).***

   Create a mental picture—or a statement—of your goal exactly as you'd like to achieve it. Think of it as if it were already realized or fulfilled. If you design a visualization, describe what your life would look and feel like if you attained your goal, in as much detail as you can. If you design one or more affirmations, they should be positive statements in the present tense, worded as though you'd already achieved your goal. If you seek wholeness and health, for example, you might say, "I am fully whole and healthy in body and mind." See the sections on developing visualizations and affirmations below for more details on writing your own.

3. ***Acknowledge and detach from any doubts or fears.***

   This is an important step. If you have any doubts or fears about being able to have what you truly want, take time to acknowledge them but don't give them any additional energy or attention. Let yourself detach emotionally from them as best you can. If they come up, you might want to write them down to give them expression, and then resolve to move past them and refocus on your goal. The less energy you give them, the weaker such fears become until they eventually die of neglect. For example, if you're dealing with a chronic anxiety disorder, you might have doubts or fears such as, "I've had this problem twenty years; I'll never get better," or "This problem is so old and familiar that I'm scared to embrace the possibility of a new life without it." Simply notice that these attitudes come up, give them a moment of acknowledgment, and then resolve to look past them and refocus on the goal of creating wholeness and wellness. See the section below on "Overcoming Fears, Doubts, and Self-Limiting Beliefs" for further assistance with this step. It's helpful to work through self-limiting beliefs and attitudes before you sit down to practice a creative visualization or affirmation.

4. ***Relax.***

Relaxation helps you to put more energy and presence behind your visualization or affirmation. If you try to visualize or affirm something while your mind is scattered, it's hard to focus conscious energy on it because your consciousness itself is scattered. Relaxation helps you to quiet and focus your mind. Then you can hold the visualization or affirmative statement in your mind easily. Research has confirmed, in fact, that visualizations for healing illness are far more effective in a relaxed, reverie-like state than in a more active, analytical state of mind.

Before doing a visualization or working with affirmations, you might want to use progressive muscle relaxation, a guided relaxation tape, calming music, or meditation to relax.

5. ***Focus on your visualization or affirmation clearly.***

While relaxed, give yourself time to focus on your visualization in full detail. Or repeat your affirmation several times slowly, with full presence of mind. Try to be in the present moment, bringing your full, undistracted awareness to this process. This is the time to be clear and deliberate about what you are visualizing/affirming without rushing.

6. ***Energize it.***

The more you can get behind your visualization or affirmation with your whole being, the more you empower it. To put your heart and soul into it gives your visualization or affirmative statement increased power to attract exactly what you seek. Think about your goal in a positive, uplifting way and build your conviction that you truly can have it, and that it is now coming to you. As you put deeper levels of yourself (your inner being) behind your intention, you may begin to draw on resources beyond yourself (i.e., your Higher Power or God) to bring it about.

7. ***Repeat the process of visualization or affirmation daily (or until your goal manifests).***

   Repetition of your visualization/affirmation strengthens it. First, the process of persisting in refocusing away from doubts and fears toward whatever you seek helps you to release those doubts. Your conviction and commitment toward your goal increase. Second, repetition actually increases the capacity of your belief—your own picture or statement of your goal—to attract its real-life equivalent on a physical level. The principle of "mind over matter" is reinforced by perseverance.

   It's important to persevere with the process of visualizing or affirming a goal until you achieve it. This may take days, week, months, or even years.

Developing a Visualization

You may be concerned that it's difficult to visualize your goal because you don't readily "see" mental pictures in your mind. Realize that you don't need to see images in detail to utilize visualization. Some people are naturally visual, while others tend to favor auditory or kinesthetic channels of sensory experience. More important than seeing your goal in detail is your ability to *feel* a sense of conviction about it when you imagine it. The strength of your belief and commitment to your goal is the best measure of your ability to actually create it.

If you're still concerned about your capacity to visualize, work with the script below until you feel satisfied with your ability to "see" the scene involved. Have a friend read it to you or record it on tape so you can be fully relaxed when you visualize it. The more you relax, the easier it will be for you to visualize the scene in detail.

The Beach

You're walking down a long wooden stairway to a very beautiful, expansive beach. It looks almost deserted and stretches off into the distance as far as you can see. The sand is very fine and light in appearance. You step onto the sand in your bare feet and rub it between your toes. It feels so good to walk slowly along this beautiful beach. The roaring sound of the surf is so soothing that you can just let go of anything on your mind. You're watching the waves ebb and flow . . . they're slowly coming in . . . breaking over each other . . . and then slowly flowing back out again. The ocean itself is very beautiful and so relaxing just to look at. You look out over the surface of the ocean all the way to the horizon and then follow the horizon as far as you can see, noticing how it bends slightly downward as it follows the curvature of the earth. As you scan the ocean you can see, many miles offshore, a tiny sailboat skimming along the surface of the water. And all these sights help you to just let go and relax even more. As you continue walking down the beach, you become aware of the fresh, salty smell of the sea air. You take in a deep breath . . . breathe out . . . and feel very refreshed and even more relaxed. Overhead you notice two seagulls flying out to sea ... looking very graceful as they soar into the wind ... and you imagine how you might feel yourself if you had the freedom to fly. You find yourself settling into a deep state of relaxation as you continue walking down the beach. You feel the sea breeze blowing gently against your cheek and the warmth of the sun overhead penetrating your neck and shoulders. The warm, liquid sensation of the sun just relaxes you even more ... and you're beginning to feel perfectly content on this beautiful beach. It's such a lovely day. In a moment, up ahead, you see a comfortable-looking beach chair. Slowly, you begin to approach the beach chair ... and when you finally reach it, you sit back and settle in. Easing back in this comfortable beach chair, you let go and relax even more, drifting even deeper into relaxation. In a little while you might close your eyes and just listen to the sound of the surf, the unending cycle of waves ebbing and flowing. And the rhythmic sound of the surf carries you even deeper ... deeper still ... into a wonderful state of quietness and peace.

Now, write a script in which you picture yourself having achieved your goal in as much vivid detail as possible. What would a day in your life look like if you had realized your goal? What new things would you do? How would you feel? Would there be changes in your environment, and, if so, what would they look like? How would you act toward significant others in your life? How would they act toward you?

When you have developed a detailed script answering as many of these questions as are relevant, have a friend read it to you or listen to a tape recording of it while you're in a relaxed state. With practice, you should find that your ability to visualize it in detail increases.

The following is an example of a detailed visualization of an ideal day developed by one of my clients.

It's 5 A.M. and I am up and moving comfortably, without dizziness and anxiety, to the kitchen to fix breakfast for my husband, Steve, and me. My mind is clear, and I am thinking at a normal pace and moving without pain or stiffness. As I move I am talking to myself with affirmations and mentally planning my day. As I sit down to breakfast, I talk about my plans for the day and watch the animals outside our window. I am calm and enjoying breakfast at a normal pace. It is 6:15 and Steve is leaving for work. I wish him a good day and comfortably move into my early morning exercise routine. I'm looking forward to doing my daily program: yoga is helping me become stronger, more flexible, and more relaxed; aerobics is giving me stamina, strength, and energy; and relaxation and meditation are giving me inner peace and calm. I find that I have boundless energy. I'm feeling calm, at peace with the world and myself, energetic, and comfortable in my body. I'm enjoying and desiring healthy food, and am preparing a healthy snack. As I dress slowly, I am doing abdominal breathing and using affirmations to calm any anticipatory anxiety or racing thoughts. This helps me stay in the moment . . . Now I imagine that I'm at my desk, enjoying the sunlight and the view, as I plan and prioritize my day. Decision-making is easy, as is scheduling. My schedule allows me to balance all of my activities. I am excited with these items on my agenda for today and at peace with each of them. After lunch I'll give myself time to rest, read or nap, if I want to. I find it easy to move through the day comfortably, calmly, and with self-confidence. I know I am ready to handle the unusual or unexpected and can reprioritize if needed . . . Now I see myself calmly walking to the car to go to the grocery store and I feel happy to be going out. As I begin my drive, I move comfortably and with purpose, ready to do what I need to do. As I drive I remain calm and relaxed. The entire trip is easy to negotiate. It is getting easier every time to handle driving and going to the grocery store. I do fine both on the trip out and on the return trip . . . Now I see myself getting ready to go to the golf course to practice. This is something I like to do. I enjoy what the game of golf teaches me about myself. Today I will learn more about life from golf—things such as "easy does it," "go with the flow," "laugh and enjoy," "less is more," and "life is an ongoing process, not a task to always be completed." I'll watch my childlike, playful self get stronger. What a nice way to meet and talk with people in a peaceful setting . . . On my way home I plan dinner, the evening, and think about what I might do to help others through my experience with anxiety/panic/depression. I'm excited that I might help someone overcome or cope better with anxiety through my experiences. Walking through the door to our house, I thank God for a wonderful day and the blessings I have. I calmly move through my tasks after being out for the day. I'm sitting on the floor, having a mini-break and playing with my dog, Boggs. What a good and loving friend he is. He makes me laugh and think often that life's greatest pleasures are the little things. As I fix dinner I think of what I experienced today, what lessons I learned and what I can glean from those lessons. I have had a full, productive, and enjoyable day and am enjoying dinner with Steve. After dinner, I'll get ready for bed and read or listen to the tapes I've been working with. Or I may just take a long, relaxing bath or sit on the patio and watch the animals in the yard.

Write a Visualization of Your Goal

Write a detailed visualization of what achieving your goal would look like in the space below (or on a separate sheet of paper).

Please note that if your healing visualization involves overcoming a phobia, you may need to do *imagery desensitization* first. This will be necessary if you find that you become anxious when you first imagine approaching your phobic situation. Break the visualization down into a series of steps, starting with the easiest and proceeding to the most difficult. For example, if you have a fear of flying, you might visualize going to the airport first, then checking in your bags, and then going to the gate. When you're comfortable with these scenes, visualize each aspect of a flight separately, beginning with boarding the plane, then finding your seat, then waiting until the door to the aircraft is closed, then taxiing down the runway, then taking off, etc. Visualize each scene repeatedly until you get fully comfortable with it, then proceed to the next scene. For detailed instructions on how to do imagery desensitization, see chapter 7 in *The Anxiety & Phobia Workbook*.

Developing Affirmations

Much of what goes on in your mind is based on the basic or "core" beliefs that you've gained from parents, peers, and society at large. Many of these beliefs can be counterproductive—in fact, such beliefs are often the source of much of the anxiety and stress you experience. Beliefs such as "I'm powerless to change my circumstances," "There is something very wrong with me," or "I don't really deserve to have what I want" are common examples of such unhelpful beliefs.

An affirmation is a way to "make firm" something you would *like* to believe. The practice of using affirmations enables you to begin replacing some of the negative, conditioned beliefs from your past with more constructive ideas about yourself, others, and life in general. Utilizing affirmations will help you, first, to overcome any depressed or anxious feelings that stem from your negative beliefs. More than this, *affirmations will help draw to you circumstances that reflect their positive content*. You can use them to help you create the goals you seek.

Here are some examples of affirmations:

- I am becoming prosperous.
- I have all the financial resources I need.
- I now have a well-paying, satisfying job.
- I now have a loving, fulfilling relationship.
- I am vibrantly healthy and whole.
- I love myself the way I am.
- I respect and believe in myself.
- My relationship with _________ is growing happier and more fulfilling all the time.
- Whatever I truly need comes to me.

In writing an affirmation to reflect a goal you wish to attain, observe the following guidelines:

1. Keep affirmations in the *present tense* ("I am prosperous") or *present progressive tense* ("I am becoming prosperous"). Telling yourself that some change you desire will happen in the future always keeps it one step removed.
2. *Avoid negations.* Instead of saying "I'm no longer afraid of public speaking," try "I am learning to enjoy public speaking" or "Public speaking comes easily to me."

3. An affirmation should be *short*, *simple*, and *positive*. "My mind and body are healthy and whole" is preferable to "I am overcoming my problem with panic attacks."

4. An affirmation should be framed in terms of a new goal rather than an old problem. As in the preceding example, state the goal you wish to achieve rather than overcoming some problem in the past.

5. It's important that you have *some* belief in—or at least a willingness to believe in—your affirmations. It's by no means necessary, however, to believe in an affirmation 100 percent when you first start out. The whole point is to shift your beliefs and attitudes in the direction of the affirmation.

Write Affirmations of Your Goal

Write a list of positive statements affirming your goal in the space below.

Ways to Work with Affirmations

Once you have developed one—or preferably several—affirmations that reflect your goal, you can work with them in one of three ways:

1. Write the affirmation slowly, with your awareness fully present, five to ten times. Try to build conviction about your positive statement as you write it again and again. On the opposite side of the paper, write down any doubts or fears that come up in the process (if they do). See the following section on "Overcoming Fears, Doubts, and Self-Limiting Beliefs" to deal with these.

2. Record the affirmation on tape, five times in the first person—e.g.,"I am healthy and whole," and five times in the second person, "You are healthy and whole." Leave five to ten seconds between each reiteration of the affirmation so that you have time to reflect and meditate on it. Your recording should take about a minute or two. Listen to this recording once or twice per day when you are in a relaxed, focused state for at least thirty days. It's okay to play the tape at any time, while you're cleaning the house or driving your car. However, doing so in a relaxed, aware state will increase the power of the process considerably.

3. Take one affirmation describing your goal into quiet meditation. Repeat this affirmation slowly and with conviction when you feel relaxed and centered. Continue this process for five to ten minutes. The more you can put your deepest conviction—your "heart and soul"—behind your affirmation, the more you empower it to attract what you seek. Should doubts or fears come up, clear them (using the guidelines in the following section) before you repeat the process.

Overcoming Fears, Doubts, and Self-Limiting Beliefs

Many of us want to heal limiting circumstances in our bodies, minds, and lives, and yet we harbor doubts and fears. Various forms of resistance stand in our way. You may be afraid to have what you truly want or else you feel you don't deserve to have it. Often your doubts and fears are unconscious. By making them conscious, you can work through them and free the way for your visualizations or affirmations to be effective.

Some of the most common ways you can obstruct your own progress follow:

1. ***Fear of change.***

   It may feel safer to cling to what's familiar, even if it's uncomfortable, than to venture into unknown territory (which is always necessary if you truly want to change). Living with panic and phobias—or obsessions and compulsions—can be miserable, but at least it's familiar. To imagine yourself without them might be such a major change that you balk (perhaps unconsciously) at the prospect.

2. ***Reluctance to give up a problem's hidden benefit or "payoff."***

   Remaining ill often affords the opportunity to receive a lot of attention and be taken care of. It may also provide reasons not to have to work, not to have to deal with the outside world, or not to have to leave an unhappy relationship and risk being alone. In short, there can be many hidden (or not so hidden) benefits to staying ill. In such cases it becomes easy to complain and imagine that you would *like* to recover, when deep inside you don't really want to.

3. ***Being "lost" without your problem.***

   Perhaps you derive your sense of identity from having an anxiety disorder or from some other misfortune such as strained family relations, financial problems, or job dissatisfaction. You might ask yourself whether you feel like a "victim" of your circumstances. If you get your sense of who you are from your problem, it may be difficult to let it go. To do so would mean giving up your very identity. To truly change means relinquishing your habitual way of seeing yourself.

4. ***Fear of giving up control.***

   A close cousin to the fear of losing your sense of self is the fear of giving up control. If you're always busy trying to manipulate circumstances in order to "conquer" your problem, it may be difficult to relinquish control to allow others or your Higher Power to assist. It's certainly important to develop a sense of responsibility for yourself in order to overcome an anxiety disorder (or any other problem). However, a sense of responsibility can be carried to an extreme when you become unwilling to relinquish control enough to accept outside help. The chapter on "Letting Go" addresses this issue in depth.

5. ***Low self-esteem.***

   If you haven't learned to accept, respect, and believe in yourself, you may unconsciously feel that you don't deserve what you want most. Often it's important to deal with guilt or shame from the past, to forgive yourself for what you perceive to be past mistakes or failings. As you let go of shame and learn to truly love yourself, you can begin to believe in your right to be well, happy, and successful. See chapter 5, "Address Your Personality Issues," for further assistance with this.

6. ***Specific mistaken beliefs.***

   All of the above points of resistance involve certain mistaken, limiting beliefs that can interfere with your capacity to attain your goals and resolve your problems in general. What follows are examples of specific mistaken beliefs that can obstruct the process of visualizing or affirming your goal. The list was adapted in part from Louise Hay's *You Can Heal Your Life* (1984), a book I highly recommend if you are serious about healing your anxiety or any other problem.

Beliefs That Hold You Back from Growth and Change

- It's not right for me to try that.
- It's too much work.
- It's too expensive.
- It will take too long.
- It's not practical.
- My family never did that.
- Ordinary people don't do that.
- Ordinary men/women don't do that.

Others Won't Let Me

- It isn't the right environment.
- They won't let me change.
- My doctor doesn't want me to.
- I can't get time off from work.
- *They* have to change first.
- My spouse, family, friends . . . wouldn't approve.
- I don't want to hurt them.

Negative Self-Concept

- I'm too: old, young, fat, thin, short, tall, weak, dumb, smart, poor, messed up, scattered, lazy, stuck

Stalling Tactics

- I'll do it later.
- I don't have the time right now.

- I have too many other things to do.
- As soon as ________________ happens, I'll do it.

Fear

- I might fail.
- They might reject me.
- I might get hurt.
- What would my spouse, friends, boss, etc., think?
- I might have to change.
- I don't have the energy.
- Who knows where I might end up?
- It might hurt my image.
- I'm not good enough (don't deserve it).
- God doesn't care about my little problem.

General Self-Limiting Beliefs

- I feel powerless or helpless.
- Often I feel like a victim of outside circumstances.
- Life is very difficult—it's a struggle.
- I am unworthy. I feel that I'm not good enough.
- My condition seems hopeless.
- There is something fundamentally wrong with me.
- I feel like I'm nothing (or can't make it) unless I'm loved.
- What others think of me is very important.
- People won't like me if they see who I really am.
- I can't rely on others for help.
- If I let someone get too close, I'm afraid of being controlled.
- I'm the only one who can solve my problems.
- I'm just the way I am—I can't really change.

How to Clear Self-Limiting Beliefs

After having reviewed the preceding list, you may have a better idea about those negative attitudes and beliefs that might obstruct your ability to create your goal. To get even more specific, try the following exercise.

Release Your Limiting Beliefs Exercise

In the space below write the statement, "The reason I can't have ______*(your goal)*______ is . . ." Then list all of the reasons that come to mind. When you are done, take some time to think about what you've written. *How strongly do you believe it?*

The more energy and conviction you give to negative attitudes that are contrary to attaining your goal, the harder it will be to realize that goal. Identify the particular attitudes and beliefs that you think are most getting in your way and jot them down on a separate piece of paper. Add any additional negative beliefs from the list of self-limiting beliefs above. Now you're ready to work on clearing and releasing your problem beliefs. You may be surprised to find how well the following step-by-step process works if you follow it carefully and with sincere intention.

1. ***Accept that you have the negative belief.***
   Don't try to deny it or "beat yourself up" for having it. You probably didn't consciously choose the belief but were conditioned to believe it long ago by your parents, peers, or society at large. Before you can let a belief go, it's important to simply accept that it's been a part of your life.

2. ***Acknowledge any fearful or hurtful feelings you have around the belief.***
   Painful feelings have a way of holding a negative belief in place. If, for example, you've held a belief that you don't deserve to have your goal, you need to identify and *express* any feelings of guilt or shame that surround that belief. Or, if you are afraid to truly have what you want, it's important that you express that fear. Of all the steps in the clearing process, this is the one where you're most likely to benefit from working with a counselor or a trusted friend. It's often easier to acknowledge long-standing, painful feelings in the presence of a supportive other. If

you choose to do clearing on your own, however, you can express your feelings on paper or into a tape recorder.

A key to expressing your painful feelings is to have compassion toward yourself—to forgive yourself—especially for any negative feelings of fear, shame, or anger that may have blocked your ability to believe in yourself. Again, having a compassionate counselor or friend to assist may help this process along.

3. ***Ask yourself whether you're ready and willing to let go of the negative belief.***

   Is there some way in which holding on to the self-limiting belief(s) can still serve you? Is there some unconscious benefit or payoff you get from keeping the belief(s)? Can you accept—are you ready for—a life that is not based on such a belief? Review the list of reasons for resisting change above and decide whether you are fully *ready* and *willing* to let go of your self-limiting belief(s). Realize that while you may or may not release a long-standing, negative belief in an instant, your sincere readiness and *willingness* to let it go will assure that you do so—sooner or later.

4. ***Perform a ritual to release the negative belief.***

   To symbolize the process of releasing a negative belief, you can tear up the piece of paper on which it is written—or perhaps throw that piece of paper into a fire. In addition, you can repeat affirmations to encourage letting go, for example:

   "I now dissolve any negative, self-limiting beliefs."

   "I release and let go of any fear, shame, or guilt that stands in my way."

   "I am now free and clear of any attitude that I don't need."

   "All of my negative attitudes are now fully dissolved and released."

By going through the preceding steps, you have prepared a "place" in your mind and heart to go forward with visualizing or affirming the goal you wish to create. Keep in mind that the process of creating something new in your life may take place over time. It may be necessary to repeat the clearing process frequently until you feel you've completely released a particular limiting belief. Think of it as if you were pulling weeds from a garden. You may need to do weeding more than once in the process of watching your "plants" grow to full maturity.

Including Your Higher Power in the Creative Process

Relying on the presence of your Higher Power can deepen the process of creating your goal. By putting your heart and soul behind what you visualize or affirm, you're already moving it to a deeper level within yourself. However, the process can be taken even further by including your Higher Power as a resource to assist you. What I'm talking about is very close, if not the same, as common prayer. When you pray with conviction, consistency, and faith for something that you truly want, you have a great likelihood of bringing it about. In praying, you solicit the energy of your Higher Power to help you create something. It's my impression that *sincere* prayers are answered (see chapter 9), *if* the request is for the highest good of the person making the prayer *and* for the highest good of everyone else involved. However, the *form* in which a prayer is answered may be unexpected and possibly differ in some ways from what was originally requested (in order to assure that it's for the highest good of everyone). It's not for any of us to fully know in advance how a given prayer might be answered.

The process outlined below is the one I've often used when I want to create a particular goal. It's not necessary for you to utilize this process in creating your own goal, but, in my own experience, I've found it to be quite powerful. The process has been called "affirmative prayer" by many people, because it *affirms* a desired outcome instead of asking for it. Other terms often used for this process are "spiritual manifestation" and "cocreation," the latter because God or Spirit is invoked to participate in the process of creating a goal. I prefer to think of the process simply as bringing God into the creative process.

Before using the following five-step process, it's important to have worked through all of the steps outlined in the previous section "How to Create Your Goal." Identifying and releasing your own self-limiting beliefs is important at the outset. Relaxing and centering yourself before you begin the process greatly increases its effectiveness. Finally, this process should be repeated daily until you're satisfied with the results.

Five Steps of Affirmative Prayer

1. ***Identify the spiritual "quality" that can best overcome your problem situation.***

   What is the highest possible good you could ask for to heal or resolve the problem situation you face? What spiritual quality is needed in the situation to fully remedy it?

   "Spiritual qualities" are experienced subjectively. They are those qualities of experience through which you might experience reverence, awe, or a sense of something larger than yourself: the love of a small child, the wisdom of a famous poem, the beauty of a magnificent sunset, the peace of an alpine meadow or deep meditation, or those moments of joy when life seems nearly perfect. What makes these qualities spiritual is that they contain a certain element of perfection. In experiencing them, we are moved beyond our everyday concerns into a deeper, wider state of appreciation. Like the sun penetrating clouds, they are points through which a larger, universal reality breaks through into our personal world.

   Spiritual qualities include ideal love, peace, wholeness, harmony, order, wisdom, abundance, joy, and beauty. Recognizing the spiritual quality that could best heal or overcome a difficult situation is the first step in turning it around. In simply recognizing that quality, you turn away from the immediate appearance of the situation toward a higher reality. For example, to affirm perfect love in the midst of conflict, or perfect peace in the midst of turmoil is to invite the presence of your Higher Power (God) to help overcome your own limited beliefs and perceptions about the situation. In the case of illness, perfect wholeness (in mind and body) might be the spiritual quality that overcomes the condition.

2. *Unify in consciousness with your Higher Power.*

   In this step you enter into an attunement with your Higher Power. This can be done by meditating, in which you become silent and simply ask to enter into the presence of God. For example, you might say to yourself, "Great Spirit, I ask for your support and guidance in this moment." (The Lord's Prayer and the Twenty-third Psalm are well-known forms of coming into the presence of your Higher Power in the Judeo-Christian tradition.)

   Another way to facilitate unification is to write out statements that affirm a state of oneness with Spirit, such as "I know that I am in the perfect presence of Spirit now," or "God is working in my life right now for my highest good." It's helpful to write several of these affirmative statements until you actually feel a deepening sense of connection with your Higher Power.

3. *Affirm the spiritual quality that overcomes your problem.*

   At this point you simply affirm the spiritual quality you identified in the first step. This can be done silently in meditation or by writing out two or three affirmative statements. For example, if you're ill, the divine attribute you might want to affirm is Wholeness. You might say: "I know that I'm whole and healthy in mind and body. I am well, strong, and vital in every respect. In this moment, I realize my right to be fully healthy and whole."

   It's important at this stage to put aside, as far as possible, any fear or worry about whatever circumstances you face. No matter what circumstances and limitations you confront, you turn your attention away from them and resolve to affirm the highest good. This does not mean you deny or ignore the limitations of your situation. The point is to stop giving undue attention and energy to the problem. Instead, you focus on affirming the highest good in the situation. In so doing you line up with the creative power of your Higher Power—the universal resource that is God—to effect a change for the better.

4. *Express gratitude.*

   At this point you give thanks to God (your Higher Power) in advance for the fulfillment of whatever you've affirmed. Remember that from the standpoint of your Higher Power, there is no time. To give thanks in advance for wholeness, peace, abundance, or love is to strengthen your conviction that it's already present at the highest level (i.e., in Universal Consciousness). Expressing gratitude gives impetus to the process whereby whatever good you've affirmed can actually manifest in the physical world.

Expressing gratitude also acknowledges, in humility, that your personal will or ego is not the ultimate source of healing and resolution.

5. ***Release.***

   After giving thanks, it's time to let the process go. You do not, at this point, need to hold on in anxious concern about whether the process will "work." Having affirmed the highest good in faith, you can now relinquish the fulfillment of your affirmation to your Higher Power.

   For example, you might say:

   - "I now entrust this affirmation to the Creative Spirit."
   - "I let go and allow God to work on the realization of this goal, for the highest good of everyone concerned."

   It's time to simply trust the process of creation by letting go and getting on with the business at hand. However, it's appropriate, whenever you feel your conviction wavering, to repeat the preceding five steps. It's important to persist in the process until you actually experience a healing or resolution of the problem, whether this takes days, weeks, months, or even years. Your persistence will eventually bear fruit.

The following example of an affirmative prayer illustrates the five-step process just described.

An Affirmation for Restoring Wholeness

There is One Healing Power in the Universe—
a pattern for Perfect Wholeness that exists beyond all separation or discord.
I acknowledge this One Omnipresent Power—
present in all things and in myself.
Spirit is a force for wholeness that knows no obstacles or limits.

I now experience this all-loving presence of Spirit.
Right where I am, God is working in my life for my highest good.
I now let go of all perceptions and judgments of limitation and allow my will to align fully with the Divine Will.

I am steadfast in faith regardless of what appears in my life.
No matter what has happened in the past, I now realize, as I speak these words, a renewed conviction and confidence that healing is taking place in my life.
I am becoming whole and at peace in all aspects of my life.

I reclaim my Divine inheritance, which is wholeness and the fullness of life in body, mind, and spirit.

I give thanks to Spirit for the power to disperse all appearances and bring healing into my life.
I give thanks to the power of Spirit to release doubt and fear and restore my faith.
I am grateful for the new directions in my life, which are revealed through Spirit.

I now release this affirmation to the universe, knowing that its perfect realization is in process.
I let go and allow Spirit to move in new and mysterious ways for my highest good and the highest good of all others.
And so it is.

Feel free to use this prayer to affirm your own recovery, or write your own prayer incorporating the five steps just described. For an outstanding collection of short affirmative prayers, see the book *Heart Steps* (1997).

Write Your Own Affirmative Prayer

In the space below, write your own affirmative prayer following the five-step process.

Summary: Attitudes That Empower Creating Your Goal

The following six attitudes will help you to succeed in affirming your recovery or creating any other goal in your life.

Acknowledge and Release Feelings

Fear, anger, and feelings of victimization about a problem tie you to it rather than opening the door to healing and resolution. For this reason it's very important to *acknowledge* and *express* your feelings about a difficult situation. Do this with a counselor, a trusted friend, or your journal or tape recorder. Then you can clear a space for the kind of serenity from which your affirmation or visualization can be powerful.

Meditation practice can be very helpful in the process of learning to acknowledge and release feelings. See chapter 7 for a discussion of the usefulness of meditation.

Courage

When a problem frightens you, it takes courage to affirm the possibility of healing and resolution. Courage means that after being frightened or even overwhelmed by some difficult situation, you don't knuckle under. Instead you get back up on your feet and believe in the possibility of moving forward no matter how tough the road has been. To affirm your belief in your goal in spite of fear, despair, or outrage takes considerable courage. Yet it is also one of the most empowering things you can do. Asking for assistance from your Higher Power when you experience a setback will help to keep you on course and likely ease your journey.

Trust

Genuine trust means you *believe* in the possibility of creating—and recreating—your reality. You trust that your visualization or affirmation actually helps to attract your goal, even though you can't *see* how it does. Earlier in this chapter I presented a model of how the creative process might actually work. However, this model is far from complete, and it may or may not be particularly convincing or plausible to you. In the last analysis, none of us can fully understand exactly how the process of creating your reality works. Trusting that it does ultimately needs to come not from an intellectual understanding but from personal experience.

If you feel skeptical about the possibility of creative visualization or affirmation being effective, I invite you to try it out for yourself, following all the guidelines suggested in this chapter. To give it a fair trial, be willing to keep working with the process toward a specific goal until you obtain what you regard as genuine results. The direct experience of success with the creative process is the best way to gain trust in its potential.

Perseverance

Repeating what was just said, it's important to persevere with a visualization or affirmation until a problem resolves in one way or another. It's especially important to persevere at those times when worry or doubt cloud the initial resolution you felt at the time you first initiated your visualization, affirmation, or prayer. It took time to manifest the negative problem situation that you seek to overcome. And so it may take time to create something new. For example, if your struggle with anxiety involves not only conditioned thoughts and reactions but also a long-standing neurobiological problem, it may take time to create a high level of recovery. Months or even years may pass for the complete realization of healing to occur, but your willingness to persist over time—both in direct efforts (the "footwork" part) as well as consistently affirming your recovery—will assure the highest possible outcome.

Faith

Faith can help you to persevere. Faith means believing in the ultimate triumph of "good" over limitation in the long run, no matter what happens. Much has been written on the subject of faith, but in essence it simply means believing you live in a benevolent universe where, despite appearances, all things ultimately work out for the highest good. There is no way to logically argue the case for a benevolent universe. Such a belief develops from personal experience and direct intuitive perception in relation to your Higher Power.

Being Proactive

Taking action—doing what you can—to realize your goal is a way in which you strengthen and empower your intention. You're not merely fantasizing or talking about your goal; you're sincerely going after it. When you do your part, you make yourself available to receive assistance and guidance from your Higher Power in new ways. When you take the first step toward a goal, ideas about the next step often will come to you. The proverbial saying "God helps those who help themselves" reflects a fundamental truth about the creative process.

In closing, I would like to offer an example that illustrates the power of intention. This excerpt was written by a physician who has explored Native American healing practices, and it demonstrates what's possible when an intention to heal is held with courage, perseverance, and faith.

Wesley was a Native American living in Duluth, about one hundred miles from the reservation where he had grown up. When I met him, Wesley's face was gaunt and he moved very slowly, wincing at the effort of rising from his chair. He looked like a man in his late sixties.

Doctors at the University Medical Center in Duluth had diagnosed Wesley's illness as lymphoma, cancer of the lymph nodes. Wesley's concern had spread rapidly into his abdomen and chest, and his doctors told him he had no more than six months to live. They advised him to put his affairs in order. Wesley sought out an Ojibway medicine woman from northern Minnesota and asked her to conduct a ceremony for him. Carolyn, the woman, told him to come at the waxing of the moon. She told him to bring anyone who might help with his healing.

At first Carolyn worked alone with Wesley, using what psychologists would call hypnosis to prepare him for the ceremony. The Arikara of North Dakota have a phrase for Carolyn's brand of hypnosis; literally it means "putting him to sleep so he thinks he sleeps when he's really awake."

After she had prepared Wesley, Carolyn took us all into the sweat lodge to pray for four straight nights. On the fifth day she took Wesley outside and walked with him. She told him that he might not think so yet, but he would still bend many bows before he died. She told him an eagle would be his sign of wellness.

When Wesley spotted an eagle later that day, he was ecstatic. Carolyn performed a ceremony on the spot, sanctifying the ground by sprinkling tobacco and cornmeal. Then she burned sage to chase away evil, singing sacred songs and smoking the sacred pipe and speaking to the spirits. Finally, she told Wesley that the White Buffalo Woman had told her he was well. When he returned to the city, Wesley's doctors could find no trace of his lymphoma—and they could give no explanation of its disappearance, which was simply recorded on his chart as one of those rare, baffling spontaneous remissions. The doctors were not as quick as Carolyn had been to declare him well; because lymphomas sometimes go into remission and then reappear, judgment on a lymphoma cure is withheld for five years. When Wesley had remained cancer-free for the required five-year interval, his physicians came around to the White Buffalo Woman's position and declared Wesley well.

What You Can Do Now

1. Decide on a goal that you'd like to create. Use the seven-step process in the section "Creating Your Goal" to begin working on bringing it into your life. Develop a visualization, a series of affirmations, or both, to define your goal. Repeat the process on a regular basis until you achieve the results you seek.

2. Review the section "Overcoming Fears, Doubts, and Self-Limiting Beliefs." Think about what obstacles you might be putting in the way of achieving whatever goal you seek. Work through the four-step process in the section "How to Clear Self-Limiting Beliefs" to release unhelpful attitudes. Rehearse the visualization or affirmations two or three times when letting go of attitudes or beliefs you've held for many years. Seek out the assistance of a counselor if you need help working through feelings of sadness, anger, or shame that surround particular negative beliefs.
3. If you feel inclined, use the five-step process in the section "Including Your Higher Power in the Creative Process" to create your goal. I have found this to be a very powerful approach when used on a regular basis. Write out an affirmative statement that corresponds to each step at first. Then read through what you've written in a relaxed, focused state each time you repeat the process. Work on building conviction and faith that you will eventually attain the goal you seek. See the following references to increase your understanding about the process of creating your vision.

References and Further Reading

Cameron, Julia. 1997. *Heart Steps.* New York: Tarcher/Putnam. (More than one hundred affirmative prayers for all purposes.)

Chopra, Deepak. 1994. *The Seven Spiritual Laws of Success.* San Rafael, Calif.: New World Library. (A concise summary of Dr. Chopra's spiritual philosophy.)

Dyer, Wayne. 1997. *Manifest Your Destiny.* New York: HarperCollins.

Gawain, Shakti. 1995. *Creative Visualization, Revised Edition.* San Rafael, Calif.: New World Library.

Hay, Louise. 1984. *You Can Heal Your Life.* Santa Monica, Calif.: Hay House.

Holmes, Ernest. 1988. *The Science of Mind.* New York: Putnam. (The classic text on affirmative prayer.)

———. 1995. *How to Use the Science of Mind.* Los Angeles: Science of Mind Publications.

Mehl-Madrona, Lewis. 1997. *Coyote Medicine.* New York: Scribner. (A Stanford-trained physician bridges conventional medicine with Native American healing. Excellent reading.)

Redfield, James. 1993. *The Celestine Prophecy.* New York: Warner Books.

11

Love

Love and fear are opposites. Fundamentally, they move in opposite directions. In love, we are drawn to connect with someone or something other than ourselves. In fear, we want to move away from or avoid the object of our fear. None of us exists in total isolation; we all live in relationship to loved ones, community, nature, and the cosmos. Love is an innate force in the human heart that moves us toward unity with the "Other" in its multiple forms.

Fear, on the other hand, is a part of our instinctive nature that propels us away from a perceived threat. It's a separating force intended to preserve our individual integrity from threats to survival. In some cases fear serves us, but in many more cases it's a false alarm. Fear debars us from feeling either love or peace whenever we imagine a threat, whether or not that threat actually exists. Because we've been hurt—even traumatized—before, we're conditioned to easily project imaginary scenarios of disaster. Such fearful projections take us away from the immediate moment, from our deeper selves, and from the matrix of life that supports us. Unfounded fears separate and alienate us, while genuine love reunites us with others and heals our fear.

Love, in its most essential form, is not something you have to learn. It's a gift of the soul—an innate potential within you that's always there no matter what is going on nearer the surface of your awareness. What *can* be learned and practiced are ways to bring out and reveal the love that lies within. *Learning* to love means learning how to release the obstacles to the natural, innate flow of love within your heart—a potential that you brought with you into the world. That potential was very visible when you were an infant, coexisting with your more instinctive needs. No matter what has happened to you since infancy, your potential to give and receive love is still there, always ready to be evoked and nurtured.

Fear can run deep, but not as deep as your potential for love. Love is at the very core of your innermost being and ultimately derives, I believe, from your Higher Power, God, Spirit, the Infinite Field of Possibilities—whatever you choose to call it. I'm not talking about human forms of love such as romance, passion, or affection (although these certainly may be exalted to a high level), but the highest forms of love that you experience in moments of genuine forgiveness, compassion, kindness, or altruism. Sometimes this kind of love is referred to as "unconditional love"—a spontaneous love for another that has no conditions or expectations attached to it. In a manner of speaking, you might view unconditional love as a "gift from heaven"—a bit of God reflected in each human's soul. Fear, on the other hand, is not part of our inheritance from heaven. It's a survival mechanism that all animals need to thrive in a physical world. It's a part of our earthly existence that may help or hinder us. Fear may reside deep in your subconscious, but not at the very source of your being. Love, however, does exist at the source. Because it lies deeper, love can ultimately overcome any form of fear, no matter how entrenched. When you call upon love to help you heal fear, you are bound, sooner or later, to succeed.

There is much more to be said about the various forms of love. The Greeks distinguished two forms of love: Eros and agape. *Eros* referred to the passionate or romantic love you feel when physically attracted to another. *Agape* is the kind of love you feel when you genuinely care for someone, apart from any personal attraction to them. Either form of love can take on spiritual dimensions when it moves you beyond yourself into something larger. (Just because Eros is more physical does not render it less potentially "divine" than agape, in the Greek view of things.) Other forms of love include filial love—the love between close friends or brothers and sisters—and maternal love, which has certain elements in common with agape. Compassion, a form of love that plays an important role in Eastern philosophy, particularly Buddhism, is also closely related to agape. Compassion is an unselfish concern for another born out of empathy or understanding of their particular life situation (especially if that situation involves suffering). Any of these forms of love can be conditional or unconditional, depending on whether there is any personal agenda or expectations involved in extending one's love. True compassion closely approximates unconditional love; when you feel compassion you are not usually concerned about taking care of your own needs. Conditional love falls short of this ideal. If you extend your love primarily out of a need to get something from another, or out of a motive to control or manipulate them, your love is less likely to have a healing impact on the other person or yourself. The other person will likely experience your own personal agenda mixed in with whatever apparent love you offer.

How Love Can Heal Fear

If extending your love arises out of a self-imposed expectation that you "should" give—rather than out of a spontaneous desire—once again your act is less likely to heal or empower. Codependent or selfishly motivated acts of love are distortions of genuine love that ultimately create resentment within you. If you sacrifice yourself too much in the process of giving to another, you'll eventually resent it. It is the unconditional forms of love—compassion, kindness, forgiveness, generosity and altruism—that can heal fear. Opening your heart to cultivate such forms of love in your life is a very powerful way to move beyond fear.

How can you do this? *It begins with learning to love yourself.* If you're lacking love for yourself, how can you possibly extend love toward others? *Genuine* love for others cannot be willed—it cannot arise out of a self-imposed "should." It is a spontaneous overflow of whatever love you feel within and toward yourself. What you give to yourself first is what you have to give to others.

Loving Yourself

Loving yourself can be defined as *accepting*, *respecting*, and *believing* in yourself. *Accepting* yourself means you can live comfortably with both your personal strengths and weaknesses without excessive self-criticism. You can be okay with yourself just the way you are. *Respecting* yourself means you know your own worth and dignity as a unique human being. You value yourself and do not allow anyone to use or take advantage of you. *Believing* in yourself means you feel you deserve to have what you want out of life. You feel confident that you can fulfill your personal dreams and goals.

To love yourself is the opposite of being selfish or self-centered. Selfishness comes from a feeling of insufficiency or inadequacy within yourself that leads you to try to grab or manipulate to get what you want. Loving yourself, on the other hand, is associated with an inner confidence and self-regard that naturally overflows into expressions of caring toward others. Selfishness is associated with inner lack; self-love with inner fullness and security.

You begin life with a limitless capacity to give and receive love. As you go through childhood, you make decisions about yourself that often cause you to lose that capacity. If your parents overly criticized you, you may have made a decision such as "I'm unlovable." If you lost a parent due to death or divorce, you may have decided "I've got to go it alone—it's too painful to get close and then lose someone I love." Or, if you were physically abused, your decision might have been "It's dangerous to trust." Trauma and mistreatment close down our hearts and propel us to defend and withhold our inner selves from others. We may grow up finding it difficult to love anyone, least of all ourselves.

Fortunately, loving yourself is something that can be *learned*—or relearned, since you had the capacity at the outset of your life. You can learn to love yourself through specific changes in the way you perceive, think about, talk to, and act toward yourself. You can also learn through having close relationships with other persons who *model healthy self-love*. This can include partners, friends, counselors, or mentors. At least eight approaches to building healthy self-love are described elsewhere in this book. They include:

- Taking good care of your physical body

- Practicing small acts of kindness toward yourself each day
- Discovering and expressing your unique talents and gifts
- Recognizing your personal needs and giving them equal time relative to others' needs
- Becoming assertive: asking for what you want; saying "no" to what you don't want (having boundaries)
- Letting go of perfectionism—setting realistic standards
- Building a healthy support system in your community; cultivating relationships with people who have healthy self-regard
- Recognizing that your beauty and worth as a unique human being is a gift from your Higher Power

I'll say a little about each of these and indicate the section of this book where you can find some further discussion.

Taking good care of your physical body means you make time to give your body adequate rest, relaxation, exercise, and nutrition. Your body will respond to your efforts by giving you more energy, pleasure, and an enhanced feeling of well-being. See chapters 3 and 4 of this book, which offer a variety of approaches for taking care of your physical self. See also chapters 4 and 5 of *The Anxiety & Phobia Workbook*, which cover the basic topics of relaxation and exercise.

Practicing small acts of kindness toward yourself on a daily basis is a simple but powerful way to cultivate a more loving relationship with yourself. Loving yourself is quite similar to loving another person—the relationship prospers when you give it time and attention. See the list of self-nurturing activities in chapter 5.

Discovering and expressing your unique gifts and talents. Each of us has a unique purpose—something we came here to do and can offer to others. When you're expressing your unique purpose, you will feel more alive, creative, and fulfilled within yourself. See chapter 6, "Find Your Unique Purpose," if you feel this is an area you wish to work on.

Recognizing your personal needs—and giving them equal time relative to others' needs—is certainly one way you might define the concept of "self-love." As long as pleasing others is more important than pleasing yourself, you'll likely have low regard and respect for yourself. If you tend to be a "people pleaser" at your own expense, see the section "The Excessive Need for Approval" in chapter 5.

Becoming assertive means you not only give attention to your personal needs but are willing to ask others to help you meet them. Assertiveness also implies an ability to set limits in response to unreasonable demands or requests—the ability to say "no" when you need to. It's hard to build self-respect unless you recognize and can exercise your basic rights as a human being. Again, the section "The Excessive Need for

Approval" in Chapter 5 has more information on developing assertiveness. So does the chapter "Asserting Yourself" in *The Anxiety & Phobia Workbook.*

Letting go of perfectionism and setting realistic standards is an important part of learning to love yourself. As long as you are never quite satisfied with your own achievements or actions, it's difficult to be comfortable with yourself. Being overly critical of yourself about mistakes and errors also tends to undermine your self-worth. There are several ways to ease up with perfectionism, including creating more fun and recreation in your life, cultivating a sense of humor, learning to enjoy the journey as much as the destination, and countering "should" and "must" self-talk. See the section on perfectionism in chapter 5 as well as chapter 8, "Letting Go," for further discussion.

Building a healthy support system means you have a circle of friends beyond your immediate family. These are people you can trust and confide in. Such friends can provide objectivity, feedback, support, and validation in ways that may not be possible with intimate family members. They also are likely to be reliably there, through crises or major transitions in your life. Having a healthy support system is an important way in which you can better care for yourself. If you don't presently have such a group, you can build one through getting more involved with a church, service organizations in your community, or intentional support groups for persons dealing with anxiety, codependency, recovery from an abusive childhood, or 12-step "anonymous" groups.

Recognizing that your value is inherent can go a long way toward fostering a greater sense of self-worth and self-respect. Ultimately you did not create yourself—you were born into this world with a unique value and purpose. Your own judgments of yourself, however negative, do not change your inherent worth as a person. Even your behavior, no matter how unenlightened, does not alter your innate worth. Believing that there is a higher purpose to your life will help you to see your own limitations and mistakes not as failings, but as part of a greater plan for the evolution of your soul. See chapter 9, "Spirituality," for further discussion about how spirituality can transform your estimation of yourself.

Use the following guided meditation to help you affirm the power and significance of love in your life. Have someone read it to you or else record it. You may also want to try it with "I" statements instead of "you" statements.

Guided Meditation

You deserve love.

You deserve to feel loved, accepted, and valued for the good person you are.

As you come to understand that you deserve love, you're more and more willing to receive love from others.

You find yourself increasingly willing to be open to receive love from those people you're closest to.

As you release and let go of old hurts and defenses, you discover a growing awareness of love inside. For you have much love to give.

There is no need to struggle for love—it exists completely and perfectly within you.

Each day you are learning more how to love yourself.

And as you love yourself, you experience more natural ability to love others. No longer do you deprive yourself of the free expression of love. You find you feel wonderful when you express love.

As you heal the past and learn to love yourself, you find it easier to give and receive love.

You find how much the special people in your life want to give you love, and you find it easier to allow them to.

It is becoming easier to open to more love in your life.

In this moment, you are willing and ready to embrace more love in your life.

If you have learned how to love yourself—to accept, respect, and believe in yourself—then opening your heart to various forms of unconditional love becomes easier. The remainder of this chapter considers three forms of love which, when unconditional, carry a tremendous capacity to heal both yourself and others: forgiveness, compassion, and generosity. At the end of the description of each type of love there is an exercise to help cultivate that particular form. Doing the exercises will ensure you get the most benefit out of this chapter.

Forgiveness

Forgiveness is one of the greatest acts of healing possible between two persons. It opens channels for love to be expressed again, no matter what has gone before. In forgiving another, you liberate yourself from any resentment or hurt you may have been withholding—painful emotions that only result in causing you further stress. In forgiving yourself (for past or present mistakes), you come to accept and respect your own worth. You make a space in your life to move toward a positive future unfettered by your past.

Why is it so often difficult to forgive? One of the biggest obstacles, I believe, is in trying to forgive someone or something before you feel ready to. It's impossible to genuinely forgive another when it's something you feel you *should* do. Forgiveness can't be forced—it's an experience that needs to emerge naturally after you've had the opportunity to acknowledge and express any feelings of anger or hurt. If I'm angry with you over something you said, I'm unlikely to be ready to forgive you until I've communicated my angry feelings. This is best done in a nonblaming way; I simply let you know that what you did made me angry (and perhaps hurt me as well), without putting you down. Then I can come to a place of clarity where it is possible to forgive.

If the person you need to forgive is no longer around or alive, you can still work through any unresolved anger or pain by writing a letter to that person disclosing all of your feelings in detail. It doesn't matter whether they ever receive the letter—what's important is expressing your unfinished feelings. Only then can you be open to the possibility of genuine forgiveness.

Another aid to forgiveness is empathy. It's easier to forgive if you can take the role of the other person and understand where they are (or were) coming from. Forgiveness is difficult when another person's hurtful action is unintelligible. If you don't understand them, what they did may seem arbitrary, unfeeling, or possibly even cruel. In attempting to understand what led another to act as they did, you may not agree with their position, but at least their behavior becomes comprehensible. Perhaps what they did arose out of considerable suffering on their part—in which case you may be able to feel some compassion.

Understanding the abusive backgrounds of unhappy parents who abuse their children does not condone their ugly behavior. Yet it may allow enough insight to open the door to compassion and eventually forgiveness. Sometimes, of course, even understanding may not be sufficient to allow for forgiveness. In such cases it's important simply to *accept* that what happened did happen. Acceptance is the first step. Then you can grieve your consequent loss and put what happened in the past, where it belongs, so that you're free to go on with the present.

For example, if you were physically harmed or sexually molested by a parent, you may still be angry to the point that it feels difficult to forgive. Simply acknowledging and expressing your anger about the past in the presence of a counselor or a supportive friend can help you to accept that what happened—happened. Then you can grieve the fact of your parent's inability to offer you the love you needed. Perhaps you can even have some understanding of your parent's predicament based on knowledge about their childhood. Whether or not you get to forgiveness, going through such a process empowers you to finish with your past so that you can get on with your life in the present.

Coming to terms with your past is a powerful means for opening yourself to a greater experience of love in your life. In truth, the past cannot be changed—it can only be released.

When you do reach the point where you can forgive another, you're no longer likely to be angry or afraid of them. Forgiveness frees you of inner stress or turmoil you've felt toward someone and also frees them to make amends to you. Forgiveness is a sacred act—it reaches beyond the limitations of human personality and behavior to the spiritual essence that all of us share.

Forgiveness Exercise

- Think about a person who hurt you or did something you find difficult to forgive (whether this person is alive or dead).
- What did this person do that you find most difficult to forgive? If there are many things, start with the most difficult first.
- Write a letter to this person, speaking from your heart about all of your feelings toward them and toward what they did. Take time to do this and do not hold anything back—you may need several pages. It isn't necessary and may not be appropriate to send the letter.
- When your letter is done, share it with a person you're close to and trust (or else a professional counselor). Feel free to express any feelings that come up aloud to the person you're confiding in. Give yourself at least one hour for this.
- Now think about the person who hurt you again. Do you feel ready to forgive them—in all sincerity—or do you feel you're not ready? If you're not ready to forgive, it's time to work on *accepting* the fact of what happened so that you can let go of the past and move on. Working with statements such as "It happened and it's over" or "It's in the past and I can go on" may facilitate the process. If you feel sadness and grief in the process of doing this, accept that it's part of the healing.
- If you feel you're ready to forgive the person, take time to relax, close your eyes and visualize that person (whether they're alive or not) standing before you. Then speak to them *as if they were present right now*, telling them that you forgive them for what they did in whatever words feel appropriate. If you're able to truly forgive them, you will feel as though a weight has been lifted. (Note: If you feel you need to forgive yourself for something in the past, visualize yourself and follow the same instructions.)

Compassion

Compassion involves having concern for another person's difficulty. You feel for another's suffering—and wish that they might be free of that suffering—without judging them.

The path to developing compassion is simple, although it's not always easy. Compassion begins with *acknowledging that adversity exists for everyone*. Although suffering certainly is not all there is to life, no one is immune to times of hardship and challenge. Much of our current society appears to be based on the need to deny pain and suffering as much as possible. Material consumption, TV, overeating, analgesics, and alcohol are some of the many strategies used to avoid pain. Those persons who are ill, disabled, and elderly are consigned to places where they are largely forgotten and out of sight. Youthful vitality, beauty, and virility are the ideals promoted by the media. A willingness to look beyond surface appearances and acknowledge the fragility and mortality of life is where compassion begins.

True compassion requires not just acknowledging the mortality and limitations of life but opening your heart to it. The ability to do so is something that develops with maturity and life experience. (Sometimes it happens only after having gone through a period of personal suffering.) In the moment when you stop running from your own inner pain—letting go of persons, substances, or activities that shield you from it—you find that you have more space to open your heart. To be sure, life is full of moments of joy and beauty where your heart opens naturally, without perceiving any pain. Yet, in my experience, opening deeply to compassion for others requires a willingness to bear witness to your own personal afflictions. When you have acknowledged and accepted your own difficulties in life, you can be fully present for another's. Having compassion for others is a gift to yourself. In bearing witness to your own inner discomfort, you allow it to emerge and move on. You release it instead of holding it—or hiding it—within your soul.

Beyond acknowledging suffering and opening your heart, compassion requires *understanding* another. You seek to understand the conditions that led the person into their predicament. You try seeing their situation from *their* point of view rather than your own. This particular aspect of compassion is closely related to empathy—the ability to take another person's perspective—to "walk in their shoes." Once you genuinely understand another's difficulty, you can stop judging them and feel concern for them instead. Even the most reprehensible behavior can be understood (although not condoned) if you fully understand the conditions that led up to it. As your capacity for compassion grows, you learn to stop judging people so quickly and seek instead to understand them.

When you fully understand someone—to the point where you're truly able to feel for their predicament—then that person is no longer likely to threaten you. Compassion for another diminishes the possibility of being afraid of them. Instead you see them as another fallible human being who has suffered just like yourself. To be compassionate, however, does not mean you allow another to take advantage of you or wield their inner distress in destructive ways at your expense. Compassion always comes from a position of strength. It may require you to set limits, and even use force, if necessary, to redirect another away from hostile or destructive behavior. In being compassionate you hold the highest vision for another; you see their suffering and acknowledge their potential. If another person's behavior is destructive or violent, the most compassionate act toward them is one that calls them to change their ways. You call them to take responsibility for being true to their full potential as a human being—anything less is unacceptable. A popular expression for this form of compassion is "tough love." Concern for another's distress does not include allowing destructive expressions of that distress to hurt you. Compassion for yourself is always included in compassion for another.

Compassion Exercise

Close your eyes and take a few deep breaths until you feel relaxed and centered. Now think about a person you know who is experiencing physical or mental suffering. Reflect on their situation without judgment and allow your heart to open to them. Do this for two or three minutes. If it helps, you might want to silently repeat a phrase such as "May you be free of your pain and suffering" or perhaps "May you be at peace." (Pick your own phrase if you prefer.) If feelings other than compassion arise, such as fear, despair, anger, or sorrow, focus on your breathing and allow these feelings to arise and move through. You may want to write them down if they start to distract you. When your feelings pass, refocus on the person you've chosen and allow yourself to settle down into a place where you simply feel concern for their ultimate well-being. In learning to perceive another's adversity without getting lost in fear or sorrow, you will begin to transform the way you relate to your own pain. Developing compassion leads to more equanimity within yourself.

Optional: Try this same exercise with someone you strongly dislike, or even someone who is causing harm in the world. As you reflect on this person, make an effort to understand what kind of conditions/circumstances might have led them to behave the way they do. Even if there is no way to know the background of this particular person, acknowledge that there are certain reasons and conditions that led them to act as they do. Reflect on the truth that hurtful behavior usually arises out of suffering (often fear) and ultimately only adds further suffering to the perpetrator's situation.

If you find judgment of—or anger at—the person coming up, focus on your breathing and allow the judgments to arise and pass through you, while staying with the exercise. If you need to write down your negative feelings do so, but then return to the exercise. See if you can reframe the way you perceive the other person. Instead of judging them as "bad" or "evil," try instead seeing their *behavior*—what they did—as unenlightened or ignorant. Imagine how this person might act if they lived up to their full potential as a human being—if they could learn to act from a position of love instead of fear or anger.

Generosity

Generosity is the desire to extend yourself in order to benefit or bring joy to someone else. It is one of the earliest expressions of unconditional love. Small children are known to engage in simple acts of generosity spontaneously. Generosity usually arises from a feeling of contentment, joy, or love within yourself. It's an overflowing of an inner abundance you already feel, not something done out of a sense of obligation or compulsion.

Generosity is not emphasized in modern society, except perhaps at holidays and birthdays. The prevalence of consumer values conditions most of us to want, need, and seek to acquire things rather than to think about giving. True generosity requires a fundamental shift in perception: to move from a stance of "What can I get?" to one of "How can I help or give to someone else?" This shift from getting to giving in fact brings joy to the giver. Whether giving is a spontaneous impulse or a conscious choice, acts of generosity often lighten your spirit by moving you beyond immediate preoccupation with your own concerns. This is how generosity (like other forms of unconditional love) can free you from fear. Fear is a defensive posture where you contract—or move away—from something you perceive to be threatening. Generosity reverses the sequence—you transcend your own avoidance and contraction in the moment you give to someone else. Generosity overcomes separation and reconnects you with someone or something larger than yourself.

You can cultivate generosity with practice. Each of us has an innate potential to be generous, but sometimes that potential needs to be nurtured. The place to begin is to stop stifling your impulses to be generous out of fear. Sometimes you may worry about another's reaction to your generous act or perhaps whether they'll like what you plan to give. The adage we all grew up with, "It's the thought that counts," still holds true. People generally respond more to your thought of them than to what you give. When you think of giving something away, you might also worry about whether you really want to part with it. Remember always to check in with yourself first with the question: "Do I really need this?" If the answer is "no," you'll likely benefit both the other person as well as yourself by giving. Developing generosity means following through with spontaneous desires to give, in spite of any resistance your mind tries to throw up. In this respect it's not unlike developing courage; you learn by simply moving past your resistance and doing it anyway.

There are many different ways to be generous. The simplest is to be present for another person—to genuinely listen to what they have to say. Hearing a person out without interrupting them, advising them, or judging them lets the other know that you value what they have to say and, by extension, that you value them. Listening is one of the simplest of gifts, but it takes presence of mind and skill to do it well. Beyond listening, you can praise, support, encourage, validate, uplift, amuse, serve, and help others in a variety of ways. You can also give to someone on a more physical level by hugging them, touching them, giving them material gifts, anticipating their needs, cooking for them, and so on. Others seem to appreciate our gifts most when we surprise them—offering them something other than what they might expect to receive.

Unexpected gifts are sometimes called "random acts of kindness." As you look down the following list, think about which items you would consider giving to 1) your partner or spouse, 2) your child, 3) your parent(s), 4) other relatives, 5) friends, 6) an acquaintance at work, and 7) your community. Which ones are you willing to take action on this week? this month?

Random Acts of Kindness

- Listen to someone well—be present for them.

- Buy someone a special gift.
- Give someone a hug.
- Offer to help someone with a chore.
- Show interest in someone's favorite pastime.
- Give someone a back rub.
- Make something for someone.
- Cook for them.
- Spend time outdoors with them (taking a walk, going to a park).
- Offer support when they're upset.
- Praise someone for an accomplishment.
- Offer them encouragement when they're feeling challenged.
- Teach someone what they need to know.
- Thank someone for doing something you usually take for granted.
- Smile and say something pleasant to a stranger or a clerk.
- Put money in a parking meter for someone whose time ran out.
- Make a donation to your favorite charity or cause.
- Donate time to a volunteer organization or project.
- Donate things you don't need anymore.
- Your own idea of a generous act.

In bringing out your own potential for generosity, there are two important things to keep in mind. First, don't worry if you don't always feel a spontaneous desire to give. Try giving just to give. Sometimes by doing the behavior first without the feeling, the feeling comes along later. Be willing to "prime the pump" by doing random acts of kindness even at times when you don't feel like it. Second, it's self-contradictory to act generously out of a motive for personal gain or out of a sense of obligation. Be careful to distinguish true generosity from codependency. If you do something for someone because you want to win their approval, placate them, or avoid their anger, your action is primarily for yourself rather than the other. If you give because you think you should, but your heart's not in it, you're merely satisfying your own internalized standard rather than truly extending yourself. There is always some element of desire—"I want to"—in a generous act, even in the instance where you simply want to cultivate your capacity to give by practicing it. There is also usually an element of altruism—"I want to do it for them."

Remember that any sincere gift to another is always a gift to yourself. When you shift your perception from yourself to how you can benefit another, you transcend your own personal needs and the concerns that go with them. This is how practicing generosity can overcome fear. Fear and anxiety are based on separation from others—generosity reconnects you with them.

In fact, all forms of unconditional love—forgiveness, compassion, generosity, caring, kindness, and unconditional affection—overcome fear by reconnecting you with a larger sense of life that begins with your nearest loved ones and extends to your friends, community, country, the entire planet, and ultimately the Cosmos. Fear is only an illusion of separation that you temporarily believe. Acts of genuine love reconnect you with a Source to which you've always belonged and which exists forever beyond all types of fear. As was said long ago: "Perfect love casts out fear."

What You Can Do Now

1. Review the section "Loving Yourself." Several different ways to care for and value yourself were described. Which one(s) would you be willing to make time to work on?

2. Choose one of the three forms of unconditional love discussed in this chapter: forgiveness, compassion, or generosity. Make a commitment to work on cultivating that particular form for one month, beginning with doing the relevant exercise in this chapter.

3. Love begins at home. Perhaps the best place to start opening your heart is with your closest relationship—your spouse or partner (or perhaps a parent, child, or close friend). Consider the following ways that you might cultivate greater love toward that person.

    - Be willing to share all of your deepest feelings and thoughts (including your greatest fears) with them openly. Let go of withholding yourself from them out of fear.
    - Be willing to make time to really listen to them. Hear what they say for fifteen minutes without interrupting them, judging them, or advising them. Repeat back to them the most important elements of what they say so that they know you've truly heard them. Do this at least once per week.
    - Show an interest in those activities and goals they most value. Support them in developing and expressing their creative gifts—their "life purpose(s)."
    - Hug them spontaneously at a time when they're not expecting it. Tell them you love them.
    - Help them with a project or chore prior to their asking you. Only offer help, of course, if they truly want it.

- Offer to go with them to a special place they'd like to visit. Do something playful or fun with them.
- Give them special time or attention when they're upset or having a "bad day."
- Praise them for an accomplishment.

Think about at least one thing you can do each day to demonstrate your love for this special person. Keep in mind, however, the two guidelines mentioned above. First, showing your love is something you want to do for another; not something you do for yourself, and not something you do out of a sense of obligation. Second, avoid giving more of yourself than feels natural. Giving too much at your own expense will only lead you to feel frustrated or resentful.

Finally, notice each day the ways in which the other person demonstrates love for you—however small—and let yourself feel grateful for this gift of love in your life.

References and Further Reading

Buscaglia, Leo. 1972. *Love.* New York: Fawcett Publishing.

Hendricks, Gay. 1993. *Learning to Love Yourself.* New York: Fireside Press.

Keyes, Ken. 1990. *The Power of Unconditional Love.* Coos Bay, Ore.: Loveline Books.

Jampolsky, Gerald. 1979. *Love Is Letting Go of Fear.* Berkeley: Celestial Arts.

Salzberg, Sharon. 1997. *Loving-Kindness: The Revolutionary Art of Happiness.* Boston: Shambhala.

Williamson, Marianne. 1992. *A Return to Love.* New York: HarperCollins.

12

Conclusion

Overcoming anxiety requires courage—the courage to accept, even embrace what might be easier to avoid. What does it mean to have courage? How do you acquire courage in the face of what you fear? The word "courage" derives from the word *coeur*, the French word for heart. To have courage, I believe, is closely related to what we speak of as "taking heart" or "having heart." Fear and cowardice—the opposite of courage—are sometimes referred to as being weak or "faint" of heart. By contrast, one who has courage is sometimes spoken of as being "strong-hearted" or even "lion-hearted." What does it mean, then, to be *strong of heart*?

To have strength of heart means to act from the fullness of your heart—not just your head. And also not just from your body. If you're afraid of something and "stuck" in your head thinking about it, it's easy to get lost in fearful, even catastrophic thoughts and imaginings that can paralyze action. Likewise, if you're frightened and fixated on your body, preoccupied with physical symptoms such as shaking, trembling, dizziness, heart palpitations, or shortness of breath, you can "freeze" and be unable to move forward. The moment you're able to "take heart," you move out of just your head or just your body into a wider space within yourself—a space where you have greater freedom to choose constructive action. It seems evident that the "heart"—defined not just as an organ but a place in your inner being—*is something that underlies and unifies mind and body*. Coming from your heart means to come from a larger place in yourself than just your conscious mind—a place closer to what might be called your "whole being." The heart is associated with passion, love, deep sentiment, aspiration, inspiration as well as courage. All are states of being that are larger than your mind—states where you typically feel more whole and more unified. (Such states are also more than mere emotions.) In short, the heart is a place in your being that can unify disparate parts of yourself into one.

Perhaps this inner place is very close to what is called the *soul*. The words *heart* and *soul*, in fact, are often used together, and I believe they are closely related. Feeling something "deep in your heart" or "deep in your soul" are not so far apart. Both involve experience that can go beyond your ordinary consciousness, and from which the highest states of being (pure love, peace, joy, creativity, as well as courage) can arise. I believe this "heart and soul" place deep within is your inner point of connection with Spirit. It has existed since you were born and cannot be diminished or limited by anything that happens in your life. Yet it's often hidden underneath a morass of reactions, thoughts, images, and judgments that make up the ordinary, moment-to-moment activity of your mind. Anxiety and irrational fear are reactions that arise whenever your conscious mind *believes in the possibility of danger*. When you can move into this larger place within yourself, you move beyond your conscious mind—outside the field of imagination where fearful thoughts can arise. Outside of fear, courage—the ability to move toward rather than avoid whatever frightens you—will come more naturally.

The capacity to "take heart"—to move from conditioned thoughts and reactions into a larger, more unified place in yourself—depends on how connected (some would call it integrated) you are within yourself. In fact, living from your heart and being connected or unified within yourself are really two ways of describing the same thing. The more connected you feel with your deeper self, the easier it is to overcome fear in all forms. The greater the distance that you live from your heart and soul, the more alienated you will feel and the more vulnerable you will be to fear.

I would like to conclude this book with two basic ideas:

Fear—especially irrational fear—arises from separation, alienation, or disconnection from yourself, as well as from others, nature, and the Cosmos.

Courage, unconditional love, and serenity are different faces of the same thing: a state of being which is the opposite of fear. They all arise from the same place—a place where you feel connected and unified with your own deeper self as well as with others, nature, and the Cosmos.

Restating these ideas more simply:

Anxiety and irrational fear arise out of separation from what is real, and are themselves ultimately unreal.

Reconnecting with what is real, within your deepest self and within others, will heal anxiety and irrational fear.

What I'm referring to as "real" here is not the so-called "real world" of adult society but something much deeper—something beyond the conditioned thoughts, perceptions, and reactions of your mind. It's not something you can see with your eyes; rather, it's a reality you experience in those moments when you return to your true heart and soul. You'll know it to be real when you're there.

The individual chapters of this book describe a variety of ways of returning to this inner place—ways of reconnecting with yourself and with others. All of these approaches address how to restore lost connections and overcome self-alienation. The more of these approaches you can embrace, the more naturally you will find courage—and perhaps serenity as well—to face and ultimately heal whatever may frighten you.

What follows is a summary of the major perspectives described in this book, with a brief description of how each can help you reconnect with yourself and the larger world around you.

Simplifying your life can give you the *time* to reconnect with your deeper self and live more in the moment. Fewer complications in your life allow you greater opportunities to spend quality time both in the presence of yourself and with those you care about.

Relaxation has a similar effect. Any form of stress creates internal tensions that obstruct being in touch with your inner self. When you relax and slow down, you'll find it easier to access your inner being. You'll feel your true feelings and more easily be in touch with the inspirations and intuitions that can guide you to take care of yourself and make wise decisions. *Regular aerobic exercise* also reduces stress, helping to clear muscle tension as well as fatigue, with the result that you feel more alive, whole, and connected with yourself. *Energy balance* modalities such as yoga and t'ai chi (as well as healing arts such as acupuncture and massage) can *directly* release blocks to the flow of life energy and restore the integrity—the psychophysical integration—of mind and body.

Taking care of what you eat will also contribute to reducing stress and help you to feel more light, fluid, and energetic. Avoiding foods and substances that cause indigestion, allergy, toxicity, and congestion in your body will enable you to feel more alive and vital. And when you feel energetic and alive, you're not only more connected with yourself but with larger rhythms of nature and the universe. You are empowered by not only your own physical bodily energies but by a matrix of subtler energies that influence all living things.

Developing mindfulness, through the regular practice of meditation, allows you to connect with your inner self directly. Meditation very effectively moves you to deeper ground beyond the constant play of emotional reactions, judgments, and thoughts that make up your moment-to-moment experience. When you meditate, you reconnect with a place of peace and integrity within yourself that always remains calm. The more you can connect with that still place inside, the more you will move beyond anxiety; and the more freedom you will experience simply to act in your own best interest without conflict and doubt.

Learning to let go helps you to stop struggling so much for control. You begin to develop an ability to trust the natural rhythms of life. In so doing, you learn to accept life's inevitable ups and downs, realizing that nearly all problems work themselves out in time. When you can let go of the struggle for control, you create much less resistance and conflict within yourself, making room for higher wisdom and intelligence to speak to you. At such times you may receive assistance from your Higher Power, if you choose to ask. Often it's easier to find courage when you can let go and trust in the possibility of resources beyond your own conscious mind to overcome a problem situation.

To create your vision is to believe firmly in the highest vision of yourself and your life. You do this no matter what present circumstances look like. In so doing, you stop moving to the beat of your conscious mind's fears and limitations. Instead, you align yourself with a universal intelligence that holds greater wisdom and a more hopeful intention for your life. It's my personal conviction that there is a higher purpose or "plan" for each individual's life. When you hold the highest possible vision of what you can be—whole, healthy, vital, and fulfilling your life's deepest purpose(s)—you line up with that plan. When you consistently affirm the highest vision of your life, you'll receive assistance from resources beyond your conscious mind and will. Anyone who has worked deeply with prayer or a 12-step program will attest to this.

Learning to love is the simplest and most direct way to come more from your heart—and thus from your whole being. Love cancels out fear because love is fear's opposite. Genuine love arises from a desire to overcome the separation that creates fear. It arises from a place deeper than the "mind field" where you perceive threat and imagine fear. Love always leads you to reconnect with someone or something larger than yourself. In that reconnecting you will not only feel more safe, but more in touch with who you truly are.

Each of the pathways described in this book ultimately leads to the same destination—a place of integration and self-connection where you can find the courage to face whatever you fear. The more of these paths you embrace, the easier it will be to live in alignment with your deeper self, others, and the world around you. In so doing, you line up with the rhythm and intelligence of nature and the larger universe. You find yourself more a part of the "whole" of life rather than apart from it. In truth, you never really were apart. Fear and anxiety are illusions of separation each of us creates in our minds. At the deepest level we are all safe—all parts of a common ground which knows only love and peace.

Since much of the above has tended toward the abstract, I would like to conclude with something practical. Overcoming anxiety is not a philosophy but a daily practice that requires effort and application on your part. The list on the next page enumerates ten daily practices that can all help you to overcome your anxiety and fears. You may find it helpful to photocopy the list and post it.

Ten Ways to Heal Anxiety Daily

1. Spend one half hour in deep relaxation (progressive muscle relaxation, guided visualization, or meditation).
2. Engage in twenty to thirty minutes of aerobic exercise (forty to sixty minutes of walking).
3. Work with affirmations to overcome counterproductive or fearful thinking (see appendix 5).
4. Avoid caffeine, all forms of sugar, and processed foods as much as possible.
5. Pace yourself slowly throughout the day. Give yourself more time to do fewer activities than you (or others) think you should do. Practice living simply.
6. Make quality time to be with your significant others among family or friends (remember to hug them).
7. Spend one half hour reading inspirational or uplifting material (see appendix 3).
8. Make time for a few minutes of prayer. Your prayer can be asking for support, strength, or guidance. Or it can simply be to let something go.
9. Make time for a few minutes to reinforce the vision of your recovery, using an affirmative statement, prayer, or a visualization.
10. Find humor in something (comics in the newspaper, a video, or yourself). Lighten up.

Appendices

1

Resources

The Anxiety Disorders Association of America

The Anxiety Disorders Association of America (ADAA) is a nonprofit, charitable organization founded in 1980 by leaders in the field of treatment for phobias, agoraphobia, and panic/anxiety disorders. Its purpose is to promote public awareness about anxiety disorders, stimulate research and development of effective treatments, and offer assistance to sufferers and their families in gaining access to available specialists and treatment programs.

The association publishes a quarterly newsletter and a *National Professional Membership Directory*, which lists professionals and programs throughout the United States and Canada specializing in the treatment of anxiety disorders. It also publishes several relevant books and pamphlets.

For further information about the Anxiety Disorders Association of America, its services, publications, and annual conference, as well as how to join, please contact:

The Anxiety Disorders Association of America
11900 Parklawn Drive, Suite 100
Rockville, MD 20852-2624
(301) 231-9350

For a detailed listing of professionals specializing in anxiety disorders treatment by zip code, go to www.adaa.org.

Other Resources

Agoraphobic Foundation of Canada
P.O. Box 132
Chomedey, Laval, Quebec
H7W 4K2, Canada

Agoraphobics in Action, Inc.
P.O. Box 1662
Antioch, TN 37011-1662
(615) 831-2383

Agoraphobics in Motion-A.I.M.
1719 Crooks Street
Royal Oaks, MI 48067
(248) 547-0400

Anxiety Disorders Network
1848 Liverpool Rd., Ste 199
Pickering, Ontario
LIV 6M3, Canada
(905) 831-3877

CHAANGE
128 Country Club Drive
Chula Vista, CA 91911
(619) 425-3992

ENcourage Newsletter
13610 North Scottsdale Road, Suite 10-126
Scottsdale, AZ 85254

National Institute of Mental Health Information Service
Call 1-800-64-PANIC for free information on the nature and treatment of panic disorder.

Obsessive-Compulsive Foundation, Inc.
337 Notch Hill Road
North Branford, CT 06471
(203) 315-2190

Phobics Anonymous
P.O. Box 1180
Palm Springs, CA 92263
(760) 322-COPE

Terrap
932 Evelyn Street
Menlo Park, CA 94025
(800) 274-6242

For a detailed, state-by-state listing of self-help and support groups, go to www.adaa.org (the Web site of the Anxiety Disorders Association of America) and click on "self-help groups" under the category "Consumer Resources."

2

Descriptions of the Anxiety Disorders

In this short appendix, I have included only basic descriptions of the seven most common anxiety disorders. For additional information on how these disorders can be treated, please see chapter 1 of *The Anxiety & Phobia Workbook* Third Edition (2000).

Panic Disorder

Panic disorder is characterized by sudden episodes of acute apprehension or intense fear that occur "out of the blue," without any apparent cause. Intense panic usually lasts no more than a few minutes but, in some instances, can return in "waves" for a period of up to an hour or longer. During the panic itself, any of the following symptoms can occur:

- Shortness of breath or a feeling of being smothered
- Heart palpitations, pounding heart, or accelerated heart rate
- Dizziness, unsteadiness, or faintness
- Trembling or shaking
- Feeling of choking
- Sweating
- Nausea or abdominal distress
- Feelings of unreality—as if you're "not all there" (*depersonalization*)

- Numbness or tingling in hands and feet
- Hot and cold flashes
- Chest pain or discomfort
- Fears of going crazy or losing control
- Fears of dying

At least four of these symptoms are present in a full-blown panic attack, while having two or three of them is referred to as a *limited-symptom attack.*

Your symptoms would be diagnosed as panic disorder if you: 1) have had two or more panic attacks and 2) at least one of these attacks has been followed by one month (or more) of persistent concern about having another panic attack, or worry about the possible implications of having another panic attack. It's important to recognize that panic disorder, by itself, does not involve any phobias. The panic doesn't occur because you are thinking about, approaching, or actually entering a phobic situation. Instead, it occurs spontaneously and unexpectedly for no apparent reason.

A diagnosis of panic disorder is made only after possible medical causes—including hypoglycemia, hyperthyroidism, reaction to excess caffeine, or withdrawal from alcohol, tranquilizers, or sedatives—have been ruled out. The causes of panic disorder involve a combination of heredity, chemical imbalances in the brain, and personal stress. Sudden losses or major life changes may trigger the onset of panic attacks. So can the use of so-called recreational drugs, especially cocaine or methamphetamine ("crank").

People tend to develop panic disorder during late adolescence or their twenties. In many cases, panic is complicated by the development of agoraphobia (as described in the following section). Between 1 and 2 percent of the population has "pure" panic disorder, while about 5 percent, or one in every twenty people, suffer from panic attacks complicated by agoraphobia.

Agoraphobia

Of all the anxiety disorders, agoraphobia (usually referred to as "panic disorder with agoraphobia") is the most prevalent. About 5 percent of the general population suffer from varying degrees of agoraphobia. The only long-term psychological disorder that affects a greater number of people in the United States is alcoholism.

The word *agoraphobia* means fear of open spaces; however, the essence of agoraphobia is a fear of panic attacks. If you suffer from agoraphobia, you're afraid of being in situations from which escape might be difficult—or in which help might be unavailable—if you suddenly had a panic attack. You may avoid grocery stores or freeways, for example, not so much because of their inherent characteristics, but because these are situations from which escape might be difficult or embarrassing in the event of panic. Fear of embarrassment also plays a key role. Most agoraphobics fear not only having panic attacks but *what other people will think* should they be seen having a panic attack.

It's common for the agoraphobic to avoid a variety of situations. Some of the more common ones include:

- Crowded public places such as grocery stores, department stores, restaurants
- Enclosed or confined places such as tunnels, bridges, or the hairdresser's chair
- Public transportation such as trains, buses, subways, planes
- Being at home alone

Perhaps the most common feature of agoraphobia is anxiety about being far away from home or far from a "safe person" (usually your spouse, partner, a parent, or anyone to whom you have a primary attachment). You may completely avoid driving alone or may be afraid of driving alone beyond a certain short distance from home. In more severe cases, you might be able to walk alone only a few yards from home or you might be housebound altogether.

Agoraphobia affects people in all walks of life and at all levels of the socioeconomic scale. Approximately 80 percent of agoraphobics are women, although this percentage has been dropping recently. It's possible that as more women are expected to hold down full-time jobs (making a housebound lifestyle less socially acceptable), the percentage of women and men with agoraphobia may tend to equalize.

Social Phobia

Social phobia is one of the more common anxiety disorders. It involves fear of embarrassment or humiliation in situations where you are exposed to the scrutiny of others or must perform. This fear is much stronger than the normal anxiety most nonphobic people experience in social or performance situations. Usually it's so strong that it causes you to avoid the situation altogether, although some people with social phobia endure social situations, albeit with considerable anxiety. Typically, your concern is that you'll say or do something that will cause others to judge you as being anxious, weak, "crazy," or stupid. Your concern is generally out of proportion to the situation, and you recognize that it's excessive (children with social phobia, however, do not recognize the excessiveness of their fear).

The most common social phobia is fear of public speaking. In fact, this is the most common of all phobias and affects performers, speakers, people whose jobs require them to make presentations, and students who have to speak before their class. Public speaking phobia affects a large percentage of the population and is equally prevalent among men and women.

Other common social phobias include:

- Fear of blushing in public

- Fear of choking on or spilling food while in public
- Fear of being watched at work
- Fear of using public toilets
- Fear of writing or signing documents in the presence of others
- Fear of crowds
- Fear of taking examinations

Sometimes social phobia is less specific and involves a generalized fear of *any* social or group situation where you feel that you might be watched or evaluated. When your fear is of a wide range of social situations (for example, initiating conversations, participating in small groups, speaking to authority figures, dating, attending parties, and so on), the condition is referred to as *generalized social phobia.*

While social anxieties are common, you would be given a formal diagnosis of social phobia only if your avoidance interferes with work, social activities, or important relationships, and/or it causes you considerable distress. As with agoraphobia, panic attacks can accompany social phobia, although your panic is related more to being embarrassed or humiliated than to being confined or trapped. Also the panic arises only in connection with specific types of social situations.

Social phobias tend to develop earlier than agoraphobia and can begin in late childhood or adolescence. They often develop in shy children around the time they're faced with increased peer pressure at school. Typically these phobias persist (without treatment) through adolescence and young adulthood, but have a tendency to decrease in severity later in life. Recent studies suggest that social phobia affects 3 to 13 percent of adults in the U.S. at some time in their life (the prevalence rates vary depending on the threshold used to evaluate distress).

Specific Phobia

Specific phobia typically involves a strong fear and avoidance of *one particular* type of object or situation. Most often the phobic situation is avoided, though in some instances it may be endured with dread. Confronting the object or situation almost always provokes anxiety.

With specific phobia, fear is generally focused on the *phobic situation* itself and only secondarily, if at all, on having a panic attack. This is unlike agoraphobia, where the primary focus of fear tends to be on panic attacks. There is also no fear of humiliation or embarrassment in social situations, as in social phobia. Panic attacks may occur with specific phobia, but only upon confronting the feared object or situation.

While fears are pervasive, a diagnosis of specific phobia is made only when the fear and avoidance are strong enough to interfere with normal routines, work, relationships and/or to cause significant distress.

Specific phobias are classified into five different types:

- *Animal phobias* consist of fears of animals such as snakes, mice, or dogs; or insects such as bees or spiders. Typically, animal phobias originate in childhood.

- *Natural environment type*—These phobias consist of fears related to the natural environment such as heights (sometimes referred to as acrophobia), fire, or water; or natural occurrences such as thunderstorms, tornadoes, or earthquakes.

- *Blood-injection-injury type*—In this category are fears evoked by the sight of blood or seeing someone injured. Phobias of receiving an injection or other invasive medical procedure are also included. These phobias are grouped together because they're all characterized by the possibility of fainting, in addition to panic or anxiety. Blood-injection-injury phobias can develop at any age.

- *Situational type*—Situational phobias relate to a variety of situations in which a fear of being enclosed, trapped, and/or unable to exit plays a dominant role. Such situations include flying, elevators, driving, public transportation, tunnels, bridges, and other enclosed places such as shopping malls. Situational phobias tend to develop in childhood or in early adulthood (twenties).

- *Other type*—This is a residual category for specific phobias not falling into the previous four types. Included here are fears of contracting illness (such as AIDS or cancer), avoidance of situations that might lead to choking or vomiting (for example, eating solid foods), and the fear of open spaces.

Specific phobias are common and affect approximately 10 percent of the population. However, since they do not always result in severe impairment, only a minority of people with specific phobias actually seek treatment. These types of phobias occur in men and women about equally. Animal phobias tend to be more common in women, while illness phobias are more common in men.

As previously mentioned, specific phobias are often childhood fears that were never outgrown. In other instances, they may develop after a traumatic event, such as an accident, natural disaster, illness, or visit to the dentist—in other words, as a result of conditioning. A final cause is childhood *modeling*. Repeated observation of a parent with a specific phobia can lead a child to develop it as well.

Generalized Anxiety Disorder

Generalized anxiety disorder is characterized by chronic anxiety that persists for at least six months *but is unaccompanied by panic attacks, phobias, or obsessions*. You simply experience persistent anxiety and worry without the complicating features of other anxiety disorders. To be given a diagnosis of generalized anxiety disorder, your anxiety and worry must focus on two or more stressful life circumstances (such as finances, relationships, health, or school performance) a majority of days during a six-month period. It's common, if you're dealing with generalized anxiety disorder, to have a large number of worries, and to spend a lot of your time worrying. Yet you find it difficult to exercise much control over your worrying. Moreover, the intensity and frequency of the worry are always out of proportion to the actual likelihood of the feared events happening.

In addition to frequent worry, generalized anxiety disorder involves having at least three of the following six symptoms (with at least one symptom present more days than not over a period of six months):

- Restlessness—feeling keyed up
- Being easily fatigued
- Difficulty concentrating
- Irritability
- Muscle tension
- Difficulties with sleep

Finally, you're likely to receive a diagnosis of generalized anxiety disorder if your worry and associated symptoms cause you significant distress and/or interfere with your ability to function occupationally, socially, or in other important areas.

If a doctor tells you that you suffer from generalized anxiety disorder, he or she has probably ruled out possible medical causes of chronic anxiety, such as hyperventilation, thyroid problems, or drug-induced anxiety. Generalized anxiety disorder often occurs together with depression: a competent therapist can usually determine which disorder is primary and which is secondary. In some cases, though, it's difficult to say which came first.

Generalized anxiety disorder can develop at any age. In children and adolescents, the focus of worry often tends to be on performance in school or sports events. In adults, the focus can vary. This disorder affects approximately 4 percent of the American population, and may be slightly more common in females than males (55 to 60 percent of those diagnosed with the disorder are female).

Obsessive-Compulsive Disorder

Some people naturally tend to be more neat, tidy, and orderly than others. These traits can in fact be useful in many situations, both at work and at home. In obsessive-compulsive disorder, however, they are carried to an extreme and disruptive degree. Persons with obsessive-compulsive disorder can spend many hours cleaning, tidying, checking, or ordering—to the point where these activities interfere with the rest of the business of their lives.

Obsessions are recurring ideas, thoughts, images, or impulses that seem senseless but nonetheless continue to intrude into your mind. Examples include images of violence, thoughts of doing violence to someone else, or fears of leaving on lights or the stove or leaving your door unlocked. You recognize that these thoughts or fears are irrational and try to suppress them, but they continue to intrude into your mind for hours, days, weeks, or longer. These thoughts or images are not merely excessive worries about real-life problems and are usually unrelated to a real-life problem.

Compulsions are behaviors or rituals that you perform to dispel the anxiety brought up by obsessions. For example, you may wash your hands numerous times to dispel a fear of being contaminated, check the stove again and again to see if it's turned off, or look continually in your rearview mirror while driving to assuage anxiety about having hit somebody. You realize that these rituals are unreasonable. Yet you feel compelled to perform them to ward off the anxiety associated with your particular obsession. The conflict between your wish to be free of the compulsive ritual and the irresistible desire to perform it is a source of anxiety, shame, and even despair. Eventually you may cease struggling with your compulsions and give over to them entirely.

Obsessions may occur by themselves, without necessarily being accompanied by compulsions. In fact, about 25 percent of the people who suffer from obsessive-compulsive disorder only have obsessions.

The most common compulsions include washing, checking, and counting. If you're a washer, you're constantly concerned about avoiding contamination. You avoid touching doorknobs, shaking hands, or coming into contact with any object you associate with germs, filth, or a toxic substance. You can spend literally hours washing hands or showering to reduce anxiety about being contaminated. Women more often have this compulsion than men do. Men outnumber women as checkers, however. Doors have to be repeatedly checked to dispel obsessions about being robbed; stoves are repeatedly checked to dispel obsessions about starting a fire; or roads repeatedly checked to dispel obsessions about having hit someone. In the counting compulsion, you feel you must count up to a certain number or repeat a word a certain number of times to dispel anxiety about harm befalling you or someone else.

Obsessive-compulsive disorder is often accompanied by depression. Preoccupation with obsessions, in fact, tends to wax and wane with depression. This disorder may also be accompanied by phobic avoidance—such as when a person with an obsession about dirt avoids public restrooms or touching doorknobs.

It's very important to realize that as bizarre as obsessive-compulsive behavior may sound, it has nothing to do with "being crazy." You always recognize the irrationality and senselessness of your thoughts and behavior and you're very frustrated (as well as depressed) about your inability to control them.

Obsessive-compulsive disorder used to be considered a rare behavior disturbance. However, recent studies have shown that as many as *2 to 3 percent of the general population* may suffer, to varying degrees, from obsessive-compulsive disorder. The reason prevalence rates have been underestimated up to now is that most sufferers have been reluctant to tell anyone about their problem. This disorder appears to affect men and women in equal numbers. Although many cases of obsessive-compulsive disorder begin in adolescence and young adulthood, about half begin in childhood. The age of onset tends to be earlier in males than females.

The causes of obsessive-compulsive disorder are unclear. There is some evidence that an imbalance of a neurotransmitter in the brain known as serotonin, or a disturbance in serotonin metabolism, is associated with the disorder. This is borne out by the fact that many sufferers improve when they take medications that increase brain serotonin levels, such as clomipramine (Anafranil) or specific serotonin-enhancing antidepressants such as fluoxetine (Prozac), sertraline (Zoloft), and paroxetine (Paxil). Further research needs to be done.

Post-Traumatic Stress Disorder

The essential feature of post-traumatic stress disorder is the development of disabling psychological symptoms following a traumatic event. It was first identified during World War I, when soldiers were observed to suffer chronic anxiety, nightmares, and flashbacks for weeks, months, or even years following combat. This condition came to be known as "shell shock."

Post-traumatic stress disorder can occur to anyone in the wake of a severe trauma outside the normal range of human experience. These are traumas that would produce intense fear, terror, and feelings of helplessness in anyone and include natural disasters such as earthquakes or tornadoes, car or plane crashes, rape, assault, or other violent crimes against yourself or your immediate family. It appears that the symptoms are more intense and persistent when the trauma is personal, as in rape or other violent crimes.

Among the variety of symptoms that can occur with post-traumatic stress disorder, the following nine are particularly common:

- Repetitive, distressing thoughts about the event
- Nightmares related to the event
- Flashbacks so intense that you feel or act as though the trauma were occurring all over again
- An attempt to avoid thoughts or feelings associated with the trauma
- An attempt to avoid activities or external situations associated with the trauma—such as a phobia about driving after you have been in an auto accident
- Emotional numbness—being out of touch with your feelings
- Feelings of detachment or estrangement from others
- Losing interest in activities that used to give you pleasure
- Persistent symptoms of increased anxiety, such as difficulty falling or staying asleep, difficulty concentrating, startling easily, irritability, and outbursts of anger

For you to receive a diagnosis of post-traumatic stress disorder, these symptoms need to have persisted for at least one month (with less than one month's duration, the appropriate diagnosis is "acute stress disorder"). In addition, the disturbance must be causing you significant distress, interfering with social, vocational, or other important areas of your life.

If you suffer from post-traumatic stress disorder, you tend to be anxious and depressed. Sometimes you will find yourself acting impulsively, suddenly changing residence or going on a trip with hardly any plans. If you have been through a trauma where others around you died, you may suffer from guilt about having survived.

Post-traumatic stress disorder can affect people at any age. Children with the disorder tend not to relive the trauma consciously but continually reenact it in their play or in distressing dreams.

3

Inspirational Books

The following books have been uplifting to me personally and to a number of my clients.

Beattie, Melody. 1990. *The Language of Letting Go.* New York: Harper/Hazeldon.

Borysenko, Joan. 1993. *Fire in the Soul.* New York: Warner Books.

Bunick, Nick. 1998. *In God's Truth.* Charlottesville, Va.: Hampton Roads Publishing Co.

Caddy, Eileen. 1979. *The Dawn of Change.* Forres, Scotland: Findhorn Publications. (Inspired messages from the author's Higher Power.)

Hay, Louise. 1984. *You Can Heal Your Life.* Santa Monica, Calif.: Hay House. (Helpful tools and affirmations for developing self-worth.)

Jampolsky, Gerald. 1979. *Love Is Letting Go of Fear.* Berkeley, Calif.: Celestial Arts.

Miller, Carolyn. 1995. *Creating Miracles.* Tiburon, Calif.: H.J. Kramer, Inc. (As the title implies, this insightful book has many useful ideas about how to create miraculous outcomes in ordinary life.)

Mitchell, Stephen, ed. 1989. *The Enlightened Heart: An Anthology of Sacred Poetry.* New York: Harper Perennial.

Moody, Raymond. 1976. *Life After Life.* New York: Bantam. (The classic book on near-death experiences.)

Nelson, Martia. 1993. *Coming Home.* Novato, Calif.: Nataraj Publishing. (Offers deep insight into the human condition.)

Norwood, Robin. 1994. *Why Me. Why Now. Why This.* New York: Carol Southern Books. (Makes a strong case that what happens to us in life are lessons for our growth.)

Redfield, James. 1993. *The Celestine Prophecy.* New York: Warner Books.

Robinson, John. 2000. *Ordinary Enlightenment.* Unity Village, Mo.: Unity House.

Rodegast, Pat. 1985. *Emmanuel's Book.* New York: Bantam. (Very inspiring communications from a Higher Source. A personal favorite.)

———. 1989. *Emmanuel's Book II.* New York: Bantam.

Roman, Sanaya. 1989. *Spiritual Growth.* Tiburon, Calif.: H.J. Kramer.

Walsch, Neale. 1996. *Conversations with God, Book 1.* New York: Putnam. (Inspiring presentation of the author's "conversation" with his Higher Power.)

Weiss, Brian. 1996. *Only Love Is Real.* New York: Warner Books.

Williamson, Marianne. 1994. *Illuminata.* New York: Random House. (An outstanding collection of reflections and prayers for modern times.)

Zukav, Gary. 1990. *The Seat of the Soul.* New York: Fireside Books.

4

Creating Your Reality: How It Works

Everything Consists of Energy

All phenomena in the universe are forms of energy. According to modern physics, all of the things in the world are made of particles that also pose as waves. These "wave/particles" can be converted back and forth from matter to energy in accord with Einstein's well-known equation, $E=mc^2$. So, too, mental phenomena—your thoughts, desires, feelings, etc.—are all forms of energy. Some would argue that these phenomena are nothing more than patterns of electrical activity in the brain. However, it might be asked how a mere pattern of electrical activity can fully explain the content of a thought—for example, your thought about what you are reading or your feeling of interest or disinterest. Perhaps patterns of brain activity are necessary to "carry" the contents of your thoughts—much as radio waves are necessary to carry or transmit the content of the music you hear on the radio. Yet the meaning of the thoughts (or melody of the music) cannot be understood solely as a physical brain phenomenon. How do you derive meaning from neurophysiology or neurochemistry? There is no obvious way that an inspiration or sentiment can be fully reduced to patterns of electrical discharge in the neural networks of the brain. Still, if you assume that everything is some form of energy, even inspirations and sentiments must be energy phenomena, albeit very subtle ones.

Some people have proposed that thoughts and feelings, in essence, are actually energetic phenomena traveling faster than the speed of light. (Although Einstein held that nothing could exceed the speed of light, his theory of relativity applies only to material phenomena that exist in space and time.) That may be why we can't actually *see* thoughts and feelings objectively in our material world, where everything we do see, other than light itself, is traveling slower than the speed of light. If there are energies that travel faster than the speed of light, they must certainly be nonmaterial. Therefore, they cannot be localized in space, yet they *can* be directly experienced. You won't see them but you can, so to speak, *be* them. You won't find the feeling of anxiety by looking anywhere in your physical brain, but you can directly experience the quality anxiety. An interesting implication of this is that there may be a part of yourself—that part of you which *experiences the content or meaning inherent in your thoughts and feelings*—that exists independently of space and (linear) time. The religions of the world have referred to this aspect as the "soul" and propose that it goes on existing in a nonphysical realm ("heaven" or "nirvana") after your physical body dies.

It isn't necessary to accept all of the above to imagine that thoughts (including consistently held thoughts—your beliefs and attitudes) may have an independent existence apart from your physical brain. If you can entertain this one hypothesis, what follows will be easier to understand.

Consciousness is Inherently "Nonlocal"

As indicated in the previous section, the qualitative aspects of consciousness (meanings) are not material phenomena visible in space. They cannot be precisely located in space. The question "Where—in space—is the meaning of what you are reading?" has no answer, although specific patterns of neural activity in your brain enable you to experience that meaning here and now. The term "nonlocal" is used in physics to refer to a phenomenon that can't be precisely located in space. Consciousness, in its qualitative (meaning) aspect, is inherently nonlocal. Your physical brain, on the other hand, is a very complex instrument for *localizing* the qualitative aspects of consciousness. Specific thoughts, perceptions, and feelings that you have in any instant focus or "localize" the qualitative aspects of consciousness at a particular time and place. This is necessary, for example, for you to be able to have whatever thought you are having in this moment. In sum, your brain filters nonlocal reality—the field of all possibilities—into specific thoughts at a particular time. Think of thought much like the subatomic particle studied by physicists—i.e., as having both a "wave" and a "particle" aspect. The wave-like aspect cannot be specifically located in your brain; the particle-like aspect shows up as *this* particular thought process occurring in so-and-so's brain at such-and-such time. As I see it, the nonlocal, qualitative aspects of consciousness are the "software" that organizes the neurochemistry of the brain into meaningful sequences.

Sometimes the nonlocal characteristic of consciousness "peeks through" in experiences of telepathy—where you and I, even if separated by many miles, have the same thought at the same time. Remote viewing ("seeing" what is happening far away) is another example of this.

There is an experiment in physics that actually demonstrates the existence of nonlocal phenomena. It has been shown that information associated with one electron can be transferred to another electron, many miles away, *instantaneously*. If the information were actually traveling at the speed of light, the transmission would take about forty billionths of a second. Yet, mysteriously, the second electron performs exactly as the first at virtually the same time. Whatever allows the second particle to match the first must not be dependent on space. In fact, it is from experiments demonstrating this phenomenon that physicists coined the term "nonlocal."

This and the results of other experiments have led the physicist David Bohm to propose an "implicate order" of the universe that does not exist within the physical universe but is a timeless, spaceless matrix from which the physical universe arises. If such an implicate order does exist, it's not difficult to see the parallel with traditional religious concepts of heaven or nirvana; both are realms which exist outside of space and linear time.

Microcosm Reflects Macrocosm

The basic idea presented in chapter 10 is that your thoughts, beliefs, and attitudes give shape to your outer circumstances as well as your inner world. The notion "microcosm reflects the macrocosm" suggests that this *same* relationship between "mind" and "matter" holds at the level of the entire universe. Human beings (as well as animals) are not unique in having souls, minds, and bodies that work together. It would be, in fact, rather provincial to suppose that we alone are the only place in the entire universe where mind and consciousness exist. The idea here is that our own makeup *mirrors* the way the entire universe is organized. Suppose that the whole universe has something like a "soul" and a "mind," as well as the physical aspect—ranging from atoms to galaxies— that we can see and measure. This idea may perhaps seem strange, but it's only strange if we suppose that the "universal mind" is anything like our rather limited and self-centered minds. If the entire macrocosm has its own form of consciousness, such consciousness is probably well beyond our comprehension. However, such consciousness may have something to do with the Deity that the religions of the world have referred to by various names—"God," "Allah," "Jehovah," "Brahma," "Great Spirit," and so on. Of course, such a consciousness can only represent one aspect—or even a creation—of God, for God cannot be understood or grasped through any finite description. In sum, the idea here is not that the entire universe is like a human being, but that *the hierarchical relationship of mind to matter* occurs on all scales of size, from the cosmic down to the human, and on down to the cellular, molecular and subatomic. Mind—or intelligence—is not a unique aspect of higher animals but is an inherent aspect of all things on all levels, as the philosopher Spinoza proposed. Rather than recasting the universe to resemble man, the idea here is that man is a miniaturized version of the cosmos—the "microcosm reflects the macrocosm." Such an idea is epitomized in the saying: "As above, so below." It is also found in the Bible in the statement: "Man is made in God's image."

Form Follows Idea

The first idea presented above was that everything that exists—from atoms and molecules to thoughts and feelings—are various forms of energy. There is a philosophical tradition, which originated in the Far East, that proposes that the only difference among all these different phenomena is how "subtle vs. gross" the energy is that constitutes them. Material objects (actually the atoms out of which they're made) are more gross energy forms. Feelings and thoughts are very subtle energy forms, and spiritual awareness and inspiration are perhaps the subtlest of all.

An important assumption made by this same philosophical tradition is that subtle energy forms shape and determine gross energy forms to a much greater degree than vice versa.* For example, wind affects the movement of water more easily than water can affect the movement of air. In a similar fashion your beliefs, attitudes, and ideas tend to shape and determine the emotional and physical levels of your existence. The thought "I'm going to drive to the store" precedes actually doing so. So does the thought "I need to find a job" precede actually going out to look for one. The same principle holds *even if you do not take physical action* to bring about your idea. That is, if you simply hold an idea in your mind with conviction, it will tend to attract and create corresponding physical circumstances on a material level. The popular phrase for this situation is "mind over matter." It's also expressed in the popular notion "Be careful what you wish for—you just might get it." It's demonstrated most dramatically in the phenomenon of psychokinesis, the ability to move or alter physical objects without touching them. Yet, it also takes place more subtly and imperceptibly whenever you focus or concentrate your mind with consistent desire or intention.

Thoughts/Beliefs Attract Their Physical Counterparts

With the previous four points in mind, I'll offer a speculation on how thoughts might shape material circumstances. How might this actually work? Recall that everything in the universe .(including thoughts, beliefs, and attitudes) are different forms of energy. Energy, as we understand it, is not static but travels in the form of waves (visible light is a common example). Just like different colors represent different frequencies or wavelengths of light, suppose that various thoughts correspond to different "energy forms" varying possibly in frequency, wave form, or perhaps some other type of characteristic yet to be discovered. Every thought carries a particular energetic "signature." The energy forms corresponding to thoughts are not visible and possibly move faster than the speed of light, as was hypothesized above. Energies that make up physical

* The notion that ideas shape physical circumstances has also played a major role in Western philosophy, beginning with Plato. In philosophy, such a view is called "idealism" as opposed to "materialism." It is not inconsistent with causality and the physical laws of nature. Physical laws explain *how* phenomena move from one state to the next, but they do not explain the *particular* forms and patternings that happen to occur, especially for living things. Something more than physical laws is needed for that. The universe is more than a machine—an "intelligent organism" is a better metaphor to describe how the universe operates.

things, on the other hand, can take on a particle form that enables us to see them in space. One thing that differentiates various forms of energy is how fast they vibrate. Very subtle energies like thoughts and feelings vibrate very fast. More gross energies or material things (actually the subatomic particles that make them up) vibrate more slowly.

Now, if thoughts in essence are nonlocal, then whenever you dwell on a particular thought, that thought—as a particular energy form—would seem likely to "line up" with all other thoughts sharing the same energy form. The more technical word for "line up" is *resonate*—as when two musical notes at the same pitch (frequency) resonate together. Thus, if you think consistently about being healthy and whole, your thought of health lines up—resonates—with all other thoughts of health everywhere. *Your thought doesn't have to "go" anywhere to do this.* The level at which your thought exists in essence—and all other similar thoughts exist in essence—is nonlocal (nonspatial). At such a level there is no separation in terms of space. Your mind simply goes to the "place" where all other similar thoughts of health exist. That is, you tune into a particular frequency or energy configuration, much like tuning a radio to a particular station.

If you happen to "stay" in such a "place"—stay focused on healthy ideas and expectations long enough—healthy circumstances will inevitably tend to show up in your life. *This is because the idea of health in your consciousness can resonate with all other ideas of health in a much more inclusive, "universal consciousness."* *

If this happens, then you simply become part of the process whereby health is being created or manifested everywhere (from nonlocal reality into material reality). As was proposed earlier, form follows idea at all levels of reality from the macrocosm down to the subatomic. If your sincere intent can embrace the highest ideas of health at the nonlocal level of reality, sooner or later healthy circumstances are likely to show up in your life, no matter how ill you may be at present.

The More "Energized" a Belief, the Greater Its Ability to Attract

The more energy I give to a thought—say of healing—the greater the power of my thought to line up with similar thoughts of healing; that is, the more it can partake of

* The most universal level is the consciousness of the entire macrocosm, as described above. Each of our individual consciousnesses is embedded in that universal consciousness, much as a drop of the ocean is part of the larger ocean. When you hold an idea (belief) in your mind with conviction, you can potentially line up with the counterparts to that same idea in universal consciousness.

Make the further assumption now that universal consciousness is not static but continuously creative. As an active process, universal consciousness can be compared with the creative aspect of the Deity referred to in all of the religions of the world, influencing our world in subtle ways that generally converge with the laws of nature but can sometimes supersede causality and natural laws, in the instance of miracles and synchronicities.

At the point when your intention, belief, or desire for health lines up with the idea or archetype of health/wholeness in universal consciousness, you participate in the process of health/wholeness being created everywhere (from the highest, nonlocal level down to the material, spatial world). As such, healthy circumstances are bound to show up in your daily life sooner or later. In sum, *when your own mind is attuned or aligned with universal consciousness around the same ideal* (in this case, health), *the two will converge to "co-create" the highest vision of your goal.*

that "place" (in nonlocal consciousness) where healing is happening. If I now form an *intention* to heal, I can potentially access the energy of all the thought-forms associated with healing happening everywhere to bring about healing in my life. My own life, by my choice, becomes part and parcel of that "corner of reality" where healing is happening.

Unfortunately, the opposite is also true. The more energy I give to my fear, the more I may line up with all other thoughts of fear (in nonlocal consciousness). In short, the more I may tune in to that "place" in nonlocal consciousness where "fear" is happening. And, the more likely I may draw to me exactly what I fear. My fear becomes a self-fulfilling prophecy.

How can a thought, belief, or intention become energized or strengthened?

- *Repetition*—by dwelling on it repeatedly. Repeating an idea over and over strengthens it in your mind.

- *By putting your "heart and soul" into it.* Just thinking about something doesn't energize it, because you don't invest the deeper levels of your being in it. However, if you put your "heart and soul" into it, you are bringing that larger, more inclusive, more "nonlocal" aspect of consciousness to bear. When the thought is held from the more universal, nonlocal aspect of your own inner being, it enters energetically into discourse with all other thoughts like it. This gives it tremendous energy to attract/manifest corresponding circumstances.

- *By forming a clear intention.* Just thinking about something or even wishing and hoping for it only energizes it to a degree. However, when you form a specific intention, and a clear commitment to go after it, you're *focusing* your energy. And energy that's focused is generally more powerful. This is not hard to see when you think of a laser beam versus an incandescent light bulb. Light that's highly focused (the laser) is considerably more intense and powerful than light which is more diffuse. If thoughts and beliefs are indeed *energetic* phenomena, the laser analogy may well apply. As I mentioned in chapter 9, a clear intention and commitment, from the wholeness of your heart, will tend to draw to you what you seek. The power of intention is strengthened when you put your heart and soul into it. When repetition is added, when you hold your intention with conviction over time, you have what is called *commitment*. Sustained commitment to a goal is the strongest (most energized) way to actually bring that goal about.

- *"Spiritualizing" your intention.* A clear, committed intention can be energized and strengthened even further by evoking or relying on spiritual resources. There are many ways to do this, though prayer is traditionally the most popular and widely practiced. When you not only have a strong intention, but ask for spiritual assistance in bringing it about, you may access unlimited energy—the energy associated with your Higher Power or God.

Your Life Is an "Outpicturing" of Your Beliefs

The popular sayings "You get back what you put out" and "What goes around comes around" epitomize this idea. This simply puts the ideas expressed in the previous two sections together. If you put a lot of energy into something you believe in, you will tend to bring it into being. If you believe you can heal from a chronic illness and put a lot of time and energy into that belief, you will tend to draw healing to yourself. The healing might take one of three forms: First, you might actually experience—suddenly or over time—a miraculous healing; the condition is simply lifted. There are numerous records of miraculous healings in the past as well as in recent times. Second, you might draw to yourself resources that assist you in the process of bringing about healing. For example, you might read a certain magazine article, hear about a healing modality you hadn't known about, find a particular healing practitioner, or read a quote that moves you to alter some aspect of your life. All of these unforeseen events would contribute to an eventual healing of your illness. In the third form of healing your condition persists. The condition itself does not go away but your attitude changes so much that you can live with it peacefully, without the struggle and distress you once had. The "healing" is on a psychological rather than physical level.

The "good news" is that you have the capacity to recreate your life, for the better, on the basis of your intentions and beliefs, no matter how adverse the circumstances you happen to face.

The "bad news" is that if you dwell on negativity—if you keep "feeding" what you fear—you may tend to draw *that* outcome to yourself also. The popular term for this is "self-fulfilling prophecy."

Most of the time, most of us harbor a mix of hopes and fears, a combination of faith and doubt, optimism and pessimism. The result is that we don't create anything especially positive or negative because our conflicting beliefs tend to cancel each other out. When, however, you energize a *positive* belief, in the ways described in the preceding section, you can *recreate* a new life apart from whatever fears, doubts, resentments, or guilt may have been obstructing your progress.

Not Everything That Happens to You Is the Result of Your Beliefs

There is an unfortunate tendency on the part of some people to believe that whatever happens to them is simply the result of their beliefs. If you're hit by a drunk driver, somehow you "created" that misfortune or "drew it to you." Even worse, if a small child is brutally abused, somehow the child created it. The assumption is that *anything* that happens to you is created by your beliefs.

In my opinion, this is carrying the idea of creating your reality too far. It is, in fact, a gross and unfortunate oversimplification. There are two kinds of circumstances that you don't, in fact, create in accord with your thoughts, desires, and beliefs: 1) those which are the result of the beliefs in the collective consciousness of society or humanity, and 2) those that are in the "consciousness" of, for lack of a better word, "God" or the "universe." If the government decides to raise taxes, you did not single-handedly create that circumstance, but the collective consciousness of your society did. If you're injured in an accident with an intoxicated driver, you may not have "drawn" that to yourself, but you are a participant in a society (a collective consciousness) where drunkenness and drunk driving happen to occur fairly often. The collective beliefs of the larger group created it, and you, as a member of that group, happen to participate in it. If it rains on your picnic, you did not personally create that outcome—a low-pressure system related to changes in atmospheric conditions did. Being born to your parents is not something you created but is a given—something you have to work with. So may many other things that simply come into your life outside of your conscious will. A scientific-materialistic worldview would say these events are just random occurrences. A Christian viewpoint would speak of tests and trials, while a Hindu or Buddhist would speak of karma accrued from previous lifetimes. Rather than taking a position here, I would simply call such events "life circumstances"—and speculate that such events are not random but are, indeed, the outpicturing of some consciousness or intelligence incomprehensibly greater than my personal ego. Like Job, none of us can fully know the reasons for all the circumstances that happen to come our way.

In conclusion, some of what happens in your life is a result of your particular beliefs, attitudes, desires—and some is not. What is most important is that you have free will—*the ability to change your attitude and beliefs in response to whatever happens in your life, even the most unfortunate*. It is in this sense that you are the author of your destiny, even if you did not single-handedly create or attract all of the events that happen to come into your life.

5

Helpful Counterstatements and Affirmations

You may find the following counterstatements helpful when you're going through a particularly difficult time with anxiety.

Negative Self-Talk	**Positive Counterstatements**
This is unbearable.	I can learn how to cope better with this.
What if this goes on without letting up?	I'll deal with this one day at a time. I don't have to project into the future.
I feel damaged, inadequate relative to others.	Some of us have steeper paths to walk than others. That doesn't make me less valuable as a human being—even if I accomplish less in the outer world.
Why do I have to deal with this? Other people seem freer to enjoy their lives.	Life is a school. For whatever reasons, at least for now, I've been given a steeper path—a tougher curriculum. That doesn't make me wrong. In fact, adversity develops qualities of strength and compassion.
Having this condition seems unfair.	Life can appear unfair from a human perspective. If we could see the bigger picture, we'd see that everything is proceeding according to plan.
I don't know how to cope with this.	I can *learn* to cope better—with this and any difficulty life brings.

I feel so inadequate relative to others.	Let people do what they do in the outer world. I'm following a path of inner growth and transformation, which is at least equally valuable. Finding peace in myself can be a gift to others.
Each day seems like a major challenge.	I'm learning to take things more slowly. I make time to take care of myself. I make time to do small things to nurture myself.
I don't understand why I'm this way—why this happened to me.	The causes are many, including heredity, early environment, and cumulative stress. Understanding causes satisfies the intellect, but it's not what heals.
I feel like I'm going crazy.	When anxiety is high, I *feel* like I'm losing control. But that feeling has nothing to do with going crazy. Anxiety disorders are a long way from the category of disorders labeled "crazy."
I have to really fight this.	Struggling with a problem won't help so much as making more time in my life to better care for myself.
I shouldn't have let this happen to me.	The long-term causes of this problem lie in heredity and childhood environment, so I didn't cause this condition. I *can* now take responsibility for getting better.

You may wish to record the following list of "antianxiety affirmations" or the "script for overcoming fear" on tape. Then listen to them daily, when relaxed, to reinforce a positive attitude toward overcoming anxiety.

Antianxiety Affirmations

I am learning to let go of worry.

Each day I'm growing in my capacity to master worry and anxiety.

I am learning not to feed my worries—to choose peace over fear.

I am learning to consciously choose what I think, and I choose thoughts that are supportive and beneficial for me.

When anxious thoughts come up, I can slow down, breathe, and let them go.

When anxious thoughts come up, I can make time to relax and release them.

Deep relaxation gives me the freedom of choice to move out of fear.

Anxiety is made of illusory thoughts—thoughts I can let go of.

When I see most situations as they truly are, there is nothing to be afraid of.

Fearful thoughts are usually exaggerated, and I'm growing in my ability to turn them off at will.

More and more, it's becoming easier to relax and talk myself out of anxiety.

I keep my mind too busy thinking positive and constructive thoughts to have much time for worry.

I'm learning to control my mind and choose the thoughts that I think.

I am gaining more confidence in myself, knowing I can handle any situation that comes along.

Fear is dissolving and vanishing from my life. I am calm, confident, and secure.

As I take life more slowly and easily, I have more ease and peace in my life.

As I grow in my ability to relax and feel secure, I realize that there is truly nothing to fear.

More and more, I'm growing in confidence, knowing that I can handle any situation that comes up.

Script for Overcoming Fear

Focusing on a fear always makes it worse.

When I can relax enough, I become able to change my focus. . . . I can put my mind, on loving, supportive, constructive ideas.

I can't make fearful thoughts go away. Struggling with them makes them loom larger.

Instead, I can redirect my mind to more peaceful, calming thoughts and circumstances. Every time I do this, I am choosing peace instead of fear. The more I choose peace, the more it becomes a part of my life.

With practice, I get better at redirecting my mind.

I learn how to spend less time focusing on fear.

I grow stronger in my ability to choose wholesome, helpful thoughts over fearful ones.

I make time to relax . . . to reconnect with that place deep within myself that is always at peace. When I make the time to do this, I can choose to move away from fearful thoughts.

I can allow my mind to expand into a wider place that is much larger than my fearful thoughts. Fear requires a narrow, small focus of my mind. When I relax or meditate, my mind becomes deep enough—and large enough—to transcend fear.

I'm learning to see that my fearful thoughts grossly overestimate risk or threat.

The true risk I face in most situations is actually very small.

True, it's impossible to eliminate risk from life altogether.

Being in a physical body in the physical world necessitates some risk.

Only in heaven is there an eternal risk-free state.

I'm learning to recognize my tendency to exaggerate risks—to blow them out of proportion.

Every fear involves both overestimating the risk of danger—and underestimating my ability to cope.

If I take the time to examine my fearful thoughts, I'll discover that in most cases they are unrealistic.

When I choose to see most situations as they truly are, I see that they are not dangerous.

If I practice replacing my fearful thoughts with real thoughts, eventually my fearful thoughts will diminish.

Every time I feel afraid, I recognize the unreality of my fearful thoughts and let go of them more easily.

The important thing is not to feed fear . . . not to dwell on it or give it energy.

Instead I can practice redirecting my attention to something—anything—that makes me feel better.

I can focus on talking to a friend, reading something uplifting, working with my hands, listening to a tape, or any number of activities which help me take my mind off fear.

With practice, I become more and more adept at moving away from fearful thoughts—of not indulging in them.

I begin to become master rather than victim of my mind.

I learn that I have more and more choice about fear.

I can step into it or out of it.

And, as time passes, I learn to step out of it.

About the Author

Dr. Edmund ("Ed") Bourne, Ph.D., has specialized in treating anxiety disorders and related problems for two decades. He is author of the highly regarded *Anxiety & Phobia Workbook*, which has helped hundreds of thousands of persons in the United States and other countries. For many years, Dr. Bourne was director of the Anxiety Treatment Center in San Jose and Santa Rosa, California. Currently he resides and practices in Kona, Hawaii and California.

Personal telephone consultations with Dr. Bourne may be arranged by calling 808-334-1847. Information on intensive therapy programs in Kona, Hawaii is also available by calling this number. If you would like to find a therapist who specializes in treating anxiety disorders in your local area, please contact the Anxiety Disorders Association of America for a referral (301-231-9350).

Some Other New Harbinger Titles

Freeing the Angry Mind, Item 4380 $14.95
Living Beyond Your Pain, Item 4097 $19.95
Transforming Anxiety, Item 4445 $12.95
Integrative Treatment for Borderline Personality Disorder, Item 4461 $24.95
Depressed and Anxious, Item 3635 $19.95
Is He Depressed or What?, Item 4240 $15.95
Cognitive Therapy for Obsessive-Compulsive Disorder, Item 4291 $39.95
Child and Adolescent Psychopharmacology Made Simple, Item 4356 $14.95
ACT on Life Not on Anger,* Item 4402 $14.95
Overcoming Medical Phobias, Item 3872 $14.95
Acceptance & Commitment Therapy for Anxiety Disorders, Item 4275 $58.95
The OCD Workbook, Item 4224 $19.95
Neural Path Therapy, Item 4267 $14.95
Overcoming Obsessive Thoughts, Item 3813 $14.95
The Interpersonal Solution to Depression, Item 4186 $19.95
Get Out of Your Mind & Into Your Life, Item 4259 $19.95
Dialectical Behavior Therapy in Private Practice, Item 4208 $54.95
The Anxiety & Phobia Workbook, 4th edition, Item 4135 $19.95
Loving Someone with OCD, Item 3295 $15.95
Overcoming Animal & Insect Phobias, Item 3880 $12.95
Overcoming Compulsive Washing, Item 4054 $14.95
Angry All the Time, Item 3929 $13.95
Handbook of Clinical Psychopharmacology for Therapists, 4th edition, Item 3996 $55.95
Writing For Emotional Balance, Item 3821 $14.95
Surviving Your Borderline Parent, Item 3287 $14.95
When Anger Hurts, 2nd edition, Item 3449 $16.95
Calming Your Anxious Mind, Item 3384 $12.95
Ending the Depression Cycle, Item 3333 $17.95
Your Surviving Spirit, Item 3570 $18.95
Coping with Anxiety, Item 3201 $10.95
The Agoraphobia Workbook, Item 3236 $19.95
Loving the Self-Absorbed, Item 3546 $14.95
Transforming Anger, Item 352X $12.95
Don't Let Your Emotions Run Your Life, Item 3090 $18.95

Call **toll free, 1-800-748-6273,** or log on to our online bookstore at **www.newharbinger.com** to order. Have your Visa or Mastercard number ready. Or send a check for the titles you want to New Harbinger Publications, Inc., 5674 Shattuck Ave., Oakland, CA 94609. Include $4.50 for the first book and 75¢ for each additional book, to cover shipping and handling. (California residents please include appropriate sales tax.) Allow two to five weeks for delivery.

Prices subject to change without notice.